NOV 2 6 2007

Checks and Balances

The Three Branches of the American Government

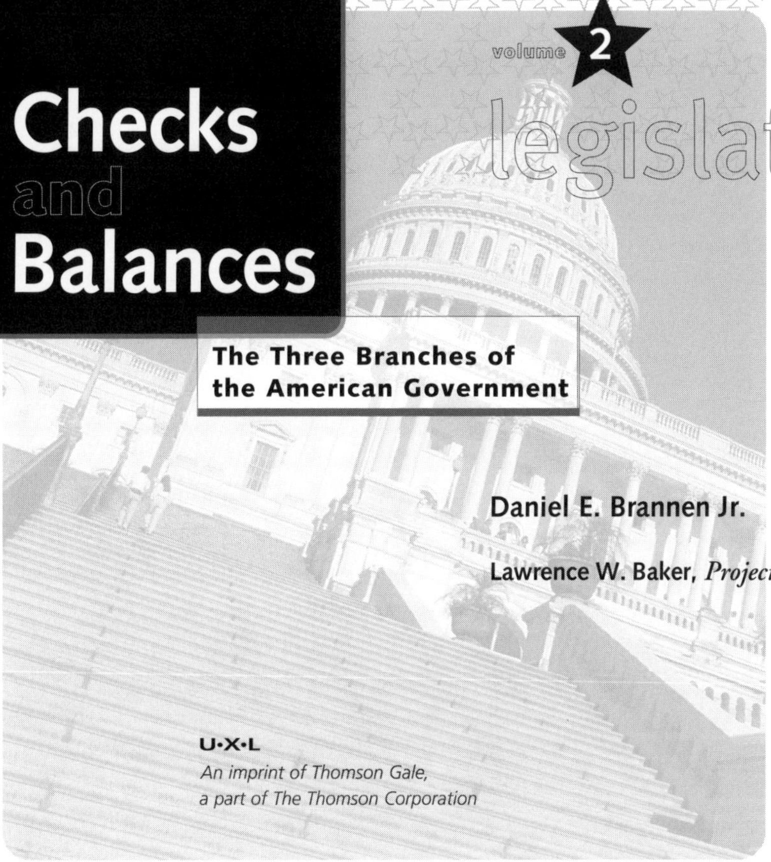

Checks and Balances

The Three Branches of the American Government

volume 2
legislative

Daniel E. Brannen Jr.

Lawrence W. Baker, *Project Editor*

U•X•L
*An imprint of Thomson Gale,
a part of The Thomson Corporation*

Detroit • New York • San Francisco • San Diego • New Haven, Conn. • Waterville, Maine • London • Munich

Checks and Balances:
The Three Branches of the American Government

Daniel E. Brannen Jr.

Project Editor
Lawrence W. Baker

Editorial
Michael Lesniak

Rights Acquisition and Management
Jacqueline Key, Ronald Montgomery, Sheila Spencer

Imaging and Multimedia
Randy Bassett, Lezlie Light, Denay Wilding

Product Design
Kate Scheible

Composition and Electronic Prepress
Evi Seoud

Manufacturing
Rita Wimberley

Thomson and Star Logo are trademarks and Gale is a registered trademark used herein under license.

For more information, contact:
Thomson Gale
27500 Drake Rd.
Farmington Hills, MI 48331-3535
Or you can visit our Internet site at
http://www.gale.com

ALL RIGHTS RESERVED
No part of this work covered by the copyright hereon may be reproduced or used in any form or by any means—graphic, electronic, or mechanical, including photocopying, recording, taping, Web distribution, or information storage retrieval systems—without the written permission of the publisher.

For permission to use material from this product, submit your request via Web at http://www.gale-edit.com/permissions, or you may download our Permissions Request form and submit your request by fax or mail to:

Rights Acquisition and Management Department
Thomson Gale
27500 Drake Rd.
Farmington Hills, MI 48331-3535
Permissions Hotline:
248-699-8006 or 800-877-4253, ext. 8006
Fax: 248-699-8074 or 800-762-4058

Cover photographs and internal artwork, © Digital Stock Corporation.

While every effort has been made to ensure the reliability of the information presented in this publication, Thomson Gale does not guarantee the accuracy of data contained herein. Thomson Gale accepts no payment for listing; and inclusion in the publication of any organization, agency, institution, publication, service, or individual does not imply endorsement by the editors or publisher. Errors brought to the attention of the publisher and verified to the satisfaction of the publisher will be corrected in future editions.

LIBRARY OF CONGRESS CATALOGING-IN-PUBLICATION DATA

Brannen, Daniel E., 1968–
    Checks and balances : the three branches of the American government / Daniel E. Brannen, Jr. ; Lawrence W. Baker, project editor.
      p. cm.
    Includes bibliographical references and index.
    ISBN 0-7876-5409-4 (set hardcover : alk. paper) — ISBN 0-7876-5410-8 (v. 1) — ISBN 0-7876-5411-6 (v. 2) — ISBN 0-7876-5412-4 (v. 3)
    1. United States—Politics and government. I. Baker, Lawrence W. II. Title.
    JK271.B6496 2005
    320.473—dc22
                                                      2005009975

This title is also available as an e-book.
ISBN 1-4144-0468-9
Contact your Thomson Gale sales representative for ordering information.

Printed in the United States of America
10 9 8 7 6 5 4 3

Contents

Reader's Guide **vii**

Timeline of Events **ix**

Words to Know **xxvii**

volume 1 **executive branch**

1: American Government: An Overview **1**

2: Historic Roots of the Executive Branch **19**

3: Constitutional Role of the Executive Branch **37**

4: Changes in the Executive Branch **61**

5: Key Positions in the Executive Branch **89**

6: Daily Operations of the Executive Branch **113**

7: Executive-Legislative Checks and Balances **131**

8: Executive-Judicial Checks and Balances **159**

volume 2 **legislative branch**

1: American Government: An Overview **179**

2: Historic Roots of the Legislative Branch **197**

3: Constitutional Role of the Legislative Branch **217**

4: Changes in the Legislative Branch **239**

5: Key Positions in the Legislative Branch **265**

6: Daily Operations of the Legislative Branch **283**

7: Legislative-Executive Checks and Balances **309**

8: Legislative-Judicial Checks and Balances **337**

Contents

volume 3 judicial branch

1: American Government: An Overview **359**

2: Historic Roots of the Judicial Branch **379**

3: Constitutional Role of the Judicial Branch **395**

4: Changes in the Judicial Branch **415**

5: Key Positions in the Judicial Branch **435**

6: Daily Operations of the Judicial Branch **455**

7: Judicial-Executive Checks and Balances **473**

8: Judicial-Legislative Checks and Balances **493**

Appendix: Constitution of the United States of America; Constitutional Amendments **xxxvii**

Where to Learn More **lxi**

Index **lxv**

Reader's Guide

Checks and Balances: The Three Branches of the American Government offers relevant, easy-to-understand information on the inner workings of the American federal government, from its earliest beginnings to its current structure. The eight chapters of each volume focus on the American government and a particular branch: Volume 1, executive; Volume 2, legislative; and Volume 3, judicial. The first chapter of each volume begins with an identical overview of the American government. The other seven chapters focus on the following aspects of the specific branch:

★ Historic roots

★ Constitutional role

★ Changes through the years

★ Key positions

★ Daily operations

★ Checks and balances with each of the other two branches (two chapters)

Each of the "checks and balances" chapters appears twice in the set. For instance, the "Executive-Legislative Checks and Balances" chapter in the executive branch volume is duplicated as the "Legislative-Executive Checks and Balances" chapter in the legislative branch volume. Illustrations and sidebars vary in those chapters, however.

All chapters include "Words to Know" boxes that provide definitions of important words and concepts within the text. Other sidebars highlight significant facts and describe other related governmental information. A timeline of events, a general glossary, reprints of the U.S. Constitution and the Constitutional Amendments, a general bibliography, and a cumulative index are included in each volume. Approximately 150 black-and-white photos help illustrate *Checks and Balances*.

Acknowledgments

Many thanks go to copyeditor Rebecca Valentine, proofreader Amy Marcaccio Keyzer, indexer Dan Brannen, and the folks at Integra Software Services for their fine work.

Comments and suggestions

We welcome your comments on *Checks and Balances* and suggestions for other topics to consider. Please write: Editors, *Checks and Balances,* UXL, 27500 Drake Rd., Farmington Hills, Michigan 48331-3535; call toll free: 800-877-4253; fax to 248-699-8097; or send e-mail via http://www.gale.com.

Timeline of Events

6th century • Emperor Justinian I of the Byzantine Empire oversees the compilation of the *Corpus Juris Civilis,* or Body of Civil Law. This enormous collection and organization of the laws and legal opinions from emperors and jurists of the Roman Empire affects the development of legal systems in Europe after the Dark Ages (476–1000), and eventually affects the development of American legal systems.

1100s–1200s • England establishes three permanent courts to hear cases that affect the interests of the monarch. The courts, called superior common law courts, influence the development of law in America.

June 1215 • King John of England signs the Magna Carta, a document that proclaims and protects the political and civil liberties of English citizens.

1300s • Political philosopher Niccolò Machiavelli writes *Discourses on the First Ten Books of Titus Livius.* Machiavelli champions the Roman Republic system of government, which influences the convention delegates in Philadelphia, Pennsylvania, nearly five hundred years later.

1648 • British Parliament member Clement Walker writes of a British government that divides its power into three branches.

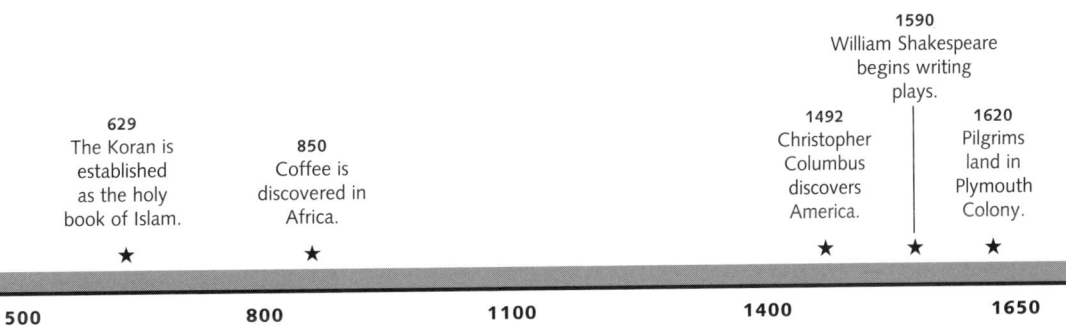

Timeline of Events

1689 • British Parliament adopts the English Bill of Rights, strengthening Parliament's power in the constitutional monarchy.

1689 • English philosopher John Locke publishes *Two Treatises of Government.* In it, he argues that the legislative branch of government should be separate from the executive branch.

1696 • British Parliament establishes the Board of Trade to oversee Great Britain's commercial interests worldwide. The Board of Trade has the power to review and strike down colonial laws that violate British law. In this way, the Board of Trade resembles the U.S. Supreme Court.

1748 • French philosopher Charles Montesquieu publishes *The Spirit of Laws,* influencing the authors of the U.S. Constitution four decades later.

1765–69 • English legal scholar Sir William Blackstone publishes *Commentaries on the Laws of England,* a thorough description of English law at the time. In it, he celebrates the checks and balances of the British system. Most of the men who write the U.S. Constitution two decades later were familiar with Blackstone's work.

1773 • American colonists express their displeasure over taxes by dumping tea into the harbor during the famous Boston Tea Party.

1774 • The thirteen American colonies first send delegates to the Continental Congress.

1775 • The American Revolutionary War begins.

1776 • Revolutionary figure Thomas Paine criticizes the British system of checks and balances in his pamphlet *Common Sense.*

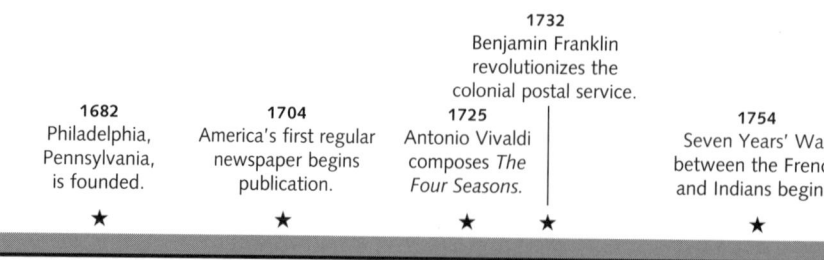

Timeline of Events

July 1776 • The United States of America is born when representatives from the thirteen American colonies join together to break from English rule by signing the Declaration of Independence.

1777 • Delegates serving in the Continental Congress write the Articles of Confederation, one year after America declared independence from Great Britain.

1777 • Pennsylvania physician and political leader Benjamin Rush publishes *Observations on the Government of Pennsylvania*, in which he alludes to a checks and balances form of government. He supports men of moderate wealth having representation in one chamber and men of great wealth having representation in another chamber.

1781 • The states adopt a new form of government with the Articles of Confederation. The articles provide for only a Congress, with no president or judiciary.

1783 • The American Revolutionary War ends.

1786 • Farmers protest debtor laws in Massachusetts in Shays's Rebellion.

1787 • Fifty-five state delegates meet at the Constitutional Convention to frame a Constitution for a federal government.

1787 • In the draft of the Constitution, delegates James Madison and Elbridge Gerry suggest changing Congress's power to "make war" to "declare war."

1787 • The Constitution is presented to the states for approval.

May–June 1787 • Virginia delegate Edmund Randolph proposes that the free men of the states elect members to the

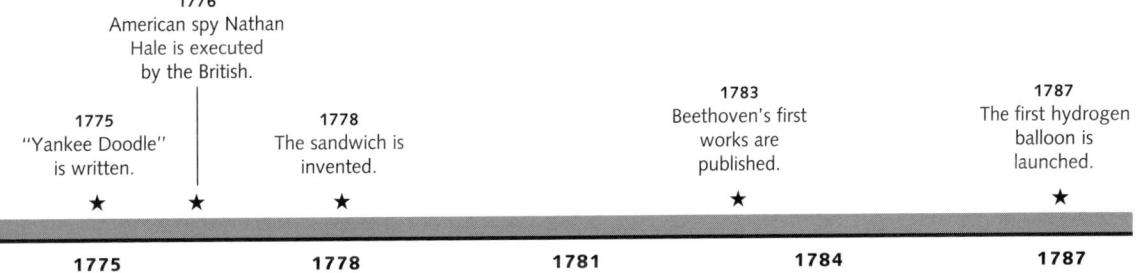

Timeline of Events

House of Representatives. In turn, members of the House would choose the members of the Senate from nominations made by the state legislatures. Most of the large states, however, want free men to control elections to Congress. They also want state population to be the basis for determining how many members each state would have in each chamber. Most of the small states want at least one chamber of Congress to be elected by the states, and they want that chamber to provide equal representation to each state. A set of compromises leads to the delegates agreeing that free men will elect the members of the House and state legislatures will elect the members of the Senate; also, representation in the House will be based on population, while representation in the Senate will be equal for each state.

1787–88 • New York politician Alexander Hamilton and Secretary of Foreign Affairs John Jay write a series of essays called "The Federalist," an attempt to convince Americans to adopt the U.S. Constitution.

1788 • Virginia delegate and future U.S. president James Monroe writes *Observations upon the Proposed Plan of Federal Government,* in which he states that a preamble would be an important part of the Constitution.

June 1788 • The Constitution becomes law in the United States following ratification.

1789 • The new federal government begins to operate under the Constitution, with George Washington as the country's first president.

1789 • The Judiciary Act of 1789 creates a federal judiciary with trial courts (district and circuit courts) and appellate courts to serve under the Supreme Court, as well as the position of attorney general, who is the lead attorney for the United States, and U.S. attorneys to assist the attorney general with the government's caseload. Congress sets the number of

---

1787
The dollar currency is introduced in the United States.
★

1788
New York City becomes the temporary U.S. capital.
★

1789
The U.S. Army is established.
★

1787   1788   1789

Supreme Court justices at six, a number that is raised and lowered seven times until 1869, when it settles on nine justices.

1789 • Congress creates four departments to oversee certain aspects of the government: State, Treasury, War, and Navy.

1789 • President George Washington signs the first appropriations law for the United States. He approves of $568,000 to fund the Departments of War and Treasury, as well as to fund government salaries and pensions.

January 1790 • President George Washington delivers the nation's first annual message, as required by the Constitution.

1790 • Maryland donates land to the U.S. government to be used as the location for the federal capital. The new city is called Washington, D.C., or the District of Columbia.

1791 • The states approve the first ten constitutional amendments, often called the Bill of Rights.

1794 • President George Washington helps end the Whiskey Rebellion by granting a full pardon to rebels involved in the skirmish. The rebellion was a protest by grain farmers against a tax on whiskey.

1797 • The House of Representatives impeaches U.S. senator William Blount of Tennessee, the only time in U.S. history a member of Congress has been impeached. Blount is accused of conspiring to conduct military activities for the king of England; the Senate opts not to conduct an impeachment trial, reasoning that it does not have power under the Constitution to conduct an impeachment trial of a senator.

1798 • Congress passes and President John Adams signs into law the Sedition Act. The new law makes it a crime to say or write anything "false, scandalous and malicious" against the government.

1789	1792	1794	1796	1798
	1792 *Farmer's Almanac* is first published. ★	1794 The cotton gin is patented. ★	1796 Edward Jenner introduces the smallpox vaccination. ★	

Timeline of Events

1798 • The Eleventh Amendment is officially declared part of the Constitution, nearly three years after it was ratified. The amendment decrees that a citizen of one state (or foreign country) may not use the federal court system to sue the government of another state.

1800 • Congress creates the Library of Congress; one year later, it receives its first collection of materials.

1800 • Vice President Thomas Jefferson and New York politician Aaron Burr receive the same number of electoral votes in the presidential election, forcing the House of Representatives to break the tie vote, as required by the Constitution (even though the electors clearly intended Jefferson to be president and Burr to be vice president). Jefferson wins on the thirty-sixth ballot.

1801 • President Thomas Jefferson begins the tradition of delivering his messages to Congress in written form. This form of communication between president and Congress continues for 112 years.

1801 • President Thomas Jefferson repeals the Sedition Act.

1801 • The Federalist-controlled Congress lowers the number of Supreme Court seats from six to five so that the new president, Democratic-Republican Thomas Jefferson, would be unable to appoint a replacement if Justice William Cushing, who was ill at the time, died.

1802 • The Democratic-Republican Party gains control of Congress, and raises the number of justices back to six.

1802 • Congress assigns one Supreme Court justice to travel to each circuit to hear trials.

1803 • In *Marbury v. Madison,* the U.S. Supreme Court rules that a federal law giving the Supreme Court the power to hear cases for compelling government action is unconstitutional.

1799 The Rosetta Stone is found in Egypt.

1800 John Adams is the first president to live in the White House.

1803 The United States nearly doubles, following the Louisiana Purchase.

1798 — 1799 — 1800 — 1801 — 1803

Under the Constitution, such cases must begin in a lower federal court, with the Supreme Court permitted to review them only on appeal.

1803 • Federal district court judge John Pickering is the first judge to be impeached. He is convicted of drunkenness and removed from office.

1803 • Judicial review becomes a permanent part of the federal judiciary after the U.S. Supreme Court announces its power to strike down congressional laws that violate the U.S. Constitution.

1804 • The House of Representatives impeaches Supreme Court justice Samuel Chase; the Senate, however, votes not to convict him.

1804 • The Twelfth Amendment to the Constitution is adopted, requiring that electors label their two votes: one for president and the other for vice president. Previously, electors voted for their top two choices, with the leading vote-getter becoming president and the runner-up being elected vice president. In 1800, this flawed system resulted in a tie vote between two members of the same party.

1812 • Congress uses its constitutional right by declaring war (the War of 1812).

1824 • None of the presidential candidates receives a majority of electoral votes, forcing the U.S. House of Representatives to choose between the leading three vote-getters. Secretary of State John Quincy Adams wins the election after the candidate who was no longer eligible, Speaker of the House Henry Clay, convinces the states that had voted for him to support Adams. Later, Clay becomes Adams's secretary of state, leading many to believe that Adams had promised Clay the position in exchange for his votes.

1804 Napoléon Bonaparte is crowned emperor of France.

1806 *Webster's Dictionary* is first published.

1814 Francis Scott Key writes the "Star Spangled Banner."

1825 The New York Stock Exchange opens.

1834 The Braille system for the blind is invented.

Timeline of Events

April 1841 • President William Henry Harrison dies after only a month in office. His vice president, John Tyler, insists that the Constitution allows him to fill the office of the presidency for the remainder of Harrison's term. Evidence to the contrary does not exist, so Tyler stays on as president, establishing a line-of-succession tradition.

1846 • Congress uses its constitutional right by declaring war (the Mexican War).

1857 • In *Scott v. Sandford,* the U.S. Supreme Court rules that former slave Dred Scott is not a citizen of the United States because African Americans could not be citizens under the U.S. Constitution.

1860 • Congress creates the Government Printing Office, which serves as a printer for Congress and collects and publishes information about the federal government for all three of its branches.

1861 • The American Civil War begins.

1862 • U.S. district judge West H. Humphreys of Tennessee is impeached by the U.S. House of Representatives and removed by the Senate, on charges of joining the Confederacy without resigning his judgeship.

1862 • President Abraham Lincoln creates the U.S. Department of Agriculture.

1863 • Congress raises the number of justices on the U.S. Supreme Court to ten. This allows President Abraham Lincoln to appoint a new justice at a time when he is stretching his constitutional powers to conduct the American Civil War.

1865 • The Thirteenth Amendment bans slavery.

1865 • The American Civil War ends.

1844	1852	1856	1862	1865
Samuel F. B. Morse transmits the first telegraph message.	The Otis safety elevator is invented.	Neanderthal man fossils are found.	Jefferson Davis becomes president of the Confederacy.	President Abraham Lincoln is assassinated.
★	★	★	★	★

| 1841 | 1847 | 1853 | 1859 | 1865 |

Timeline of Events

1866 • Congress reduces the number of U.S. Supreme Court seats from ten to seven. Congress fears that President Andrew Johnson, who is against many of Congress's Reconstruction Acts for rebuilding the country after the American Civil War, will appoint justices who will strike down the acts as unconstitutional.

1868 • The states adopt the Fourteenth Amendment, which declares that all people born or naturalized in the United States are citizens of the country and of the state in which they live.

1868 • Andrew Johnson is the first U.S. president to be impeached. He escapes removal from office by a single vote in the U.S. Senate.

1869 • Congress raises the number of Supreme Court seats from seven to nine, shortly after the inauguration of Ulysses S. Grant. The number has been fixed there ever since.

1870 • The Fifteenth Amendment makes it illegal to deny a person the right to vote based on race or color.

1870 • The attorney general becomes head of the U.S. Department of Justice.

1873 • England combines common law and equity courts into one court. U.S. federal courts would later do the same thing.

1875 • Congress passes the Civil Rights Act of 1875, making discrimination illegal in places of public accommodation, such as inns and theaters.

1875 • Congress reorganizes the judiciary by passing the Judiciary Act of 1875. It shifts some kinds of trials from the circuit courts to the district courts and gives the circuit courts more responsibility for hearing appeals.

1866	1868	1870	1874	1876
The first U.S. oil pipeline is completed.	Louisa May Alcott publishes *Little Women*.	The first African American congressmen take office.	The first American zoo opens in Philadelphia.	Alexander Graham Bell invents the telephone.
★	★	★	★	★

1866 — 1869 — 1872 — 1875 — 1878

Timeline of Events

1883 • The U.S. Supreme Court strikes down the Civil Rights Act of 1875, saying the Fourteenth Amendment only made discrimination by states illegal, not by private persons in their businesses.

1891 • Congress passes the Circuit Courts of Appeals Act, finishing the judicial branch reorganization that began in 1875. The act transfers most federal trials to the district courts, creates nine new circuit courts of appeals, and requires the Supreme Court to hear only certain kinds of appeals from the district and circuit courts and from the circuit courts of appeals.

1896 • The U.S. Supreme Court decides in *Plessy v. Ferguson* that the Fourteenth Amendment does not prevent states from requiring whites and blacks to use separate railway cars. The Court rules that "separate but equal" facilities satisfy the "equal protection" requirements of the Fourteenth Amendment.

1898 • Congress uses its constitutional right by declaring war (the Spanish-American War).

1899 • The U.S. House of Representatives names its first official whip.

1912 • The number of members of the U.S. House of Representatives reaches 435, a total that has not changed in subsequent years.

1913 • President Woodrow Wilson revives the practice of delivering his annual address to Congress orally.

February 1913 • The Sixteenth Amendment is ratified, giving Congress the power to collect an income tax.

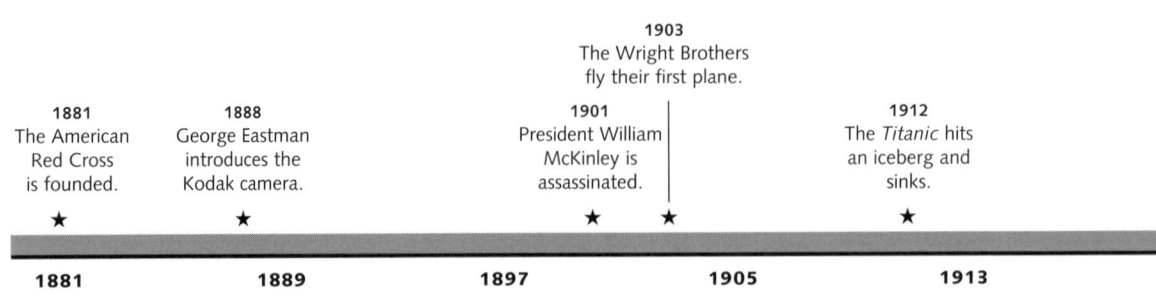

Timeline of Events

May 1913 • The Seventeenth Amendment is ratified, which changes the way U.S. senators are elected to office. Instead of state legislatures electing them, citizens vote them in.

1917 • Congress uses its constitutional right by declaring war (World War I).

January 1919 • The Eighteenth Amendment is ratified, making the manufacture, sale, and transportation of alcoholic beverages illegal.

1920s • U.S. senators of both the Republican and Democratic parties began to elect official majority and minority leaders.

August 1920 • The Nineteenth Amendment is ratified, giving women the right to vote.

1921 • Congress passes the Budgeting and Accounting Act. The act gives the president the job of preparing an initial budget plan each year, and also creates the Bureau of the Budget (later renamed the Office of Management and Budget), a governmental office for helping the president prepare the budget.

1923 • President Calvin Coolidge is the first president to broadcast his annual address to Congress on the radio.

1933 • The Twentieth Amendment is ratified, changing the dates the president, vice president, and members of Congress take office, following the November election. The amendment also states that the vice president–elect becomes president in the event of the death of the president-elect.

1933 • The Twenty-first Amendment is ratified, ending nationwide prohibition by repealing the Eighteenth Amendment.

1937 • President Franklin D. Roosevelt tries to change the philosophical makeup of the Supreme Court by asking Congress to increase the number of seats on the Supreme Court from nine to fifteen and allow Roosevelt to fill the new seats

---

1913
The first Charlie Chaplin silent movie is released.
★

1920
Joan of Arc is canonized a saint.
★

1923
Edwin Hubble identifies galaxies beyond the Milky Way.
★

1929
The Great Depression begins.
★

1933
German Nazis build the first concentration camps.
★

1913 — 1919 — 1925 — 1931 — 1937

Timeline of Events

whenever a justice over seventy years of age does not resign. (Four justices who regularly voted against Roosevelt's New Deal program were already over seventy, and the president wanted to appoint new justices who would support his New Deal.) The plan is controversial, and is proved to be unnecessary; the Court winds up approving much of Roosevelt's New Deal legislation and the president names five replacement justices through 1940 as a result of three retirements and two deaths. Congress does not approve of Roosevelt's "court-packing."

1939 • President Franklin D. Roosevelt creates the Executive Office of the President to help the president manage the executive branch. Four of the most important positions in the department are the chief of staff, director of the Office of Management and Budget, director of the National Economic Council, and national security advisor.

1940 • President Franklin D. Roosevelt tells Democratic Party officials he will not run for a third term unless they select Secretary of Agriculture Henry A. Wallace as his vice presidential running mate. The party grants Roosevelt's wish, thus beginning the tradition of presidential candidates choosing their running mates.

1941 • Congress uses its constitutional right by declaring war (World War II).

1947 • President Harry S. Truman is the first president to broadcast his annual address to Congress on television.

1947 • The War Department, Navy Department, and Department of the Air Force combine to form the Department of Defense.

1947 • The National Security Council is created to advise the president on national security affairs.

1939	1942	1945	1948
The Baseball Hall of Fame is established.	Humphrey Bogart stars in *Casablanca*.	The United States drops two atomic bombs on Japan.	Jews in Palestine form the State of Israel.
★	★	★	★

1937　　　1940　　　1943　　　1946　　　1949

Timeline of Events

1949 • Congress passes a law making the vice president an official member of the National Security Council.

March 1951 • The Twenty-second Amendment is ratified, limiting presidents to a maximum of two terms, or two terms and two years if the president was finishing no more than half of his predecessor's term.

1954 • The U.S. Supreme Court unanimously decides in *Brown v. Board of Education of Topeka* that separate public services are not equal under the Fourteenth Amendment. This is an example of an amendment not changing but the Supreme Court's *interpretation* of it changing.

1961 • The Twenty-third Amendment is ratified, allowing Washington, D.C., to select a number of electors equal to the number of senators and representatives it would have if it were a state, but no more than the number of electors allowed for the least populous state. This gives electors from Washington, D.C., the chance to vote in a presidential election.

January 1964 • The Twenty-fourth Amendment is ratified, making it illegal for the United States or any state to charge a poll tax for participating in presidential and congressional elections.

July 1964 • President Lyndon B. Johnson signs into law the Civil Rights Act, making discrimination illegal in public places, such as motels and restaurants. Congress says it passed the act using its power under the Interstate Commerce Clause. Later, in *Heart of Atlanta Motel v. United States* and *Katzenbach v. McClung,* the U.S. Supreme Court rules that the Civil Rights Act is lawful under the Constitution because Congress can outlaw private discrimination under its power to regulate interstate commerce, but not under the equal rights provisions of the Fourteenth Amendment.

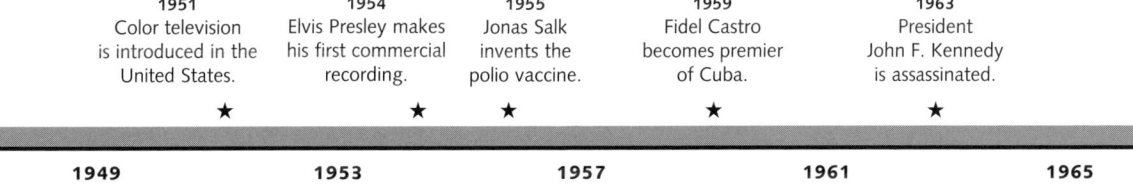

Timeline of Events

1967 • The Twenty-fifth Amendment is ratified, officially providing for the vice president to become president "in case of the removal of the president from office or his death or resignation." Prior to the adoption of this amendment, the vice president's swearing-in to office—which had happened seven times before—was by tradition only.

1967 • The Department of Transportation is established.

1968 • Congress passes the Federal Magistrates Act, giving district courts the power to appoint magistrate judges to help district court judges do their jobs.

July 1971 • The Twenty-sixth Amendment is ratified, lowering the voting age to eighteen.

1972 • The U.S. Supreme Court rules in *Roe v. Wade* that states cannot ban abortions completely because women have a constitutional right to have abortions in some cases. After that decision, some states rewrite their abortion laws to ban abortions in situations allowed under the Supreme Court's ruling. This is an example of a legislative check on judicial power.

1973 • Congress passes the War Powers Resolution to try to strengthen the constitutional separation of military powers. President Richard Nixon vetoes the bill, but both chambers of Congress vote to override the veto. The resolution says presidents should commit troops only with congressional consultation and authorization.

1973 • President Richard Nixon tries to use executive privilege to hide information about the Watergate scandal from Senate investigators.

October 1973 • Spiro T. Agnew resigns as vice president after it is divulged that he failed to report almost $30,000 on his federal income tax return in 1967 while he was governor of

1967	1969	1970	1972	1973
The first human heart transplant takes place.	Neil Armstrong is the first astronaut to walk on the moon.	Four Vietnam War protesters are killed at Kent State University.	The United States reestablishes relations with the People's Republic of China.	U.S. troops pull out of Vietnam.

Maryland. He is also accused of taking bribes while serving as a county official in Maryland.

December 1973 • The Twenty-fifth Amendment is invoked for the first time when U.S. representative Gerald Ford is approved by Congress as the new vice president.

1974 • Congress passes the Budget and Impoundment Control Act, which creates the Congressional Budget Office and standing budget committees in both chambers of Congress.

August 1974 • President Richard M. Nixon resigns from office, the first president in history to do so. The House was almost certainly about to impeach him for his role in covering up a 1972 burglary of the offices of the Democratic National Committee by members of the Republican Party, a scandal known as Watergate. Gerald Ford succeeds him, becoming the only person to serve as both president and vice president without being elected to either office.

September 1974 • President Gerald Ford pardons former president Richard Nixon for any involvement he had in the Watergate scandal. Ford reasons that a long trial involving Nixon would not allow the country to move beyond the scandal.

1980 • Congress creates the Department of Education.

1981 • Sandra Day O'Connor becomes the first female U.S. Supreme Court justice.

1983 • The U.S. Supreme Court decides in *INS v. Chadha* that the legislative veto violates the Constitution. The Constitution says the only way Congress can pass a bill or resolution is when both chambers approve it and present it to the president for executive veto consideration. Legislative vetoes violate this by giving either one or both chambers of

1974	1976	1978	1982
Hank Aaron passes Babe Ruth as baseball's all-time home run hitter.	The United States celebrates its bicentennial.	John Paul II begins his reign as pope.	The compact disc (CD) is introduced.
★	★	★	★

1973 — 1976 — 1978 — 1981 — 1983

Timeline of Events

Congress the power to take official action that the president cannot veto. Despite the Court's ruling, Congress continues to include the legislative veto power in the nation's laws.

1984 • U.S. congresswoman Geraldine Ferraro of New York becomes the first female vice presidential candidate on a major party ticket, running unsuccessfully with the Democratic presidential contender, former vice president Walter Mondale.

1992 • More than two hundred years after it was first proposed by Congress, the Twenty-seventh Amendment is ratified. It says that if Congress passes a law changing the salaries for senators or representatives, the law cannot take effect until after at least one House election passes. This prevents representatives from giving themselves pay raises while in office.

1993 • The National Economic Council is created to help the president develop and implement economic policies, both domestic and international.

1996 • Congress passes the Line Item Veto Act, allowing the president to strike specific dollar amounts and tax benefits from appropriations bills passed by Congress. Congress can override the line item veto only by passing another bill containing the portions the president has stricken.

1997 • Madeleine Albright becomes the first female secretary of state.

1998 • The U.S. Supreme Court strikes down the 1996 Line Item Veto Act. The Court rules that it violates the Constitution, which states that the president may use his veto power to veto only an *entire* bill.

1998 • President Bill Clinton becomes the second president to be impeached. He is charged with perjury and obstruction of justice relating to an Arkansas real estate deal, a sexual

---

1985 Microsoft introduces Windows to the market. ★

1989 The Berlin Wall is torn down. ★

1993 Toni Morrison becomes the first African American to win the Nobel Prize for literature. ★

1994 Nelson Mandela becomes the first black president of South Africa. ★

1999 The euro is accepted as legal tender in Europe. ★

1984 — 1988 — 1992 — 1996 — 2000

Timeline of Events

harassment case, and a relationship with a White House intern. The U.S. Senate vote leaves him in office, however.

2000 • In the extremely tight presidential election of 2000 between Texas governor George W. Bush and Vice President Al Gore, a narrow victory for Bush in Florida leads Gore to sue to have votes in certain counties recounted. Bush appeals one of the cases from the Florida Supreme Court to the U.S. Supreme Court. The U.S. Supreme Court issues a decision in December, stopping the recounts in Florida, giving Bush Florida's twenty-five electoral votes and, therefore, making him the presidential victor.

September 2001 • President George W. Bush delivers a special message to Congress following the terrorist attacks of September 11, 2001. Aside from their annual addresses to Congress, it is rare for presidents to speak to the complete Congress.

October 2001 • The Office of Homeland Security is created following the terrorist attacks of September 11, 2001. A year later, it becomes a full department in the executive branch.

2001	2002	2003	2004	2005
Terrorists attack the World Trade Center and the Pentagon.	Washington, D.C., snipers kill ten, wound others.	The United States declares war on Iraq.	A powerful tsunami in the Indian Ocean kills hundreds of thousands.	George W. Bush begins his second term as president.
★	★	★	★	★
2001	2002	2003	2004	2005

Words to Know

appropriations bill: A bill, or law, that assigns money to a government department or agency.

Articles of Confederation: The document that established the federal government for the United States of America from 1781 to 1789.

bicameralism: The practice of dividing the legislative, or law-making, power of government into two chambers.

Bill of Rights: The first ten amendments to the U.S. Constitution, proposed in 1789 and adopted in 1791. The Bill of Rights contains some of the rights of citizens of the United States of America.

cabinet: A group of executive officials who advise the president on important policy matters and decisions. By law, the cabinet includes the heads of the executive departments. Presidents can also include other important executive officials in their cabinets, such as the vice president.

casework: Work that a member of Congress does to help a voter with a personal governmental problem.

checks and balances: The specific powers in one branch of government that allow it to limit the powers of the other branches.

Words to Know

circuit court of appeals: A court in the federal judicial system that handles appeals from the trial courts, called federal district courts. The United States is divided into twelve geographic areas called circuits, and each circuit has one court of appeals that handles appeals from the federal district courts in its circuit. A party who loses in a circuit court of appeals may ask the Supreme Court to review the case.

civil case: A case that involves a dispute between private parties or a noncriminal dispute between a private party and a government.

cloture rule: A rule that allows senators to end a filibuster, or prolonged speech, by a vote of three-fifths of the Senate.

common law: A law developed by judges in England and America on a case-by-case basis for governing relationships between private parties. Examples of common law include contract law and tort law.

Congress: The legislative, or lawmaking, branch of the federal government. Congress has two chambers, the Senate and the House of Representatives.

constituents: The voters who are in a representative's district or a senator's state.

Constitution of the United States of America: The document written in 1787 that established the federal government under which the United States of America has operated since 1789. Article I covers the legislative branch, Article II covers the executive branch, and Article III covers the judicial branch.

Constitutional Convention of 1787: Convention held in Philadelphia, Pennsylvania, from May to September 1787, during which delegates from twelve of the thirteen American states wrote a new Constitution for the United States.

Continental Congress: The main body of American government from 1774 until 1779.

courts of appeals: Federal appellate courts that review district court trials to correct serious errors made by judges and juries.

criminal case: A case in which a person is charged with violating a criminal law.

district courts: The courts in the federal judicial system that handle trials in civil and criminal cases. Each state is divided into one or more federal judicial districts, and each district has one or more federal district courts. A party who loses in a federal district court may appeal to have the case reviewed by a circuit court of appeals.

executive branch: The branch of the federal government that enforces the nation's laws. The executive branch includes the president, the vice president, and many executive departments, agencies, and offices.

executive departments: Departments in the executive branch responsible for large areas of the federal government. As of 2005, there are fifteen departments: Agriculture, Commerce, Defense, Education, Energy, Health and Human Services, Homeland Security, Housing and Urban Development, Interior, Justice, Labor, State, Transportation, Treasury, and Veterans Affairs. The heads of the departments, called secretaries, make up the president's cabinet.

executive privilege: A privilege that allows the president to keep information secret, even if Congress, federal investigators, the Supreme Court, or the people want the president to release the information. The privilege is designed to protect information related to national security, or public safety.

federalism: A principle of government under which independent states join to form a central government to serve their collective needs.

filibuster: A tactic used by one or more senators who speak for a prolonged period of time so that the time for considering a bill runs out before a vote can be taken on the Senate floor.

Words to Know

Founding Fathers: General term for the men who founded the United States of America and designed its government. The term includes the men who signed the Declaration of Independence in 1776 and the Constitution of the United States in 1787.

impoundment: The presidential practice of refusing to spend money that Congress appropriates for an executive department, agency, or program.

income tax: A tax on the money and property that a person earns during the year.

Interstate Commerce Clause: The clause in Article I, Section 8, of the Constitution that gives Congress the power "to regulate commerce ... among the several states."

iron triangle: The three-way relationship between congressional committees, executive agencies, and private interest groups that all specialize in the same area of government.

judge: A public official who presides over a court and who often decides questions brought before him or her.

judicial interpretation: The process by which federal courts interpret the meaning of laws passed by Congress.

judicial review: The process by which federal courts review laws to determine whether they violate the U.S. Constitution. If a court finds that a law violates the Constitution, it declares the law unconstitutional, which means the executive branch is not supposed to enforce it anymore. Congress can correct such a defect by passing a new law that does not violate the Constitution.

judiciary: The branch of the federal government that decides cases that arise under the nation's law. The federal judiciary includes the Supreme Court of the United States, circuit courts of appeals, and federal district courts.

justice: One of nine jurists who serve on the U.S. Supreme Court. The chief justice serves as the head of the Supreme Court; the other eight are called associate justices.

legislative courts: Courts created by Congress to handle some of its lawmaking powers under Article I of the U.S. Constitution.

lobbying: Meeting with members of Congress to convince them to pass laws that will benefit businesses, citizen's groups, or other organizations.

monarchy: A government under which power is held by a monarch, such as a king or queen, who inherits power by birth or takes it by force.

natural law: The idea that human laws must conform to a higher law—one of nature, often believed to come from God.

Necessary and Proper Clause: The clause in Article I, Section 8, of the Constitution that gives Congress the power "to make all laws which shall be necessary and proper" for exercising the other powers of the federal government.

personnel floor: A congressional minimum on the number of employees a governmental department, agency, or program must employ.

plutocracy: A government under which power is held by the wealthy class of society.

president: The highest officer in the executive branch of the federal government, with primary responsibility for enforcing the nation's laws.

Words to Know

quorum: The number of members of Congress who must be present for Congress to conduct business, such as voting on bills. The U.S. Constitution says a chamber has a quorum when a simple majority of its members is present.

ratification: The process of formally approving something, such as a treaty, constitution, or constitutional amendment.

reception provisions: Laws passed by some of the new American states around 1776 to define which parts of the common law, English statutes, and colonial statutes continued to apply in the states after they separated from Great Britain.

reprogramming: The practice of using money that Congress appropriates to one governmental program for a different program.

republicanism: Theory of government under which power is held by the people, who elect public servants to represent them in the bodies of government.

separation of powers: Division of the powers of government into different branches to prevent one branch from having too much power.

suffrage: The right to vote.

Supreme Court: The highest court in the federal judiciary. The judiciary is the branch of government responsible for resolving legal disputes and interpreting laws on a case-by-case basis.

unicameralism: The practice of placing the legislative, or law-making, power of government in one chamber.

veto: Rejection of a bill, or proposed law, by the president of the United States. If the president vetoes a bill, it does not become law unless two-thirds of both chambers of Congress vote to override the veto.

vice president: The second highest officer in the executive branch of the federal government. The vice president replaces the president if the president dies or becomes unable to serve. The vice president also serves as president of the Senate, with power to break tie votes when the whole Senate is equally divided on an issue.

Checks and Balances

The Three Branches of the American Government

American Government: An Overview

The Constitution is the framework for the federal government of the United States of America. Written in 1787 and adopted in 1788, it carves the federal government into three branches. Generally, the legislative branch makes America's laws, the executive branch enforces the laws, and the judicial branch decides cases under the laws. The Constitution also gives the three branches duties outside the realm of the nation's laws.

The division of government into branches is what political scientists call the separation of powers. The separation of powers prevents the same person or branch of government from having full power to make, enforce, and interpret the nation's laws. The separation set up by the Constitution, however, is not absolute. Each branch has powers that allow it to affect the affairs of the other branches. These checks and balances prevent the branches of government from being completely separate. Indeed, some observers believe the checks and balances make the federal government one of shared powers, not separate powers.

The legislative branch: Congress

The Constitution contains six parts called articles and, as of 2005, twenty-seven parts called amendments. Amendments are changes made since the original six articles were adopted in 1788. The first three articles cover the three branches of government, and the very first article covers the legislative branch. It begins, "All legislative Powers herein granted shall be vested in a Congress of the United States, which shall consist of a Senate and House of Representatives."

American Government: An Overview

Words to Know

checks and balances: The specific powers in one branch of government that allow it to limit the powers of the other branches.

Congress: The legislative, or lawmaking, branch of the federal government. Congress has two chambers, the Senate and the House of Representatives.

judicial interpretation: The process by which federal courts interpret the meaning of laws passed by Congress.

judicial review: The process by which federal courts review laws to determine whether they violate the U.S. Constitution. If a court finds that a law violates the Constitution, it declares the law unconstitutional, which means the executive branch is not supposed to enforce it anymore. Congress can correct such a defect by passing a new law that does not violate the Constitution.

president: The highest officer in the executive branch of the federal government, with primary responsibility for enforcing the nation's laws.

separation of powers: Division of the powers of government into different branches to prevent one branch from having too much power.

Supreme Court: The highest court in the federal judiciary. The judiciary is the branch of government responsible for resolving legal disputes and interpreting laws on a case-by-case basis.

The powers of Congress The legislative power is the power to make laws, so Congress is the nation's main lawmaker. Article I, Section 8, lists Congress's lawmaking power, including the power to:

- ★ collect taxes and other money for paying the nation's debts and providing for its common defense and general welfare

- ★ regulate commerce, or business, that crosses the boundaries of states, Indian lands, and foreign nations

- ★ establish rules for naturalization, which is the process by which people from other countries can become citizens of the United States

- ★ create money and punish counterfeiters (people who make fake money to be used as real money)

- ★ raise and support armies and navies and provide rules for regulating them

In the Constitution, this list ends with a general clause that says Congress has the power "to make all Laws which shall be necessary and proper for carrying into Execution the foregoing

Powers, and all other Powers vested by this Constitution in the Government of the United States, or in any Department or Officer thereof." In other words, Congress has the general power to make all laws the government needs to exercise its specific powers.

The chambers of Congress The very same section of the Constitution that makes Congress the lawmaker divides it into two chambers, the Senate and the House of Representatives. The Senate contains two senators from each state of the United States, for a total of one hundred as of 2005. Delegates from small states, such as New Jersey and New Hampshire, insisted on this arrangement when they met to write the Constitution in steamy Philadelphia, Pennsylvania, in the summer of 1787. The delegates from small states feared that the large states would control the federal government without a legislative chamber that gave each state equal representation. Two senators from each state—regardless of geographic size or population—means each state has equal power in the Senate.

As of 2005, the House of Representatives contains 435 members, a total that has not changed since 1912. This number comes from a law passed by Congress, not from the Constitution. The Constitution only says that each state must have at least one member in the House, and may have no more than one member for every thirty thousand people in the state.

Under the Constitution, the total number of members in the House must be divided among the states once every ten years based on the population of each state. Roughly speaking, then, each state has control in the House in proportion to the size of its population. States then divide themselves into districts, with one House member representing each district. Redistricting is the process of dividing the total number of House members for a state among its districts based on the population census taken every ten years. The most recent redistricting happened after publication of the 2000 federal census.

The Senate and the House of Representatives share most of the powers of Congress equally. Both chambers can propose changes to the Constitution, called amendments, although three-fourths of the states must approve an amendment before it becomes law. Action by both chambers is necessary to admit new states to the United States, a topic that occasionally arises

Birth of a Government

The U.S. Constitution, written in 1787, created a federal government that has lasted into the twenty-first century. The Constitution was signed by representatives, then called delegates, from twelve of the thirteen states that made up the United States in 1787: Connecticut, Delaware, Georgia, Maryland, Massachusetts, New Hampshire, New Jersey, New York, North Carolina, Pennsylvania, South Carolina, and Virginia. (Rhode Island sent no delegates to the Constitutional Convention of 1787. Its population of mostly farmers rejected the Convention's goal of creating a strong central government, which would be hard for the people to control from their communities, far away from the capital.)

The Constitution became law in the United States in June 1788 after ten of the thirteen states ratified, or approved, it. The new federal government began to operate under the Constitution in 1789.

The Constitution, however, did not create the United States of America, and was not the blueprint for its first government. The country was born on July 4, 1776, when representatives from the thirteen American colonies joined together to break from English rule by signing the Declaration of Independence.

At the time of independence in 1776, the new American states operated together as a nation in the Continental Congress. In 1781, the states adopted a new form of government with the Articles of Confederation. American government under the Articles of Confederation had only a Congress, with no president or judiciary. The weakness of this government led the men who wanted a powerful federal government to call for writing the U.S. Constitution in 1787.

concerning the District of Columbia and Puerto Rico, which are not states as of 2005. Congress as a whole shares the power to make rules and regulations for territories of the United States, which are lands that the United States controls without making them states. Examples of territories are Puerto Rico and the U.S. Virgin Islands in the Caribbean Sea, and Guam and the Northern Mariana Islands in the Pacific Ocean.

Each chamber of Congress must pass a bill for the bill to become law. Both chambers can pass bills for raising money, such as through taxes, but such bills must start in the House. If the president vetoes, or rejects, a bill, the bill dies unless two-thirds of the members of each chamber of Congress vote to override the veto. In this case, the bill becomes law despite the president's veto.

Only the House can impeach the president, vice president, and other civil officers of the United States, including judges. Impeachment is a formal accusation that someone has committed treason, bribery, or other high crimes or misdemeanors. The

American Government: An Overview

Tourists look at the U.S. Constitution at the National Archives Building in Washington, D.C.
© Richard T. Nowitz/Corbis.

Constitution defines treason as levying war against America or giving aid and comfort to its enemies. Bribery is an illegal payment to influence official action. U.S. district judge West H. Humphreys (1806–1882) of Tennessee was impeached in 1862, and removed

Checks and **Balances** *The Three Branches of the American Government* 183

by the Senate, on charges of joining the Confederacy without resigning his judgeship, but nobody has been impeached specifically for treason. Additionally, nobody has been impeached for bribery, but six of the seventeen impeachments in history to date have involved accusations that an official used his office for improper personal gain. The Constitution does not define "high crimes" or "misdemeanors." The House has interpreted the phrase loosely to mean any conduct that makes a person unfit to continue in office. The two highest-profile impeachments were presidents: Andrew Johnson (1808–1875; served 1865–69) in 1868 and Bill Clinton (1946–; served 1993–2001) in 1998.

Once accused by impeachment in the House, a civil officer stands trial in the Senate. The Senate alone can convict the officer. To convict an impeached officer, two-thirds of the senators at an impeachment trial must vote for conviction. Following their impeachment, neither President Johnson nor President Clinton were voted out of office, though Johnson missed conviction by only a single vote.

In addition to conducting impeachment trials, the Senate has two other powers that the House does not. If the president makes a treaty, or formal agreement, with another country, the treaty becomes law in America only if two-thirds of the senators present approve it. Similarly, a simple majority of senators must approve the president's selection of Supreme Court justices, ambassadors, and other important government officers, including the heads of the departments in the executive branch, such as the Justice Department.

Limits on congressional power The Constitution limits the powers given to Congress. Section 9 of Article I says Congress may not eliminate the writ of habeas corpus. A writ is a judicial order, and habeas corpus is a Latin term meaning "to have the body." The writ of habeas corpus is a procedure that prisoners can use to get released if they are being held in violation of the law. The writ requires a jailer to bring the prisoner before a court, where a judge can set the prisoner free if he or she is being held in violation of constitutional rights.

The Constitution also says Congress may not pass bills of attainder or ex post facto laws. A bill of attainder is a law that convicts a person of treason or other serious crime without a trial.

An ex post facto law is one that punishes a person for doing something that was not illegal when done.

Amendments adopted since 1789, when the federal government began to operate under the Constitution, also limit the power of Congress. The states approved the first ten of these amendments, often called the Bill of Rights, in 1791. The Bill of Rights limits but does not eliminate Congress's power to restrict the freedoms of religion, speech, and assembly (First Amendment) and the right to bear arms (Second Amendment). The Eighth Amendment prevents Congress from passing a law that would impose cruel and unusual punishment on convicted criminals.

In addition to limits imposed by the Constitution, the system of checks and balances limits congressional power, too. As chief executive of the United States, the president enforces the laws made by Congress. A president who thinks a particular law is unwise or unimportant can ignore it by devoting people and money to enforcing other laws. As commander in chief of the U.S. Army and Navy, the president controls the military that Congress establishes.

The judiciary also checks the power of Congress. The primary judicial check is judicial review, which is the power to review congressional laws to determine if they violate any of the limitations in the Constitution. Judicial review is a controversial part of the system of checks and balances, because the Constitution does not specifically say the judiciary has this power. Many of the men who wrote the Constitution, however, presumed the judiciary would exercise this power. The Supreme Court confirmed this presumption in the 1803 case of *Marbury v. Madison*. In that case, the Supreme Court decided that a federal law giving the Supreme Court the power to hear cases for compelling government action was unconstitutional. Under the Constitution, such cases must begin in a lower federal court. The Supreme Court may only review them on appeal.

The executive branch: the president

The second Article of the Constitution begins, "The executive power shall be vested in a President of the United States of America." The executive power is the power to enforce the laws made by Congress.

The president's duties Only four paragraphs in the Constitution say what the president's duties are. The power to enforce the nation's laws comes from the clause that says, "he shall take care that the laws be faithfully executed."

Making sure the laws are enforced would be impossible for one person, even in 1789. The Constitution says the president "may require the Opinion, in writing, of the principal Officer in each of the Executive Departments." This clause is a seed that has grown to give the executive branch fifteen major departments plus many more agencies. As of 2005, the fifteen departments are: Agriculture, Commerce, Defense, Education, Energy, Health and Human Services, Homeland Security, Housing and Urban Development, Interior, Justice, Labor, State, Transportation, Treasury, and Veterans Affairs. Some of the agencies are the Central Intelligence Agency (CIA), the Environmental Protection Agency (EPA), the National Aeronautics and Space Administration (NASA), the Peace Corps, and the U.S. Postal Service.

Many of the departments and agencies make and enforce laws, called regulations, that relate to their area of service. For example, under power given to it by Congress, the EPA makes rules concerning the nation's air, land, and water. Executive departments and agencies also administer government programs. The Department of Agriculture, for instance, gives money to industrial farming operations that qualify for financial help under congressional laws.

The head of each of the fifteen executive departments is called the secretary (except for the head of the Department of Justice, who is called the attorney general). The fifteen department heads make up the core of the president's cabinet. Presidents also may include other officials in their cabinet, such as the vice president, the chief of staff (the person who manages the president's staff), and important directors from executive agencies, such as the Central Intelligence Agency or the Office of Management and Budget. Presidents rely on their cabinet not only to run the departments, but also to give the president information and advice for making important decisions.

Besides enforcing the nation's laws, the president is commander in chief of the U.S. Army and Navy. This means the military is ultimately controlled by a civilian, a person who is not part of the military. Putting a civilian in control of the military is supposed to prevent the military from using its power against civilians.

American Government: An Overview

Cabinet members of President James Buchanan. Seated (left to right): Jacob Thompson, John B. Floyd, Isaac Toucey, and Jeremiah Black. Back row (left to right): Lewis Cass, President Buchanan, Howell Cobb, and Joseph Holt. Cabinet members are the president's top advisors. © BETTMANN/CORBIS.

The Constitution requires the president to give Congress "information of the State of the Union" and to recommend "such Measures as he shall judge necessary and expedient [proper]." President George Washington (1732–1799; served 1789–97) delivered the nation's first annual message on January 8, 1790. Washington read his written speech to Congress. President Thomas Jefferson (1743–1826; served 1801–9) thought this practice was too formal, so he simply delivered a written copy of his messages to Congress. President Woodrow Wilson (1856–1924; served 1913–21) revived the practice of delivering the address orally in person in 1913. President Calvin Coolidge's (1872–1933; served 1923–29) message of 1923 was the first to be broadcast by radio, and President Harry S. Truman's (1884–1972; served 1945–53) 1947 speech was the first to be televised.

American Government: An Overview

President Franklin D. Roosevelt delivers his second State of the Union address to a joint session of Congress on January 4, 1935. Vice President John Nance Garner (left) and Speaker of the House Joseph Byrns are behind the president. AP/Wide World Photos.

Each year in January, the president delivers a televised State of the Union address to both chambers of Congress, with Supreme Court justices attending, too. The address gives Congress the president's view on how the country is doing, what is working, and what needs to be changed. On rare occasions, presidents appear before Congress to deliver special messages, such as when President George W. Bush (1946–) addressed Congress to explain his plan for responding to the terrorist attacks of September 11, 2001.

The president recommends "Measures" by proposing an annual budget for the federal government, which outlines how

American Government: An Overview

President George W. Bush addresses a special joint session of Congress on September 20, 2001, nine days after the September 11 terrorist attacks. Speaker of the House Dennis Hastert (left) and Senate president pro tempore Robert Byrd of Virginia are seated behind the president. © Reuters/Corbis.

the government plans to raise and spend money. The president also recommends new laws, or changes to old laws, for Congress to consider. Because the president can veto, or reject, a law passed by Congress, Congress pays close attention to the president's recommendations. It is not, however, required to do what the president wants.

Another major role for the president under the Constitution is receiving "ambassadors and other public ministers." This makes the president the head of America's relations with foreign nations.

Limits on presidential power One of the major limitations on the power of the executive branch is Congress's power to override a presidential veto by a two-thirds vote. Without this congressional

Checks and Balances *The Three Branches of the American Government* 189 power, the president would have full control over what bills become law. For example, in 1995, Congress passed a bill called the Private Securities Litigation Reform Act. The bill made it more difficult to sue private companies for misleading their investors, the people who invest money in a company. President Bill Clinton vetoed the bill in December 1995. Both chambers of Congress voted to override the veto, making the bill law.

The president can make treaties with other nations only when two-thirds of the senators approve. On May 24, 2002, for example, President George W. Bush and President Vladimir Putin (1952–) of Russia signed the Moscow Treaty on Strategic Offensive Reductions. The Moscow Treaty was an agreement to reduce the number of strategic nuclear warhead arsenals in America and Russia to between 1,700 and 2,200 each by December 2012. The U.S. Senate ratified the treaty unanimously in March 2003.

The Senate also must approve the president's selection of federal judges, ambassadors to other countries, executive department heads, and other important officers. This approval, however, need only be by a simple majority.

Both chambers of Congress check the president by playing a role in impeachment and conviction for treason, bribery, and other high crimes and misdemeanors. The House has the power to impeach, or formally accuse, a president of such misconduct. The Senate then has the power to try (put on trial) and convict a president accused of impeachable offenses.

The federal judiciary also checks the president's power, mostly by hearing and deciding cases under the nation's criminal laws. In these cases, federal courts determine whether an accused person is guilty of breaking the law. Many of these cases also involve questions of whether the executive branch has violated the accused person's constitutional rights.

The judicial branch: the Supreme Court and lower federal courts

Article III of the Constitution says, "The judicial power of the United States, shall be vested in one supreme Court, and in such inferior Courts as the Congress may from time to time ordain and establish." This means the Supreme Court is the only federal court created by the Constitution. Congress has sole authority to create federal courts underneath the Supreme Court.

Congress has used that power to create a vast federal judicial system. At the lowest level are federal district courts, the courts that hold trials. Criminal trials deal with people and businesses accused of violating the nation's criminal laws. A criminal law is a law that makes it unlawful to do something that is harmful to society, such as making illegal drugs or committing murder. Civil trials typically involve people or businesses that have private disputes to resolve, such as when one person breaks a contract, or agreement, that he or she has with another person.

As of 2005, the United States has ninety-four federal district courts. The districts cover either a portion of a state or an entire state, the District of Columbia, the Commonwealth of Puerto Rico, and the territories of the U.S. Virgin Islands, Guam, and the Northern Mariana Islands.

The next level of the federal judiciary is the circuit courts of appeals. There are twelve circuit courts of appeals, each of which covers a geographic region containing federal district courts. When a party loses a trial in federal district court, the party usually can appeal to the court of appeals in that district's circuit. The job of the courts of appeals is to review cases from the federal district courts to make sure the judges and juries there have not made significant errors.

If a party loses in the circuit court of appeals, the last place to go is to the Supreme Court of the United States, often called the court of last resort. As with the courts of appeals, the Supreme Court's job is to make sure the courts below did not make any major errors in a case.

The U.S. Supreme Court does not only hear appeals from the federal courts. It also hears appeals from the state judicial systems. Generally speaking, each state has trial courts similar to the federal district courts, courts of appeals similar to the federal circuit courts, and supreme courts similar to the U.S. Supreme Court. If a case that reaches a state supreme court involves federal laws or rights, the losing party can ask the U.S. Supreme Court to review the decision of the state supreme court. In the tight presidential election of 2000 between Texas governor George W. Bush and Vice President Al Gore (1948–), for example, an extremely narrow victory for

Bush in Florida led Gore to sue to have votes in certain counties recounted. Bush appealed one of the cases from the Florida Supreme Court to the U.S. Supreme Court. The U.S. Supreme Court issued a decision in December 2000, stopping the recounts in Florida, giving Bush the victory. Florida's twenty-five electoral votes put Bush over the top and made him the presidential victor.

There is a limited amount of work the Supreme Court can do in one year, so it has a procedure for deciding which cases to review. The losing party in a federal circuit court of appeals or in a state supreme court can begin the process by filing a document called a petition for a writ of certiorari. (A writ is a court order, and *certiorari* is a Latin word that means "to certify a court case for review.") In the petition, the party asks the Supreme Court to review the case, explaining why the case is important enough to deserve the Supreme Court's attention. If four of the nine Supreme Court justices agree to review the case, the Supreme Court issues a writ of certiorari, which allows the losing party to present its appeal to the Supreme Court. Out of the tens of thousands of petitions that the Supreme Court receives each year, it agrees to hear only around one hundred of them.

Cases and controversies: the lifeblood of the courts The federal judiciary at all levels (district courts, circuit courts of appeals, and Supreme Court) only has power to hear cases and controversies listed in the Constitution:

- ★ cases arising under the Constitution, laws, and treaties of the United States
- ★ cases affecting ambassadors and other public ministers
- ★ cases concerning the use of navigable waters
- ★ controversies in which the United States is a party
- ★ controversies between two or more states, between citizens of different states, and between citizens of the same state claiming lands under grants from different states
- ★ controversies between a state (or its citizens) and a foreign state or nation (or its citizens or subjects)

Most of the time, a case or controversy that falls into one of these categories must be brought in a federal court. State courts cannot handle these cases. One exception is cases between citizens of different states. If their dispute does not involve a federal law, they may resolve it in a state court, or they may choose to go to federal court anyway if their dispute involves an amount of money that exceeds (as of 2005) $75,000.

In cases involving ambassadors or in which a state is a party, the Supreme Court acts like a trial court and hears the case originally. In all other federal cases, the Supreme Court has appellate jurisdiction. This means the trial must first be handled by a federal district court and then might be appealed to the circuit court of appeals and, finally, to the Supreme Court by petition for certiorari.

Judicial interpretation and judicial review The plain language of Article III of the Constitution says the judiciary hears "cases and controversies." Some scholars and citizens believe that the sole power of the federal judiciary is to decide cases—that is, determine guilt or innocence in a criminal trial, and resolve a legal disagreement in a civil trial. Criminal and civil cases can both require the courts to interpret what a congressional law means, because the meaning is not always clear from the way Congress writes the laws. Such interpretation is one of the most important duties of the courts.

Federal courts, however, also exercise a power called judicial review. This is the power to review congressional and state laws that are involved in a case to decide whether the laws violate the U.S. Constitution. Some people think judicial review is necessary to prevent Congress and the president (who approves Congress's laws) from being too powerful. In other words, judicial review is part of the system of checks and balances set up by the Constitution. Others think that because the Constitution does not mention the power of judicial review, the federal judiciary should not exercise that power.

Judicial review, for example, was an important part of the case of *Elk Grove Unified School District v. Newdow*. In that case, a father named Michael Newdow sued the school district where his daughter attended public school. Newdow wanted the school to stop saying the Pledge of Allegiance because the Pledge says America is a nation "under God." Newdow, who is an atheist (a person who does not believe in God), argued that the Pledge is a religious prayer that violates the First Amendment, which prevents government from favoring one religion over others.

American Government: An Overview

The Ninth Circuit Court of Appeals agreed with Newdow, banning public schools in western states from using the Pledge. On Flag Day in June 2004, the U.S. Supreme Court reversed the ruling on a technicality. It said Newdow, who was never married to his daughter's mother and did not have custody of the child, had no power to file the lawsuit. The case, however, illustrated the controversy that arises when the Supreme Court is asked to use judicial review to strike down a widely accepted government practice based on an important constitutional right.

Because of judicial review, the federal judiciary is perhaps the branch most responsible for protecting civil liberties. These are rights that people have to be free from unreasonable governmental power. Civil liberties come primarily from the Constitution. As previously noted, the First Amendment in the Bill of Rights protects the freedoms of speech, religion, and assembly. The Fourth Amendment says the federal government may not search or arrest a person in an unreasonable fashion. The Sixth Amendment says accused criminals have a right to trial by jury and to face the witnesses against them with assistance from counsel, or a lawyer. The Eighth Amendment prevents cruel and unusual punishment. Criminal cases often require the courts to decide whether the government has violated a defendant's civil liberties.

Limiting judicial power Just as with Congress and the president, the Supreme Court and lower courts have checks on their power. One of these comes not from the Constitution, but from the makeup of the Supreme Court. Under federal law, the Supreme Court contains up to nine justices. (Nine is the accepted total, but the Court continues to function with less than nine in the event of a justice's retirement or death.) Four out of the nine must vote to hear a case by issuing a writ of certiorari in order to review it. When the justices vote on how to decide a case, five must agree in order to change the result from the courts below. This means that, in theory, one justice alone has little power, and so not much ability to abuse it.

The biggest check on judicial power is the power of Congress. If senators and representatives disagree with how the Supreme Court is interpreting a law, they can amend, or change, the law to clarify it so the Court can alter its interpretation. Congress can also pass a new law to correct a constitutional defect

American Government: An Overview

when the Supreme Court strikes a law down as unconstitutional. For example, in *Roe v. Wade* in 1972, the Supreme Court ruled that states cannot ban abortions completely because women have a constitutional right to have abortions in some cases. After that decision, states rewrote their abortion laws to ban abortions in situations allowed under the Supreme Court's ruling. For example, most states ban abortions during the last three months of pregnancy unless the abortion is necessary for the health of the mother. In addition to its lawmaking power, Congress has the power to propose constitutional amendments, which change the Constitution if approved by the legislatures or conventions in three-fourths of the states.

As for the president, when a Supreme Court justice or lower court judge retires or dies, the president gets to appoint a replacement, and the Senate confirms or rejects the president's selection. Presidents use these opportunities to fill the courts with justices and judges who agree with the president on the proper role of government and its three branches. If a majority of senators are from the same political party as the president, these appointments easily receive Senate approval. If the president and a majority of the Senate are from different political parties, the appointments can result in political battles, especially for appointments to the Supreme Court. As of 2005, presidents have nominated 148 people to the Supreme Court. The Senate has rejected twelve. The most recent rejections were during the Reagan administration with Robert H. Bork (1927–) in 1987, and twice in the Nixon administration with Clement Haynsworth Jr. (1912–1989) in 1969 and G. Harrold Carswell (1919–1992) in 1970. The Senate also has taken no action on five, and postponed voting on three, leading to unofficial rejection of these nominees.

The final significant check on the power of the judiciary is the power to remove judges from office. All officers of the federal government, including the president, vice president, and judges of the Supreme Court and lower courts, can be impeached and removed if convicted of treason, bribery, or other high crimes and misdemeanors. The House of Representatives has the sole power to impeach, or accuse, a judge of such crimes, and the Senate has the sole power to try, convict, and remove the judge from office.

As of 2005, only seven judges in the nation's history have been removed from office as a result of impeachment. The very first was John Pickering (c. 1738–1805), a federal district court judge who was impeached, convicted, and removed from office in March 1803 for drunkenness. The Pickering impeachment was a test run for Congress's real target, Supreme Court justice Samuel Chase (1741–1811), who was making speeches critical of the presidential administration of Thomas Jefferson. The House of Representatives impeached Chase in 1804. The Senate, however, voted not to convict, so Chase remained on the bench. As of 2005, he is the only Supreme Court justice to have been impeached.

For More Information

Beard, Charles A. *American Government and Politics.* 10th ed. New York: Macmillan Co., 1949.

Kelly, Alfred H., and Winfred A. Harbison. *The American Constitution: Its Origins and Development.* 5th ed. New York: W. W. Norton & Co., 1976.

McClenaghan, William A. *Magruder's American Government 2003.* Needham, MA: Prentice Hall School Group, 2002.

Roelofs, H. Mark. *The Poverty of American Politics.* 2nd ed. Philadelphia: Temple University Press, 1998.

Shelley, Mack C., II. *American Government and Politics Today.* 2004–2005 ed. Belmont, CA: Wadsworth Publishing, 2003.

Volkomer, Walter E. *American Government.* 8th ed. Upper Saddle River, NJ: Prentice Hall, 1998.

Woll, Peter. *American Government: Readings and Cases.* 15th ed. New York: Longman, 2003.

Zinn, Howard. *A People's History of the United States.* New York: HarperCollins, 2003.

Historic Roots of the Legislative Branch

The legislature is the branch in government that makes the laws. The legislature for the United States of America is called Congress. The U.S. Constitution, the blueprint for American government, divides Congress into two chambers: the Senate and the House of Representatives.

Dividing the legislature into two chambers is what political scientists call bicameralism. The word bicameralism comes from Latin words that mean "two chambers." A legislature with only one chamber is called unicameral. An example of unicameralism can be found in Nebraska, where, as of 2005, the legislature makes up the entire legislative branch of the state government.

Congress in the Constitutional Convention

In late spring and summer 1787, delegates from twelve of the thirteen American states met in Philadelphia, Pennsylvania, for a Constitutional Convention. The delegates, fifty-five white men, included Americans such as Benjamin Franklin (1706–1790), George Washington (1732–1799), James Madison (1751–1836), and Alexander Hamilton (1757–1804). At the time, America was governed under the Articles of Confederation by a unicameral Congress with no president and no judiciary, or federal court system.

The delegates to the Constitutional Convention were there to discuss how to revise America's government under the Articles of Confederation to make the government stronger. Rhode Island was the only state that refused to send delegates to the

Historic Roots of the Legislative Branch

Words to Know

Articles of Confederation: The document that established the federal government for the United States of America from 1781 to 1789.

bicameralism: The practice of dividing the legislative, or lawmaking, power of government into two chambers.

checks and balances: The specific powers in one branch of government that allow it to limit the powers of the other branches.

Congress: The legislative, or lawmaking, branch of the federal government. Congress has two chambers, the Senate and the House of Representatives.

Constitution of the United States of America: The document written in 1787 that established the federal government under which the United States of America has operated since 1789. Article I covers the legislative branch.

monarchy: A government under which power is held by a monarch, such as a king or queen, who inherits power by birth or takes it by force.

plutocracy: A government under which power is held by the wealthy class of society.

republic: A government under which power is held by the people, who elect public servants to represent them in the bodies of government.

separation of powers: Division of the powers of government into different branches to prevent one branch from having too much power.

unicameralism: The practice of placing the legislative, or lawmaking, power of government in one chamber.

---

convention. The men in control of Rhode Island wanted strong state governments, not a powerful national government.

Although they were only supposed to recommend changes to the Articles of Confederation, the delegates soon voted to recommend replacement of the Articles with a wholly new blueprint for American government. This document they would call the Constitution of the United States of America.

One of the questions the delegates faced when writing the Constitution was what kind of legislature to propose for America. History provided many examples of legislatures with more than one chamber, from the ancient Roman Republic to the British Parliament to most of the legislatures in America's first thirteen states. Political philosophers who influenced the delegates in Philadelphia had written that bicameralism was the best way to give representation in government to both the wealthy class of society and to the class of free men who did not have considerable wealth. These factors (plus the struggle between large and small states) led the delegates to recommend a bicameral legislature in the Constitution.

The Roman Republic

The Roman Republic, centered around the city of Rome (in present-day Italy), lasted from around 509 BCE to 27 BCE. The governments that ruled during this period were republican to some extent. A republican government is one in which power rests with the people, who exercise that power through elected representatives. During the Roman Republic, all free adult men were generally allowed to vote. Women and slaves could not vote, so it was not a true republic.

The Roman Republic that operated during the early part of this era is the one that most influenced the men who wrote the U.S. Constitution. Its government contained two consuls, a Senate, and two assemblies. The consuls were military generals who served as the executive heads of the Republic, much like the president of the United States. The consuls were elected by the men who served in the centuriate assembly, a body of men elected by the free adult men of the Republic. It dealt mainly with issues of war and peace.

Roman Senate The Roman Senate and the second assembly, called the tribal assembly, were the legislative bodies in the Roman Republic. The Senate was left over from the period 753 BCE to 509 BCE, when Rome was governed by a succession of seven kings. The Senate during this period acted as an advisor to the kings, who appointed the members of the Senate, mostly from the wealthy class of society. Although it was just an advisory body, the Senate, according to Marchamont Nedham in *The Excellencie of a Free-State,* insisted on having a voice in legislation:

> In old Rome, we find Romulus their first king cut into pieces by the Senate, for taking upon him to make and execute Laws at his own pleasure. And Livy tells us, that the reason why they expel'd Tarquin their last King, was, because he took the Executive and Legislative Powers both into his own hands, making himself both Legislator, and Officer, *inconsulto Senatus* without advice, and in defiance of the Senate.

Historic Roots of the Legislative Branch

When Rome became a republic around 509 BCE, the Senate remained part of its government. Just as Roman kings had appointed men to the Senate, the consuls of the republic had this power, too, so the men of the Senate continued to be drawn from the wealthy class. Although the Senate was supposed to be an advisory body without lawmaking authority, it was so powerful that its recommendations to the consuls and to the tribal assembly usually became law.

Tribal assembly The tribal assembly was the official lawmaking authority in the Republic. It was divided into geographical regions, or tribunes, where the free adult men elected their representatives to the assembly. In theory, the tribal assembly could enact laws that the people wanted without approval by the Senate. The Senate's status and power, however, effectively limited the tribal assembly's lawmaking authority to what the Senate would approve.

In the sixteenth century, a political philosopher named Niccolò Machiavelli (1469–1527; pronounced MOK-ya-VEL-lee) wrote a series of books called *Discourses on the First Ten Books of Titus Livius.* Machiavelli, whose philosophy would influence the convention delegates in Philadelphia in 1787, championed the system set up by the Roman Republic. Machiavelli said that governments have cycles that begin with monarchy (rule by one), change into aristocracy (rule by the wealthy), and change again into democracy (rule by the people). The problem with all three forms of government, he said, is that they all lead to corruption.

The Roman Republic, in Machiavelli's opinion, had solved this problem by combining in one government monarchy (the consuls), aristocracy (the Senate), and democracy (the popular assemblies):

> Fortune favored her [the Roman Republic], so that, although the authority passed successively from the kings to the nobles to the people, … yet the royal authority was never entirely abolished to bestow it upon the nobles; and these were never entirely deprived of their authority to give it to the people; but a combination was formed of the three powers, which rendered the constitution perfect, and this perfection was attained by the disunion [separation] of the Senate and the people.

Historic Roots of the Legislative Branch

Italian philosopher Niccolò Machiavelli, whose work influenced America's Founding Fathers. Time Life Pictures/ Getty Images.

The political philosophers

Unlike most Americans at the time, the delegates at the Constitutional Convention had the privilege of enjoying years of schooling and education. Classic education then involved reading the works of philosophers from western European history. These included the writings of Greek philosopher Aristotle (384 BCE–322 BCE), English philosopher John Locke (1632–1704), French philosopher Charles Montesquieu (1689–1755), and Scottish philosopher David Hume (1711–1776).

Aristotle on men of property Aristotle was a Greek scientist and philosopher whose writings defined those fields of study for

Checks and Balances *The Three Branches of the American Government* **201**

Historic Roots of the Legislative Branch

Influential Greek scientist and philosopher Aristotle, who believed government should represent three tiers of society: wealthy men, moderately wealthy men, and men without considerable wealth. © Ted Spiegel/ Corbis.

western Europe. According to Mark Roelofs in *The Poverty of American Politics,* Aristotle saw society as a collection of groups with competing interests. Those groups included extremely wealthy men, moderately wealthy men, and free men without considerable wealth. (Aristotle, like most well-known philosophers prior to the nineteenth and twentieth centuries, did not think women, children, or slaves had societal interests worthy of consideration in theories of government.)

Aristotle, says Roelofs, felt that the best way for the groups to protect their interests was for each group to have representation in government. Hence, Aristotle recommended that government have a monarch for representing the extremely wealthy, a council for representing the moderately wealthy, and an assembly for representing free men without considerable wealth. Government should not be able to pass a law or take other action, according to Aristotle, without approval by all three bodies.

The legislature proposed by the Constitutional Convention resembled Aristotle's vision in a number of respects. The House of Representatives was to be elected by people in the states who, under state law, had the right to elect representatives to their state legislatures. This generally meant free adult men who owned at least a moderate amount of property.

In contrast, the Constitution originally provided for the Senate to be selected by the legislatures of the states, not by the people. State laws usually required that the men elected to the state legislatures own a considerable amount of property. Hence, the people who would choose the senators of the United States would be men of wealth.

Finally, the U.S. Constitution generally requires that both Congress and the president approve bills for them to become law. This mirrored Aristotle's suggestion that each body of government approve governmental action in order to protect the interests of all those represented.

John Locke and the separation of powers John Locke was an English scientist and philosopher who helped launch the Age of Enlightenment. The Age of Enlightenment was a period in the seventeenth and eighteenth centuries during which men used reason to change the study of philosophy and politics. Locke's father was a country attorney, which allowed Locke to afford schooling at Christ Church college in Oxford, England.

Locke's most famous political work is called *Two Treatises of Government.* The second treatise, or essay, published in 1689, contains his theory of how government should be organized. Locke argued that the lawmaking branch of government must be separate from the executive branch, the one that executes the laws:

> The Legislative Power is that which has a right to direct how the Force of the Commonwealth shall be imploy'd for preserving the Community and the Members of it. But because those Laws which are constantly to be Executed, and whose force is to continue, may be made in a little time; therefore there is no need, that the Legislative should be always in being, not having always business to do. And because it may be too great a temptation to human frailty apt to grasp at Power, for the same Persons who have the Power of making Laws, to have also in their hands the power to execute them, whereby they may exempt themselves from Obedience to the Laws they make, and suit the Law, both in its making and execution, to their own private advantage, and thereby come to have a distinct interest from the rest of the Community, contrary to the end of Society and Government: Therefore in well order'd Commonwealths, where the good of the whole is so considered, as it ought, the Legislative Power is put into the hands of divers [diverse] Persons who duly Assembled, have by themselves, or jointly with others, a Power to make Laws, which when they have done, being separated again, they are themselves subject to the Laws, they have made; which is a new and near tie upon them, to take care, that they make them for the publick good.

The U.S. Constitution follows this advice by making the president separate from Congress. Congress, however, would grow to be in session almost year-round, contrary to Locke's opinion that legislatures need not be.

Charles Montesquieu on legislation Charles Montesquieu was a French philosopher whose *The Spirit of Laws,* published in 1748, greatly influenced the men who wrote

Historic Roots of the Legislative Branch

The title page of John Locke's Two Treatises of Government, *published in 1689.* Library of Congress.

the U.S. Constitution just four decades later. In it, Montesquieu said, "The great end of mens [sic] entering into Society, being the enjoyment of their Properties in

Peace and Safety, and the great instrument and means of that being the Laws establish'd in that Society; the first and fundamental positive law of all commonwealths, is the establishing of the Legislative Power."

Locke said much the same thing before Montesquieu. Writing in *Two Treatises of Government,* Locke said, "The great and chief end therefore, of Men's uniting into Commonwealths, and putting themselves under Government, is the Preservation of their Property."

When they used the word "Property," Montesquieu and Locke were referring not only to material wealth, but also to life and liberty, or freedom. The men who wrote the U.S. Constitution in 1787 paid particular attention to the wealth aspect of "Property" by promoting commerce, or business, through the legislative branch. The powers of Congress contained in Article I, Section 8, of the Constitution include the power to tax imports, regulate commerce and bankruptcy, coin and regulate money, punish counterfeiting (the making of fake money), and patent (protect) scientific inventions.

As for life, the Constitution of 1787 allows Congress to create an army and navy to be run by the executive branch of government for national defense.

On the subject of liberty, the Constitution prevents Congress from enacting bills of attainder or ex post facto laws. A bill of attainder is a law that convicts a person of treason or other serious crime without a trial. The Constitution defines treason as levying war against the United States or giving aid and comfort to its enemies. An ex post facto law is one that punishes a person for doing something that was not illegal when done. The Constitution also prevents Congress from eliminating the writ of habeas corpus, which is a procedure a prisoner can use to get out of jail when being held illegally. Finally, the Constitution guarantees citizens a trial by jury when accused of federal crimes, a right Great Britain sometimes denied the colonists before 1776, when America declared independence.

The Constitution of 1787 fell short of protecting liberty in one serious fashion: it protected slavery with three separate provisions. First, in calculating a state's population for determining the number of representatives the state would have in the House of

Historic Roots of the Legislative Branch

Representatives, the Constitution said each slave would count as only three-fifths of a person. Second, the Constitution prevented Congress from outlawing the importation of slaves before 1808. Third, the Constitution said that if a slave escaped to a free state, that state would have to return the slave to captivity.

David Hume on democracy David Hume was an eighteenth-century Scottish philosopher who wrote occasionally on politics. One topic that he covered was the issue of democracy. A pure democracy is a form of government in which the people themselves exercise the powers of government. Because they require the active participation of every citizen, pure democracies are impractical in large states or nations (although the Internet could conceivably change that one day).

Practicality aside, many of the Founding Fathers, the men who shaped early America, were actually hostile to the notion of democracy. John Adams (1735–1826), the country's second president, wrote in a letter to Revolutionary War leader Samuel Adams (1722–1803), "When the people, who have no property, feel the power in their own hands to determine all questions by a majority, they ever attack those who have property...."

David Hume also considered democracy dangerous. Writing in 1742 in *That Politics May Be Reduced to a Science*, Hume expressed his opinion that democracy in the Roman Republic eventually led to anarchy, the absence of law and order. Much like Aristotle, then, Hume recommended a bicameral legislature. One body, he said, should represent the nobility (men of wealth), and the other should contain representatives elected by the free men.

Charles Montesquieu on representation The Constitution established government by representation in the House of Representatives. Representation is when politicians are elected to represent the interests of citizens from a certain area. Montesquieu wrote of representation in his *Spirit of Laws:*

> As in a country of liberty, every man who is supposed a free agent ought to be his own governor; the legislative power should reside in the whole body of the people. But since this is impossible in large states, and in small ones is subject to many inconveniences, it is

Historic Roots of the Legislative Branch

Eighteenth-century Scottish philosopher David Hume, who was against democracy and for bicameralism. Library of Congress.

fit the people should transact by their representatives what they cannot transact by themselves.

The inhabitants of a particular town are much better acquainted with its wants and interests than with those of other places; and are better judges of the capacity of their neighbors than of that of the rest of their countrymen. The members, therefore, of the

Historic Roots of the Legislative Branch

legislature should not be chosen from the general body of the nation; but it is proper that in every considerable place a representative should be elected by the inhabitants.

The great advantage of representatives is, their capacity of discussing public affairs. For this the people collectively are extremely unfit, which is one of the chief inconveniences of a democracy.

Consistent with this philosophy, the Constitution provides that members are elected to the House not from the population of America generally, but "by the people of the several states." It further defines which of those "people" get to cast such a vote: "electors in each state shall have the qualifications requisite [required] for the electors of the most numerous branch of the state legislature." In other words, the right to elect representatives is governed by state law. Just as Montesquieu said only "free agents" should elect representatives, generally in 1787, only white adult men with property had the right to elect representatives under state laws and, hence, the right to elect representatives to the House.

British Parliament

The thirteen American colonies separated from Great Britain in 1776 partly because the government of Great Britain was treating them unfairly. The American Declaration of Independence from that year lists many of the colonists' complaints, primarily blaming King George III (1738–1820; reigned 1760–1820), Great Britain's monarch at the time. The king, however, was only a portion of the colonists' troubles.

The eighteenth-century legislature of Great Britain had three branches. The king and his advisory council made up one branch. The other two were the House of Lords and the House of Commons. Legislation had to be approved by all three branches to become law.

The House of Lords was often called the upper chamber of Parliament (the name for the British legislature). Its members were religious leaders, such as bishops and archbishops, and others from the noble class of English society. Instead of being elected to office, members of the House of Lords inherited their seats. This meant that the House of Lords represented the wealthiest class of English society, not the general population.

The House of Commons, also called the lower chamber, was the elective branch of Parliament. To vote in elections, though, one had to be a man who owned a certain amount of property. This meant that the House of Commons tended to represent the wealthy merchants of Great Britain.

Congress, as constructed by the Constitutional Convention of 1787, resembled Parliament in its separation of powers, its checks and balances, and its capacity to represent the wealthier members of society. It differed primarily by making office in the upper chamber (the Senate) elective rather than hereditary (passed on from one generation to the next).

Parliament and the separation of powers When Locke wrote of the separation of powers in 1689, that principle was already a celebrated feature of British government. Clement Walker, a member of Parliament in 1648, wrote that year of the way British government divided power into three branches:

> The King is the only supreme Governour of this Realme of England, to regulate and protect the people by commanding Laws to be observed and executed; and to this end He (and He alone) beareth not the Sword in vaine; yet the King by himselfe can neither make, repeal, or alter any one law, without the concurrence of both Houses of Parliament, the Legislative power residing in all three, and not in any one.

The Constitution of 1787 adopted much of this by requiring both chambers of Congress and the president of the United States to approve a bill for it to become law. An important difference, however, is that if the president rejects a bill by vetoing it, Congress can override the veto by a two-thirds vote in both chambers. In this way, the Constitution gave more lawmaking power to Congress than to the president, while in England, the power between Parliament and the monarch was equal.

Parliament and checks and balances Checks and balances refers to the ability of one branch of government, such as the

Historic Roots of the Legislative Branch

legislature, to limit the power of another branch, such as the executive. In a bicameral legislature, however, it also refers to the ability of one chamber to limit the power of the other. Writing in 1765 in *Commentaries on the Laws of England,* legal scholar William Blackstone celebrated the checks and balances of the British system:

> And herein indeed consists the true excellence of the English government, that all the parts of it form a mutual check upon each other. In the legislature, the people [House of Commons] are a check upon the nobility [House of Lords], and the nobility a check upon the people; by the mutual privilege of rejecting what the other has resolved.... Thus every branch of our civil polity supports and is supported, regulates and is regulated, by the rest; for the two houses naturally drawing in two directions of opposite interest, and the prerogative [power] in another still different from them both, they mutually keep each other from exceeding their proper limits.

Parliament and representation The House of Lords represented the nobility of Great Britain. The U.S. Constitution was written to prevent nobility from having a part in American government. Article I, Section 9, says, "No title of nobility shall be granted by the United States." The Constitution of 1787 also provided that the so-called upper chamber of Congress, the Senate, would be selected by the state legislatures every six years. Members of the Senate would not automatically hold the office for life, and the office would not be hereditary, as in the House of Lords.

Yet some of the Founding Fathers liked to think of an American nobility that would be represented by the Senate. Writing in *The Founders' Constitution,* editors Philip B. Kurland and Ralph Lerner observed, "It was generally the case that the property qualifications for electing state senators and for holding the office itself were higher and more restrictive than for electors and members of the first [lower] house." In a letter to Samuel Adams in 1790, John Adams wrote:

> The nobles have been essential parties in the preservation of liberty, whenever and wherever it has

existed. In Europe, they alone have preserved it against kings and people, wherever it has been preserved; or, at least, with very little assistance from the people.... By nobles, I mean not peculiarly an hereditary nobility, or any particular modification, but the natural and actual aristocracy among mankind. The existence of this you will not deny. You and I have seen four noble families rise up in Boston, —the Crafts, Gores, Dawes, and Austins. These are as really a nobility in our town, as the Howards, Somersets, Berties, &c., in England....

The numbers of men in all ages have preferred ease, slumber, and good cheer to liberty, when they have been in competition. We must not then depend alone upon the love of liberty in the soul of man for its preservation. Some political institutions must be prepared, to assist this love against its enemies.... The multitude [of free men], therefore, as well as the nobles, must have a check.

Colonial and state legislatures

In 1787, Americans had a century and a half of experience under state and colonial legislatures that were mostly bicameral. This history influenced the decision to propose a bicameral legislature for the new government under the Constitution.

Massachusetts England created the colony of Massachusetts by charter in 1629. A charter was a document that established the boundaries of a colony and the rules for its governance. The original charter for Massachusetts said that the free men in the colony would annually elect a governor, a deputy governor, and eighteen assistants for operating the government. The population of free men, however, would make the laws.

In 1630, the colony changed this structure so that the free men would elect only the assistants. The assistants would then elect the governor and deputy governor and be solely responsible for making the laws. In other words, Massachusetts at the end of 1630 had a unicameral legislature.

Historic Roots of the Legislative Branch

As told by Thomas F. Moran in *The Rise and Development of the Bicameral System in America,* in 1631, the men of Watertown, Massachusetts, objected to a tax law passed by the assistants. In May of the following year, some of the free men of Massachusetts met in their towns to elect two deputies from each town. The deputies were to meet in the General Court (the name for the government) to advise the governor and assistants. For the next four years, the deputies and assistants met and voted on legislation as one body of government.

In 1636, the General Court decided that the assistants and deputies should vote as separate chambers. The decision was necessary because two years earlier, a question came before the General Court that divided the assistants and deputies, namely whether the people of Newtown could move to another part of the colony. Counted together, the votes of the deputies and assistants would have approved the request. Counted alone, the votes of the assistants would have denied the request. The request was eventually resolved when the towns of Boston and Watertown gave some land to Newtown. But the deadlock over the issue made it necessary to make the deputies and assistants two chambers in a bicameral legislature.

Eight years later, sitting as a court of law, the General Court had to decide whether a pig held by a man named Captain Keayne was really owned by a poor woman named Mrs. Sherman, who claimed that the pig had wandered away. Still sitting together though counting their votes separately, the assistants and deputies divided vigorously on the question. According to Moran, "As an outcome of the controversy the General Court resolved that the two bodies should sit apart, that bills [of law] might originate in either, and that a bill having passed one house should go to the other for 'assent or dissent' [agreement or disagreement]." Hence, Massachusetts started with a unicameral legislature, but ended up with a bicameral one.

New Jersey The history of bicameralism in New Jersey is an example of the struggle between aristocracy and free men. New Jersey became a colony in February 1665. The charter was called "The Concessions and Agreement of the Lords Proprietors of the Province of New Cesarea or New Jersey to and with all and every the Adventurers and all such as shall settle or plant there." The Concessions was a contract, or agreement, between the English men, called proprietors, who would oversee the colony for Great Britain, and the free men who would settle in the colony.

The Concessions created a government composed of a governor, a council, and an assembly of deputies. The proprietors would appoint the governor, who in turn would appoint the council. The free men of New Jersey would appoint the deputies. The Concessions said that the governor, council, and deputies would serve as one body, not as three branches.

As told by Moran, the governor first called the council and deputies into session in May 1668. At the time there were seven councilors and ten deputies. The councilors insisted on sitting as a separate branch of government. Otherwise, the ten deputies could always outvote them when the free men wanted something that the proprietors did not. Although their wish was contrary to the Concessions, the councilors won the argument, at first.

By November of that year, however, the deputies refused to continue sitting separately from the council. Four years later, the free men set up a government separate from the one created by the Concessions. This led the governor and council to send two men back to England to ask the proprietors for help with the situation.

In December 1672, the proprietors signed a new document, called a Declaration. The Declaration said that under the original Concessions, the governor and council were supposed to sit together, separate from the assembly of deputies. Further, any law proposed by the deputies would have to be approved by the governor and council.

The free men of New Jersey did not like this turn of events. In October 1681, the deputies wrote a letter saying that, in their opinion, the Declaration was a violation of the original Concessions. So the deputies asked that the Declaration be nullified, or cancelled, and that the government sit as a single body.

The following month, a group of councilors visited the deputies, asking them to meet to discuss the situation. When

Historic Roots of the Legislative Branch

Benjamin Franklin and Unicameralism

Most delegates to the Constitutional Convention supported bicameralism, a legislature with two chambers. Benjamin Franklin (1706–1790), a delegate from Pennsylvania, was one of the exceptions.

One of the arguments in favor of bicameralism was that one chamber should represent the wealthy class of society, while the other should represent all free men. In 1789, the state of Pennsylvania considered a change from unicameralism to bicameralism in its government. That year, Franklin wrote *Queries and Remarks Respecting Alterations in the Constitution of Pennsylvania* to record his opposition to bicameralism.

> The Combinations of Civil Society are not like those of a Set of Merchants, who club [combine] their Property in different Proportions for Building and Freighting a Ship, and may therefore have some Right to vote in the Disposition of the Voyage in greater or less Degree according to their respective Contributions; but the important ends of Civil Society, and the personal Securities of Life and Liberty, these remain the same in every Member of the society; and the poorest continues to have an equal Claim to them with the most opulent [wealthy], whatever Difference Time, Chance, or Industry may occasion in their Circumstances. On these Considerations, I am sorry to See the Signs this Paper I have been considering [the proposed Pennsylvania Constitution] affords, of a Disposition among some of our People to commence an Aristocracy, by giving the Rich a predominancy [superior power] in Government, a Choice peculiar to themselves in one half the Legislature to be proudly called the UPPER House, and the other Branch, chosen by the Majority of the People, degraded by the denomination [name] of the LOWER; and giving to this Upper a Permanency of four Years, and but two to the lower.

Franklin felt that every member of society should have an equal say in the legislative branch of government. He disagreed with the theory of bicameralism that favored one chamber for the wealthy and another chamber for the rest of society. Pennsylvania disappointed Franklin, however, by adopting bicameralism in its new constitution.

Benjamin Franklin was a supporter of unicameralism, the practice of placing the legislative power of government in one chamber. Library of Congress.

the deputies refused, the councilors delivered a letter saying the assembly of deputies was dissolved. The letter, according to Moran, compared the deputies with the angel Lucifer, who, in Christianity, fell to hell after trying to take over heaven: "It was Lucifers Pride that Putt him upon settling himselfe where God never intended to sett him and his Presumption produced or was the forerunner of his fall."

Articles of Confederation

Beginning in 1781, the government of the United States operated under the Articles of Confederation. The Articles created a unicameral legislature, called Congress, without a separate executive and judicial branch. While the men who wrote the Constitution in 1787 rejected this structure, many of the powers of Congress under the Articles became the powers of Congress under the Constitution.

For the Founding Fathers, one of the primary purposes of federal government was to protect America in war. So the Articles of Confederation gave Congress the power to establish an army and a navy, to make the rules for their operation, and to determine questions of war and peace. Congress under the Constitution has the same powers, although the president of the United States often engages in military action without a declaration of war by Congress.

Promotion of commerce was another primary purpose of federal government for the Founding Fathers. Under the Articles of Confederation, Congress had the power to create money and post offices. It also could appoint courts for handling trials of people accused of piracy, or robbery on the high seas. Congress also had the power to regulate trade with American Indian tribes. Congress under the Constitution has all these powers, too.

Finally, Congress under the Articles had the power to make a budget and raise or borrow money for operating the nation's government. In practice, Congress had difficulty making the states contribute their share of money. This was one of the main reasons that the Founding Fathers decided to meet in 1787 to create a new federal government. The Constitution they wrote gave Congress stronger power to raise and collect money through taxes.

For More Information

BOOKS

Clark, J. C. D. *The Language of Liberty, 1660–1832.* Cambridge, Eng.: Cambridge University Press, 1994.

Kelly, Alfred H., and Winfred A. Harbison. *The American Constitution: Its Origins and Development.* 5th ed. New York: W. W. Norton & Co., 1976.

Kurland, Philip B., and Ralph Lerner. *The Founders' Constitution.* 5 vols. Indianapolis: Liberty Fund, 1987.

Lintcott, Andrew. *The Constitution of the Roman Republic.* Oxford: Clarendon Press, 1999.

Millar, Fergus. *The Roman Republic in Political Thought.* Hanover and London: Brandeis University Press and Historical Society of Israel, 2002.

Moran, Thomas Francis. *The Rise and Development of the Bicameral System in America.* Baltimore: The Johns Hopkins Press, 1895.

Nedham, Marchamont. *The Excellencie of a Free State.* London: A. Millar and T. Cadell, 1767.

Pole, J. R. *Political Representation in England and the Origins of the American Republic.* London: Macmillan, 1966.

Roelofs, H. Mark. *The Poverty of American Politics.* 2nd ed. Philadelphia: Temple University Press, 1998.

Volkomer, Walter E. *American Government.* 8th ed. Upper Saddle River, NJ: Prentice Hall, 1998.

Constitutional Role of the Legislative Branch

Fifty-five men gathered in Philadelphia, Pennsylvania, from May to September 1787 for a national convention. Their job was to propose revisions to the Articles of Confederation, the framework for American government at that time. Operating under the Articles, Congress (the only branch of the American government then) was having trouble raising money to run the government. In correspondence a year earlier between two Massachusetts politicians, Continental congressman Rufus King (1755–1827) wrote to a former Continental congressman, Elbridge Gerry (1744–1814). According to The Founders' Constitution, *King wrote, "We are without money or the prospect of it in the Federal Treasury; and the States, many of them, care so little about the Union, that they take no measures to keep a representation in Congress."*

The delegates to the Constitutional Convention were primarily from the wealthy class of society. Most were lawyers, and most either owned land and slaves or had shipping or manufacturing businesses. Half of the delegates were creditors, people who loaned money to other people. Most of them owned bonds issued by the United States, which means they had loaned money to the United States. None of the delegates were female, African American, or Native American, and none of them were poor.

Writing in *The American Constitution* in 1976, historians Alfred H. Kelly and Winfred A. Harbison said:

> The Philadelphia Convention of 1787 was one of the greatest creative assemblages [groups] of the modern

Constitutional Role of the Legislative Branch

Words to Know

Articles of Confederation: The document that established the federal government for the United States of America from 1781 to 1789.

bicameralism: The practice of dividing the legislative, or lawmaking, power of government into two chambers.

checks and balances: The specific powers in one branch of government that allow it to limit the powers of the other branches.

Congress: The legislative, or lawmaking, branch of the federal government. Congress has two chambers, the Senate and the House of Representatives.

Constitution of the United States of America: The document written in 1787 that established the federal government under which the United States of America has operated since 1789. Article I covers the legislative branch.

Constitutional Convention of 1787: Convention held in Philadelphia, Pennsylvania, from May to September 1787, during which delegates from twelve of the thirteen American states wrote a new Constitution for the United States.

federalism: A principle of government under which independent states join to form a central government to serve their collective needs.

Founding Fathers: General term for the men who founded the United States of America and designed its government. The term includes the men who signed the Declaration of Independence in 1776 and the Constitution of the United States in 1787.

ratification: The process of formally approving something, such as a treaty, constitution, or constitutional amendment.

republic: A government under which power is held by the people, who elect public servants to represent them in the bodies of government.

separation of powers: Division of the powers of government into different branches to prevent one branch from having too much power.

unicameralism: The practice of placing the legislative, or lawmaking, power of government in one chamber.

world.... It fashioned a frame of government [the U.S. Constitution] embodying the most adequate mechanism for a federal state ever achieved by man, and it produced at the same time a brilliant compromise between the requirements of adequate governmental authority and effective controls upon the exercise of political power.

In *A People's History of the United States* in 2003, historian Howard Zinn offered a different view of the convention of 1787:

The Constitution was a compromise between slave-holding interests of the South and moneyed interests of the North. For the purpose of uniting the thirteen states into one great market for commerce [business], the northern delegates wanted laws regulating interstate commerce, and urged that such laws require only a majority of Congress to pass. The South agreed to this, in return for allowing the trade in slaves to continue for twenty years before being outlawed.

The powers of Congress under the Constitution of 1787 reflect what Kelly, Harbison, and Zinn wrote. The Constitution makes Congress the lawmaking branch of the federal government. Its lawmaking powers relate mostly to either commerce or the military. While arguably making Congress the most powerful branch of government, the Constitution limits that power by creating an executive branch for enforcing the laws, and a judicial branch for deciding cases under the laws.

Separation of powers

James Madison (1751–1836) was a Virginia delegate to the Constitutional Convention who later became the fourth president of the United States. Writing in *The Poverty of American Politics,* Mark Roelofs said Madison believed the Founding Fathers faced the question of developing a government for humans, who are "prone absolutely to selfishness, competition and, no matter how disguised, a war of all against all." In other words, Madison saw government as an arrangement between the members of society, who are selfish and always competing against each other.

This attitude is reflected in the Founding Fathers' writings on the separation of powers. Separation of powers means giving the legislative, executive, and judicial powers of government to different people in different branches.

From 1787 to 1788, Madison, New York politician Alexander Hamilton (1757–1804), and Secretary of Foreign Affairs John Jay (1745–1826) wrote a series of essays called "The Federalist." They wrote the essays to convince Americans to adopt the U.S. Constitution, which had been proposed by Congress after the Constitutional Convention in September 1787. Writing in *The Federalist,* No. 47, Madison said, "The accumulation of all powers, legislative, executive, and judiciary, in the same hands, whether of one, a few, or many, and whether hereditary, self-appointed, or elective, may justly be pronounced the very definition of tyranny [dictatorship]."

John Adams (1735–1826) was a signer of the American Declaration of Independence in 1776 who would become the nation's first vice president and second president. In 1787, Adams wrote *Defence of the Constitutions of Government of the United States* to support the proposed Constitution. In it (as reprinted in *The Founders' Constitution*), Adams said that if one group of men had all three powers of government, "they would invade the liberties [freedoms] of the people, at least the majority

Washington, District of Columbia

In 1783, Congress—the governing body of America under the Articles of Confederation—met in a building called Old City Hall in Philadelphia, Pennsylvania. When the American Revolutionary War (1775–83) ended that year, Congress did not have enough money to pay all the American soldiers. In June, a large body of unpaid soldiers invaded Philadelphia to demand payment from Congress. The congressmen escaped from the capital unharmed.

Historians say this event sparked interest in setting aside a piece of land for the nation's government, a place where the government could erect forts for protection. The Constitution of 1787 approved such a plan. Article I, Section 8, said that if one or more states would cede, or give away, up to one hundred square miles of land for the federal government, Congress could accept the land and have full control over the area.

The delegates to the Constitutional Convention of 1787 offered other reasons for this plan. Speaking on July 26, Colonel George Mason (1725–1792) expressed concern that if the federal government was in the same city as a state government, it might give the federal government's work a local flavor.

James Madison (1751–1836), the delegate from Virginia who would become the fourth president of the United States, agreed. Speaking at the convention on August 11, Madison said that since American government under the Constitution would be more powerful than under the Articles of Confederation, more people would need to come to the site of government for government business. As such, it would be best for the government to be unconnected with any single state.

During the fall and winter of 1787–88, there was much debate over this part of the Constitution in the state conventions for ratifying, or approving, the new government. Some people feared that giving the new government its own city was part of a plan to make the federal government dominate the state governments. Others said it would be unfair to create a city whose inhabitants would have no control over their local government. (Since the new city would not be part of any state, the residents would have no role in electing members to Congress, which was going to have full control over the city.)

After ratification of the Constitution in 1788, the states of Maryland and Virginia offered land to the federal government in 1790 amounting to one hundred square miles around the mouth of the Potomac River. In the mid-nineteenth century, the

Constitutional Role of the Legislative Branch

of them would invade the liberties of the minority, sooner and oftener than an absolute monarchy...."

Under the Articles of Confederation, Congress had power both to make the laws and to execute, or enforce, them. When the federal convention sent the proposed Constitution to Congress on September 17, 1787, Virginia delegate George Washington (1732–1799) included a letter explaining the need for a new system with separated powers:

> The friends of our country have long seen and desired, that the power of making war, peace and treaties, that of levying money and regulating

federal government returned most of Virginia's land, leaving the federal government with the sixty-eight square miles it has occupied since then. The area became Washington, District of Columbia (or simply Washington, D.C.). President John Adams moved into the White House and Congress moved into the Capitol building there in 1800.

An 1880 drawing of the District of Columbia from the Potomac River, looking north. Drawing by C. R. Parsons. Library of Congress.

Constitutional Role of the Legislative Branch

Virginia delegate James Madison was a proponent of the concept of checks and balances. © Bettmann/Corbis.

commerce, and the correspondent executive and judicial authorities should be fully and effectually vested in the general government of the Union; but the impropriety [incorrectness] of delegating [giving] such extensive trust to one body of men is evident—Hence results the necessity of a different organization.

The Constitution of 1787 separated the powers of American government by giving Congress the power to make the laws, the president and the executive branch the power to enforce them, and the judicial branch the power to decide cases under the laws.

Checks and balances

The Constitution separated the powers of American government, but not completely. Each branch has the power to allow it to control, to some extent, the powers of the other branches. This is called the system of checks and balances.

The president, for example, checks the power of Congress with his power to veto, or reject, laws passed by Congress. In turn, Congress checks the president's power with the power to override a presidential veto by a two-thirds vote in both the House of Representatives and the Senate. The judiciary, which refers to the Supreme Court and lower federal courts, checks the power of both Congress and the president with the power to review government action to make sure it does not violate the Constitution.

When Congress proposed the new Constitution in 1787, some Americans opposed the system of checks and balances because they felt it violated the principle of separation of powers. The result, they feared, would be the tyranny that results when one person or governmental body has all three powers.

James Madison responded to these concerns in *The Federalist,* No. 47, on January 30, 1788. Using the governments of Great Britain and of the thirteen American states as examples, Madison said no government in history had separated the branches completely. Instead, he argued, the separation of powers only meant "that where the *whole* power of one department is exercised by the same hands which possess the *whole* power of another department, the fundamental principles of a free constitution, are subverted [destroyed]."

Constitutional Role of the Legislative Branch

Some scholars believe that the system of checks and balances creates a government of shared powers, not of separated powers. (For more on checks and balances, see chapters 7 and 8.)

Bicameralism and representation

After agreeing to separate the powers of government into three branches, the Founding Fathers at the Constitutional Convention had to design each branch. Historically, legislatures contained one or two chambers. A legislature with one chamber is called unicameral, and a legislature with two chambers is called bicameral. The root of these words is the Latin word *camer,* which means "chamber."

The convention of 1787 proposed that America's legislature, called Congress, be bicameral. One chamber would be called the House of Representatives, and the other would be called the Senate. For a bill to become law, both chambers of Congress would have to approve it by a simple majority. (For more information on how a bill becomes law, see chapter 6, "Daily Operations of the Legislative Branch.")

Eleven of the thirteen American states had bicameral legislatures at the time, so whether to make Congress bicameral was not a point of great debate at the convention. What the delegates argued about was the composition, or makeup, of each chamber. They had to decide how many members each state would have in each chamber, and how those members would be elected. This divided the delegates of the large states from those of the small, and the delegates in the northern states from those in the south.

Big versus small On May 27, 1787, Virginia delegate Edmund Randolph (1753–1813) presented the Virginia Plan to the convention. The Virginia Plan proposed that the free men of the states elect members to the House of Representatives (called the lower chamber at first). In turn, members of the House would choose the members of the Senate (called the upper chamber) from nominations, or proposals, made by the state legislatures.

The Virginia Plan caused great disagreement and divided the delegates according to the populations of their states. Most of the large states, including Massachusetts,

Constitutional Role of the Legislative Branch

North Carolina, Pennsylvania, South Carolina, and Virginia, wanted free men to control elections to Congress. They also wanted state population to be the basis for determining how many members each state would have in each chamber. Most of the small states, primarily Delaware, Maryland, New Jersey, and New York, wanted at least one chamber of Congress to be elected by the states, and they wanted that chamber to provide equal representation to each state.

On June 7, the large states compromised on the issue of elections when the delegates agreed that free men would elect the members of the House, and state legislatures would elect the members of the Senate. Reaching agreement on how many members each state would have in each chamber was more difficult. On June 11, Connecticut delegate Roger Sherman (1721–1793) proposed another compromise. He suggested that representation in the House be based on population, and that representation in the Senate be equal for each state.

The large states initially rejected this proposal, and there was vigorous debate on the question for a few weeks. James Madison argued that the small states had no reason to fear the large states in Congress because the large states had different economies: Massachusetts's was based on fish, Pennsylvania's on flour, and Virginia's on tobacco. Sherman argued that just as a poor man has the same single vote as a rich man, so the small states should have votes equal to the large ones. Alexander Hamilton said it was a question of neither liberty nor equality, but of power.

Debate eventually led to the compromise originally suggested by Sherman. While the delegates from the large states had enough votes not to compromise, they worried that the small states would refuse to adopt the Constitution if it did not give them equal power in one chamber. Hence, the delegates wrote the Constitution to give the states equal representation in the Senate, with two senators per state.

Looking back at the compromise almost two centuries later in *The American Constitution,* Kelly and Harbison said it proved to be harmless for the large states. In their opinion, important issues in the Senate tend to divide the senators by regions, not by the size of their states.

Constitutional Role of the Legislative Branch

Connecticut delegate Roger Sherman, who proposed that representation in the House be based on population and that representation in the Senate be equal for each state. Getty Images.

North versus South The preamble to the Constitution says one of its purposes is to "secure the blessings of liberty" for the "People of the United States." The term "people," however, did not include African Americans or other slaves. Rather than strike down slavery, the Constitution protected it.

Constitutional Role of the Legislative Branch

The three-fifths compromise on representation in the House of Representatives was one way the Founding Fathers protected slavery. The delegates to the Convention agreed that state populations would determine the number of representatives a state got in the House: at most, one representative for every thirty thousand people. The question that arose was whether slaves would count as people for calculating representation.

Delegates from the northern states, where slavery was not essential to the economy, argued that slaves should not count toward representation in the House. They said that since slaves were property, only free people should count.

The southern delegates agreed that slaves were property, but still wanted them to count for representation. That way their slave populations would increase the number of representatives they got in the House.

Under the three-fifths compromise, the delegates agreed that each slave would count as three-fifths of a person for calculating representation, as well as for calculating a state's share of direct taxes. The Constitution also protected slavery by prohibiting Congress from outlawing the importation of slaves from foreign countries until at least 1808. Finally, the Constitution required free states to return escaped slaves captured in their boundaries.

Elections

The right to vote is essential to democracy, which is government of, by, and for the people. Writer Thomas Paine (1737–1809) said this in 1795 in *Dissertation on the First Principles of Government:* "The true and only basis of representative government is equality of rights. Every man has a right to one vote, and no more in the choice of representatives. The rich have no more right to exclude the poor from the right of voting, or of electing and being elected, then the poor have to exclude the rich...."

The Constitution of 1787 failed to protect the right to vote in elections for both the House of Representatives and the Senate.

Election in the House of Representatives Benjamin Rush (1745–1813) was a physician and political leader in Pennsylvania. In 1777, he published *Observations on the Government of Pennsylvania.* One of Rush's observations was that men of moderate wealth should have representation in one

Constitutional Role of the Legislative Branch

Pennsylvania delegate Benjamin Rush, who believed that men of moderate wealth deserved representation in government, separate from those who were very wealthy.

chamber of the legislature, separate from a chamber for men of great wealth: "By a representation of the men of middling [moderate] fortunes in one house, their *whole* strength is collected against the influence of wealth."

The delegates to the Constitutional Convention designed the House of Representatives to represent free men of "middling fortunes." Article I, Section 2, says, "The House of Representatives shall be composed of members chosen every second year by the people of the several states, and the electors in each state shall have the qualifications requisite for the electors of the most numerous branch of the state legislature." This meant that only people who had the right under state law to elect members to the state House of Representatives would have the right to elect members to the federal House.

Constitutional Role of the Legislative Branch

Every state at the time had laws giving voting rights only to free white men. In addition, almost every state required a man either to own a certain amount of property or to pay a property or poll tax to have the right to vote. As of 1791, for example, Massachusetts required a voter to own property that was worth 60 pounds (a type of currency at the time) or that produced an annual income of 3 pounds. South Carolina required its voters to own either 50 acres of land or a town lot, or else to have paid a tax of 3 shillings (another currency) toward support of the government within six months of the election. The result of the various state requirements was that mostly free white men of moderate to great wealth would be electing the members of the nation's House of Representatives. Poor men, women, and slaves would not get to vote.

Madison, nonetheless, celebrated the constitutional provision for election of the House. Writing in *The Federalist,* No. 57, he said: "Who are to be the electors of the Foederal Representatives? Not the rich more than the poor; not the learned more than the ignorant; not the haughty [arrogant] heirs of distinguished names, more than the humble sons of obscure and unpropitious [unfavorable] fortune. The electors are to be the great body of the people of the United States."

To be elected to the House of Representatives, the Constitution requires only that a person be twenty-five years old, a citizen of the United States for at least seven years, and a resident of the state to be represented. Representatives serve for a term of two years, so all seats in the House are up for election every other year.

Election in the Senate Designing Congress was not just about large states against small states, or northern states against southern states. Writing in *Defence of the Constitutions of Government of the United States,* John Adams said it was a matter of rich people against poor people:

> It is agreed that "the end of all government is the good and ease of the people, in a secure enjoyment of their rights, without oppression;" but it must be remembered, that the rich are *people* as well as the poor; that they have rights as well as others; that they have as clear and as *sacred* a right to their large

Constitutional Role of the Legislative Branch

New York delegate Alexander Hamilton published The Federalist, *in which he supported a strong federal government.* Library of Congress.

property as others have to theirs which is smaller; that oppression to them is as possible and as wicked as to others; that stealing, robbing, cheating, are the same crimes and sins, whether committed against them or others. The rich, therefore, ought to have an effectual barrier in the constitution against being robbed, plundered, and murdered, as well as the poor; and this can never be without an independent senate. The poor should have a bulwark [protection] against the same dangers and oppressions; and this can never be without a house of representatives of the people.

The Constitution of 1787 provided that the two senators for each state would be chosen by the state legislatures instead of by popular elections. State laws generally required members of their legislatures to own a certain amount of property, usually even more than was required to vote in state elections. This meant that the state legislators who would be choosing the nation's senators would be mostly from the wealthy class of society.

The Constitution requires that to be a senator, a person must be at least thirty years old, a citizen of the United States for at least nine years, and a resident of the state to be represented. Senators are elected to serve for periods of six years. For election purposes, the senators are divided into three groups, so that approximately one-third of the seats in the Senate are up for election every two years.

Powers of Congress

Alexander Hamilton was a delegate from New York to the Constitutional Convention and would be the nation's first secretary of the treasury. The secretary of the treasury is the head of the Department of Treasury, which is the unit in the executive branch that is responsible for the nation's monetary policies.

On December 18, 1787, Hamilton published *The Federalist,* No. 23, which contained his defense of the need for a strong federal government. In it, Hamilton said, "The principal purposes to be answered by Union are these—The common defence of the members—the preservation of the public peace as well against internal convulsions [disturbances] as external attacks—the regulation of commerce with other nations and between the States—the superintendence [supervision] of our

Property as Liberty

When John Adams wrote of liberty in *Defence of the Constitutions of Government of the United States,* he was referring mainly to the freedom to acquire and keep property:

> The original meaning of the word *republic* could be no other than a government in which the property of the people predominated and governed; and it had more relation to property than liberty. It signified a government, in which the property of the public, or people, and of every one of them, was secured and protected by law. This idea, indeed, implies liberty; because property cannot be secure unless the man be at liberty to acquire, use, or part with it, at his discretion, and unless he have his personal life and limb, motion and rest, for that purpose. It implies, moreover, that the property and liberty of all men, not merely of a majority, should be safe; for the people, or public, comprehends more than a majority, it comprehends all and every individual; and the property of every citizen is a part of the public property, as each citizen is a part of the public, people, or community. The property, therefore, of every man has a share in government, and is more powerful than any citizen, or party of citizens; it is governed only by the law.

John Adams wrote of property as liberty in his Defence of the Constitutions of Government of the United States. Library of Congress.

intercourse [interaction], political and commercial, with foreign countries."

Commerce The Founding Fathers were concerned that American commerce was too restricted under the Articles of Confederation. At the time of the Constitutional Convention, commerce was being regulated separately by the thirteen American states. In *Vices of the Political System of the United States* (as reprinted in *The Founders' Constitution*), James Madison wrote, "The practice of many States in restricting the commercial intercourse with other States, and putting their productions and manufactures on the same footing with those of foreign nations, though not contrary to the federal articles, is certainly adverse to the spirit of the Union...."

George Washington agreed. In a letter to Massachusetts politician James Warren on October 7, 1785 (as reprinted in *The Founders' Constitution*), he said, "We have abundant reason to be convinced, that the spirit for Trade which pervades these States is not to be restrained; it behooves us then to establish just principles; and this, any more than other matters of national concern, cannot be done by thirteen heads differently constructed and organized. The necessity, therefore, of a controlling power is obvious." Writing a year later to John Jay, who would be the first chief justice of the U.S. Supreme Court, Washington said, "Experience has taught us, that men will not adopt and carry into execution, measures the best calculated for their own good, without the intervention of a coercive power."

In 1787, many of the Founding Fathers felt America desperately needed such a coercive power. Great Britain, at the time, was preventing American businesses from exporting (sending) their goods for sale in the former motherland. Americans, however, were spending lots of money on goods imported from (sent from) Great Britain and its colonies. In the *Continentalist* in 1782, Hamilton wrote that one advantage of letting Congress control commerce with other nations would be to help America enjoy a better balance of trade. By taxing or restricting imports from Great Britain, America could pressure Great Britain to allow more commerce to come from America.

Tax revenue was another benefit to be obtained from national regulation of commerce, according to Hamilton. This was especially attractive because America still had large debts from the American Revolution (1775–83). Hamilton wrote:

> No mode can be so convenient as a source of revenue to the United States. It is agreed that imposts [taxes] on trade, when not immoderate [too large], or improperly laid, is one of the most eligible species [types] of taxation. They fall in a great measure upon articles not of absolute necessity, and being partly transferred to the price of the commodity [object of commerce], are so far imperceptibly [unknowingly] paid by the consumer. It

is therefore that mode which may be exercised by the foederal government with least exception or disgust.

At the Constitutional Convention, the delegates debated the wisdom of giving Congress the power to regulate commerce. The northern states, which had manufacturing businesses being restricted by Great Britain's policies, tended to favor giving the power to Congress. The southern states, especially cotton-producing South Carolina and Georgia, were not as interested in the idea. They were not having trouble exporting cotton, a raw material, to other countries. They also did not want Congress to be able to outlaw or regulate the slave trade.

Writing in *The Federalist,* No. 42, in January 1788, Madison argued that Congress needed more than the power to regulate commerce with foreign nations. He said it also needed power to regulate commerce between the individual states. Otherwise, states that imported goods from foreign countries could add further taxes to ship the goods to other states.

The northern states got their commercial wishes in the Constitution. The powers of Congress under Article I, Section 8, include the power to tax imports, regulate commerce between states and with foreign nations and Indian tribes, coin and regulate money, punish counterfeiting (the making of fake money), and patent, or protect, scientific inventions. In exchange, the southern states got a promise in the Constitution that Congress would not outlaw the slave trade before 1808. (Many of the Founding Fathers, including Thomas Jefferson [1743–1826] and Patrick Henry [1736–1799], knew slavery was wrong and had to be outlawed eventually, even though they owned slaves, too.)

Military The Founding Fathers wanted a strong army and navy for America. They were not concerned only about defending America from attack by foreign nations and Native Americans. American commerce relied heavily on water transportation, and a strong navy was important for defending commercial vessels from piracy, or robbery on the high seas.

The Founding Fathers also wanted a strong army for crushing protests and rebellions by American citizens. Shays's Rebellion of 1780 in Massachusetts was one of the most famous. As told by Howard Zinn in *A People's History of the United States,* farmers in western Massachusetts were upset with the state legislature in

Constitutional Role of the Legislative Branch

Massachusetts farmer Daniel Shays and his supporters occupy a Massachusetts courthouse in protest of the state government's handling of financial issues pertaining to farmers. The protest became known as Shays's Rebellion. © Bettmann/Corbis.

Boston, because a new state constitution in 1780 had raised the property qualifications for voting. They were also upset that the legislature was refusing to issue paper money for helping farmers get out of debt. Some of the farmers, including Daniel Shays (1747?–1825), were in debt because the United States did not have money to pay them for their service in the American Revolutionary War.

Local authorities began to put farmers in jail and to seize their cattle and lands for failure to pay their debts. Farmers responded by gathering in groups of hundreds, marching to county courthouses, and forcing judges to delay trials until the farmers could go to Boston to seek relief from the legislature. The farmers sometimes released their jailed neighbors from prison.

Checks and **Balances** *The Three Branches of the American Government*

Constitutional Role of the Legislative Branch

On September 19, 1780, eleven leaders of the rebellion were charged in the Supreme Judicial Court in Boston with violating the law. This is when Shays entered the story, organizing a group of protesters to march to Springfield, Massachusetts, where the court planned to try the leaders for their crimes. The state rallied its militia to confront the protesters, resulting in fighting and bloodshed that lasted into the winter, when the outnumbered farmers gave up. Many were put on trial and imprisoned, and some were hung for the rebellion. Shays escaped to Vermont, returning to Massachusetts only after being pardoned, or officially forgiven, for his crimes.

When the Constitutional Convention met in the summer of 1787, many delegates, including Alexander Hamilton, wanted to give the federal government strong military powers. Writing in *The Federalist,* Hamilton referred to the danger of Shays's Rebellion.

In 1776, the authors of the American Declaration of Independence had complained of the tendency of British king George III (1738–1820; reigned 1760–1820) to keep standing armies in America even during times of peace. The colonists felt these armies were there to deprive them of their freedoms, or at least to prevent them from protesting or rebelling against the British government. Opposition to standing armies was a large part of opposition to the Constitution during the fall and winter of 1787–88, when state conventions were considering whether to ratify it. Writing in October 1787, a man who called himself a "Democratic Federalist" said that standing federal armies were entirely unnecessary because the state militias could do the job of defending a region from unexpected attack.

Hamilton disagreed. He argued that once people decided to create a government for common defense, they had to give it all powers necessary for defense. Hamilton wrote in *The Federalist,* No. 23, "These powers ought to exist without limitation: Because it is impossible to foresee or define the extent and variety of national exigencies [emergencies], or the correspondent extent & variety of the means which may be necessary to satisfy them."

Influential philosophers had advised against giving all power over the military to one branch of government. In *Wealth of Nations* in 1776 (as reprinted in *The Founders' Constitution*), for instance, Scottish economist Adam Smith (1723–1790) reminded readers how British statesman Oliver Cromwell (1599–1658) used the military to run the British Parliament out of office in the seventeenth century. The delegates took this advice to heart, proposing to separate the power to create and fund the military and the power to declare war from the power to operate the military. Under Article I, Section 8, of the Constitution, Congress has all of these powers except the power to operate the military. The president is the one who operates the military as commander in chief under Article II, Section 2.

Taxation A government needs money to operate. Taxation is how a government raises most of its money. Congress's powers of taxation under the Articles of Confederation were not very strong. It could not collect a tax on goods imported into the country. It could not collect taxes directly from the citizens, but instead had to ask the states to contribute their share of the federal government's expenses. These taxes, called requisitions, were often ignored by the states, according to James Madison in his *Preface to Debates in the Convention of 1787* (as reprinted in *The Founders' Constitution*):

> It was seen that the public debt rendered so sacred by the cause in which it had been incurred [the Revolutionary War] remained without any provision for its payment. The reiterated [repeated] and elaborate efforts of Cong. to procure from the States a more adequate power to raise the means of payment had failed. The effect of ordinary requisitions of Congress had only displayed the inefficiency of the [authority] making them; none of the States having duly [timely] complied with them, some having failed altogether or nearly so; and in one instance, that of N. Jersey, a compliance was expressly refused....

The Constitution of 1787 changed this. Article I, Section 8, says, "Congress shall have power ... to lay and collect taxes, duties, imposts and excises...." Duties and imposts are taxes on goods imported into the country. Excises are taxes on the manufacture, sale, or consumption of goods within the country.

The Constitution specifically forbids Congress from taxing exports. Delegates from southern states insisted on this provision. Their cotton and rice growers did not want to face an export tax to sell their crops to people in foreign countries.

Constitutional Role of the Legislative Branch

The state conventions adopted the Constitution despite vocal opposition to Congress's proposed powers of taxation. Some people feared that federal taxation would prevent state governments from collecting taxes, too. A person called "Brutus" wrote (as reprinted in *The Founders' Constitution*) that Congress's new taxes would "include poll [voting] taxes, land taxes, excises, duties [postage] on written instruments, on every thing we eat, drink, or wear; they take hold of every species of property, and come home to every man's house and packet. These are often so oppressive, as to grind the face of the poor, and render the lives of the common people a burden to them." (People writing public letters in the eighteenth century often used fake names to protect themselves from being punished for speaking harshly of the government.)

At Connecticut's ratifying convention in 1788, delegate Oliver Ellsworth (1745–1804) argued (as reprinted in *The Founders' Constitution*) that Congress would not, as Brutus feared, use its tax powers to oppress the states: "They [Congress] are the head, and will take care that the members do not perish."

Other powers The Constitution gives many other powers to Congress. Congress alone can admit new states into the United States. Congress also has sole authority to make rules and regulations for American territories that are not states, such as Puerto Rico and Guam (which have been territories since America captured them during the Spanish-American War in 1898).

If it wants to change the Constitution, Congress, by a two-thirds vote in each chamber, can propose amendments. Amendments can also be proposed by two-thirds of the state legislatures. For a proposed amendment to become part of the Constitution, three-fourths of either the state legislatures or state conventions must ratify it. Congress gets to make the determination between state legislatures or conventions.

Necessary and Proper Clause The last paragraph of Article I, Section 8, of the Constitution contains a highly controversial provision called the Necessary and Proper Clause. It gives Congress the power "to make all laws which shall be necessary and proper for carrying into execution … all other power vested by this constitution in the government of the United States, or in any department or officer thereof."

When the state conventions were debating whether to ratify the Constitution, the Necessary and Proper Clause received a lot of newspaper coverage. Writing that fall of 1787, a person called the "Centinel" argued that the clause would allow Congress to strike down any state laws it did not like. Another person, using the name "An Old Whig," called the clause an "undefined, unbounded and immense power." (The term whig referred to a political party in England that generally supported democratic reform of English government to make it more representative of the people's interests.) Writing in October, "Brutus" said, "The powers given by this article are very general and comprehensive, and it may receive a construction [interpretation] to justify the passing almost any law. A power to make all laws ... may, for ought I know, be exercised in such a manner as entirely to abolish the state legislatures."

Alexander Hamilton wrote *The Federalist,* No. 33, to address these fears. Hamilton said the clause had been "held up to the people, in all the exaggerated colours of misrepresentation ... as the hideous monster whose devouring jaws would spare neither sex nor age, nor high nor low, nor sacred nor profane." Hamilton argued that in reality, the clause added nothing to the Constitution. Even without it, he said, Congress would have an implied power to make any law it needed to carry out its specific powers or those of the rest of the government. Three years later, in 1791, Hamilton would argue for a different interpretation of the clause as secretary of the treasury under president George Washington, an interpretation that would give Congress tremendous power. (See chapter 4, "Changes in the Legislative Branch.")

For More Information

Beard, Charles A. *An Economic Interpretation of the Constitution of the United States.* New York: Macmillan, 1935.

Kelly, Alfred H., and Winfred A. Harbison. *The American Constitution: Its Origins and Development.* 5th ed. New York: W. W. Norton & Co., 1976.

Kurland, Philip B., and Ralph Lerner. *The Founders' Constitution.* 5 vols. Indianapolis: Liberty Fund, 1987.

Levy, Leonard W. *Original Intent and the Framers' Constitution.* New York: Macmillan, 1988.

Moran, Thomas Francis. *The Rise and Development of the Bicameral System in America.* Baltimore: The Johns Hopkins Press, 1895.

Pole, J. R. *Political Representation in England and the Origins of the American Republic.* London: Macmillan, 1966.

Roelofs, H. Mark. *The Poverty of American Politics.* 2nd ed. Philadelphia: Temple University Press, 1998.

Volkomer, Walter E. *American Government.* 8th ed. Upper Saddle River, NJ: Prentice Hall, 1998.

Wolfensberger, Donald R. *Congress and the People.* Washington, DC, and Baltimore: Woodrow Wilson Center Press and Johns Hopkins University Press, 2000.

Zinn, Howard. *A People's History of the United States.* New York: HarperCollins, 2003.

Changes in the Legislative Branch

Congress is the legislative branch of the federal government, the branch that makes the laws. The men who wrote the Constitution at a federal convention in summer 1787 created Congress to promote American commerce (business), protect property, and provide a strong military. (See chapter 3, "Constitutional Role of the Legislative Branch.") According to Howard Zinn in A People's History of the United States, *by protecting property and promoting commerce, the Constitution did "enough for small property owners, for middle-income mechanics [skilled workers] and farmers, to build a broad base of support."*

Changes in the powers of Congress since 1787 have had two main themes. One is the expansion of power through the interpretation of Congress's role under the Constitution. The other involves efforts by the American people to drive democracy, which means government of, by, and for all people, into the Constitution.

The Bill of Rights

A bill of rights is a statement of the basic rights that citizens have in a society. When the Constitutional Convention began in May 1787, each of the thirteen American states had some kind of bill of rights in its constitution. The idea of putting a bill of rights into the federal constitution, however, did not come up until near the end of the convention in September. Delegates George Mason (1725–1792) of Virginia and Elbridge Gerry

Changes in the Legislative Branch

Words to Know

Bill of Rights: The first ten amendments to the U.S. Constitution, proposed in 1789 and adopted in 1791. The Bill of Rights contains some of the rights of citizens of the United States of America.

checks and balances: The specific powers in one branch of government that allow it to limit the powers of the other branches.

Congress: The legislative, or lawmaking, branch of the federal government. Congress has two chambers, the Senate and the House of Representatives.

Constitution of the United States of America: The document written in 1787 that established the federal government under which the United States of America has operated since 1789. Article I covers the legislative branch.

Constitutional Convention of 1787: Convention held in Philadelphia, Pennsylvania, from May to September 1787, during which delegates from twelve of the thirteen American states wrote a new Constitution for the United States.

federalism: A principle of government under which independent states join to form a central government to serve their collective needs.

Founding Fathers: General term for the men who founded the United States of America and designed its government. The term includes the men who signed the Declaration of Independence in 1776 and the Constitution of the United States in 1787.

income tax: A tax on the money and property that a person earns during the year.

Interstate Commerce Clause: The clause in Article I, Section 8, of the Constitution that gives Congress the power "to regulate commerce . . . among the several states."

Necessary and Proper Clause: The clause in Article I, Section 8, of the Constitution that gives Congress the power "to make all laws which shall be necessary and proper" for exercising the other powers of the federal government.

ratification: The process of formally approving something, such as a treaty, constitution, or constitutional amendment.

republic: A government under which power is held by the people, who elect public servants to represent them in the bodies of government.

separation of powers: Division of the powers of government into different branches to prevent one branch from having too much power.

suffrage: The right to vote.

(1744–1814) of Massachusetts supported the idea, but voting by states, the delegates defeated it ten votes to zero.

After finishing the Constitution, the convention presented it to Congress, which was America's governing body under the Articles of Confederation. Congress presented the Constitution to the states, whose representatives faced the question of whether to ratify, or adopt, it as the new framework for American government. This issue divided the white men of the country into two main groups. The Federalists, led by New York delegate

Alexander Hamilton (1757–1804) and Virginia delegate James Madison (1751–1836), favored ratification. The Federalists called their opponents, those who were against ratification, Antifederalists.

Generally speaking, Federalists favored a strong national government, while Antifederalists wanted strong state governments. The Antifederalists feared that the Constitution would weaken state governments, possibly bringing statehood to an end. Men who lived near the Atlantic coast, where commerce was important, were mostly Federalists. Men who lived inside the country, on farms and the frontier, were mostly Antifederalists. (Women generally could not participate in political affairs then, so their views are not well known.)

To vote on whether to ratify the Constitution, states had to form their own conventions. They did so by having the people who could vote, mostly white men who owned a certain amount of property, elect delegates (representatives). State voting districts at the time unfairly gave greater representation to coastal areas than to the interior farms and frontiers. The combination of property requirements for voting and unfair representation of the coastal areas gave the Federalists a strong voice in the state conventions. According to Alfred H. Kelly and Winfred A. Harbison in *The American Constitution*, "Probably not more than three per cent of the male population actually balloted [voted] upon the choice of delegates to the various state conventions."

Despite their advantage, the Federalists were not assured of victory in the struggle for ratification. According to the Constitution, nine state conventions had to approve it for it to become law between those states. Seven states ratified the Constitution easily, but the vote was close in Massachusetts, New Hampshire, New York, and Virginia. (North Carolina and Rhode Island did not ratify the Constitution until after the new federal government was in operation.)

The absence of a bill of rights in the proposed Constitution led to much debate. The Federalists tried to convince the Antifederalists that a bill of rights was unnecessary because the federal government's power was limited under the Constitution. They also said that citizens' rights were inferred in the Constitution, meaning they were understood to be there without specifically being mentioned.

Changes in the Legislative Branch

A copy of the Bill of Rights.
National Archives and Records Administration.

Antifederalists disagreed. In a letter to James Madison in December 1787 (as reprinted in *The Founders' Constitution*), fellow Virginia politician Thomas Jefferson (1743–1826) said, "A bill of rights is what the people are entitled to against every government on earth, general or particular, and what no just [fair] government should refuse, or rest on inference."

The Federalists proposed a compromise. They promised that if the Antifederalists would vote for ratification, they would support amendment of the Constitution afterwards to include a bill of rights. This worked, and by the end of June 1788, ten states had ratified the Constitution. In their ratifying documents, Massachusetts and other states included a description of the rights they wanted to see in a federal bill of rights.

In 1789, Congressman James Madison of Virginia took responsibility for turning the states' suggestions into proposed constitutional amendments. His goal, as quoted in *The Founders' Constitution,* was "to satisfy the public mind that their liberties will be perpetual [ongoing], and this without endangering any part of the constitution." Madison ultimately crafted twelve

Changes in the Legislative Branch

amendments, and by 1791 the states had ratified ten. These first ten amendments came to be called the Bill of Rights. Many of them contain limitations on the power of Congress.

The First Amendment The First Amendment says, "Congress shall make no law respecting an establishment of religion, or prohibiting the free exercise thereof; or abridging [lessening] the freedom of speech, or of the press; or the right of the people peaceably to assemble, and to petition to Government for a redress [remedy] of grievances."

This Amendment contains some of America's most cherished freedoms, including the freedoms of religion and speech. The freedom of religion has come to mean that Americans can worship or not worship as they choose. In 1789, however, the amendment was designed to keep Congress out of religion in order to leave religion to the states. The Massachusetts Constitution of 1780, for example, gave the state legislature power to require people to attend public education on God and morality. The Virginia Constitution, in contrast, protected religious freedom, at least for Christians.

Freedom of speech is the right to speak and write without restriction. The freedom, however, is not absolute. According to the U.S. Supreme Court, the freedom of speech prevents the government from banning speech or writings. The government may, however, punish a person for speech or writings that injure another person or the government. For example, the government cannot stop a person from saying or printing something false about another person. But if the person makes the statement knowing it is false, the injured person can sue for damages. The person who made the false statement cannot escape responsibility by saying he or she was simply exercising the freedom of speech.

Congress, however, is allowed to regulate the time, place, and manner of speech, as long as its regulation is reasonable. Congress can also punish speech that it considers harmful. (*See* sidebar, "The Sedition Act of 1798 and the Espionage Act of 1917.") Some Americans believe Congress should be able to punish harmful speech. Others believe that the power to punish is the power to prevent speech in the first place, and that what is harmful differs from person to person.

The Second Amendment The Second Amendment says, "A well regulated Militia, being necessary to the security of a free State,

Changes in the Legislative Branch

The Sedition Act of 1798 and the Espionage Act of 1917

The First Amendment says Congress shall not abridge, or lessen, the freedom of speech. The United States adopted the amendment in 1791. Many Americans thought it would prevent Congress from punishing them for freely speaking or publishing their opinions about the government. The Sedition Act of 1798 destroyed this notion.

In 1798, John Adams (1735–1826) was president. Adams and most members of Congress were Federalists, a political party that wanted a strong national government. The French Revolution (1787–99) and rebellions in Ireland made the Federalists fearful of antigovernment speech in the United States, especially with growing numbers of French and Irish immigrants in America. Federalists were also preparing for war with France because France was interfering with American merchant vessels on the high seas.

To discourage antigovernment speech, Congress passed and Adams signed the Sedition Act of 1798. According to Howard Zinn in *A People's History of the United States*, "The Sedition Act made it a crime to say or write anything 'false, scandalous and malicious' against the government, Congress, or the President, with intent to defame them, bring them into disrepute, or excite popular hatreds against them."

Ten Americans were convicted and imprisoned under the Sedition Act. Sitting on federal courts of appeals, every member of the U.S. Supreme Court said the Sedition Act did not violate the Constitution. The First Amendment, they said, only prevents Congress from stopping people from speaking in the first place. It does not prevent Congress from punishing people for what they say if Congress thinks their speech is harmful.

The men convicted and imprisoned under the Sedition Act were mostly journalists who belonged to the Republican Party (historically known as the Democratic-Republican Party to differentiate it from the modern Republican Party). The Republican Party was the largest rival of the Federalist Party. Republicans generally supported strong state governments and limited power in the federal government. Republican Thomas Jefferson, who was vice president under Adams, secretly helped his home state of Virginia draft a resolution for protesting against the Sedition Act. After 1800, when Jefferson won election to the presidency and Republicans gained control of Congress, Congress repealed the Sedition Act.

the right of the people to keep and bear Arms, shall not be infringed." The reason for this Amendment was to make sure people could have weapons for protection. Americans wanted to protect themselves not only from attack, but also from injustice by an unfair government. They even wanted the ability to overthrow the government if necessary, as the American colonists had overthrown Great Britain in the American Revolution (1775–83).

Today the Second Amendment is primarily used to defend the right to have weapons for self-protection and for hunting and sportsmanship. Overthrowing the federal government with guns and rifles is unlikely when the government is armed with nuclear weapons. Despite the original purpose of the Second Amendment,

Changes in the Legislative Branch

In 1917, during World War I (1914–18), Congress passed the Espionage Act. The Act makes it illegal, when the United States is at war, to interfere with the enlistment of soldiers in military service.

In June 1918, a labor leader named Eugene Debs (1855–1926), who later ran for president as the Socialist Party's nominee, gave an antiwar speech outside a prison where three men were being held for opposing the military draft. According to Zinn, Debs said:

> They tell us we live in a great free republic; that our institutions are democratic; that we are a free and self-governing people.... Wars throughout history have been waged for conquest and plunder.... And that is war in a nutshell. The master [wealthy] class has always declared the wars; the subject [poor] class has always fought the battles....

Debs was convicted under the Espionage Act because it was deemed that his speech might prevent young people from enlisting in the military. He spent three years in prison until he was pardoned by President Warren G. Harding (1865–1923; served 1921–23) and released in 1921.

Eugene Debs, who was convicted under the Espionage Act of 1917 for inappropriate speech. Library of Congress.

the federal government is unlikely to allow people to have nuclear weapons for overthrowing the government if necessary, and many Americans would agree with such a restriction.

The Eighth Amendment The Eighth Amendment says, "Excessive bail shall not be required, nor excessive fines imposed, nor cruel and unusual punishments inflicted." This Amendment limits the punishment Congress can impose in its criminal laws.

The Eighth Amendment is part of the national debate over capital punishment, or the death penalty. Many people think the death penalty is cruel, is used most often to execute minorities, and sometimes results in the execution of innocent people. The U.S.

Supreme Court, however, has ruled that the death penalty does not violate the Eighth Amendment because the death penalty was widely accepted when America adopted the Bill of Rights in 1791 and has continued to be acceptable to most Americans. According to a Harris Poll in January 2004, more than two-thirds of Americans support the death penalty. Some people who support the death penalty believe it discourages people from committing murder. Whether or not this is true, some people also believe death is a just and fair punishment for killing another person.

The Tenth Amendment The Tenth Amendment says that any power not specifically given to the federal government is reserved for the state governments and for the people of the nation. Adoption of this amendment increased the importance of defining Congress's specific powers under the Constitution. Since 1789, when the federal government began to operate under the Constitution, Congress's powers have grown tremendously, especially under the Necessary and Proper Clause and the Interstate Commerce Clause of the Constitution.

The Necessary and Proper Clause: *McCulloch v. Maryland*

Article I, Section 8, of the Constitution gives Congress the general power "to make all laws which shall be necessary and proper for carrying into execution" the specific powers of Congress and the federal government. This is called the Necessary and Proper Clause.

The Necessary and Proper Clause was a source of great controversy during ratification of the Constitution. Antifederalists feared it would give Congress unlimited authority to do anything it wanted to do. They felt that listing the specific powers of Congress should be enough.

Federalist Alexander Hamilton responded to these concerns in an interesting way. Writing in 1788, he said that in reality, the Necessary and Proper Clause did not add anything to the Constitution. It only clarified that when Congress has a specific power, it can do anything it needs to do to exercise that power. Hamilton said, however, that it was important to include the clause in the Constitution so that people would not try to restrict Congress's specific powers.

Changes in the Legislative Branch

Interpretation of the Necessary and Proper Clause became important in 1791, in the middle of President George Washington's (1732–1799; served 1789–97) first term in office. Alexander Hamilton was then secretary of the treasury under Washington. The secretary of the treasury is the head of the Department of the Treasury, which is the office in the executive branch that governs the nation's monetary policies.

According to Kelly and Harbison, Hamilton "had a strong conviction that control of government should be lodged in the hands of the manufacturing, commercial, and landed aristocracies. Hamilton therefore favored an efficient, coercive, and highly centralized state [national government], which would foster commerce, manufacturing, and capitalistic development." By coercive, Kelly and Harbison meant that Hamilton wanted the federal government to have power to impose national economic plans on the states. To reach this goal, Hamilton spent much time from 1790 to 1791 devising a financial, or monetary, plan for the federal government. One of Hamilton's proposals was to ask Congress to open a national bank.

Controversy erupted in the federal government. Nowhere did the Constitution specifically give Congress the power to open a bank. President Washington asked Hamilton and Secretary of State Thomas Jefferson to give him written opinions on whether Congress could open a bank under any of its general powers, including its power under the Necessary and Proper Clause.

Jefferson submitted his opinion on February 15, 1791. He said Congress lacked the power to open a national bank. Jefferson focused on the word "necessary" in the Necessary and Proper Clause. He argued that Congress could exercise its specific powers, such as imposing taxes, borrowing money, paying national debts, and regulating commerce, without opening a national bank. A national bank, therefore, was not necessary

Hamilton responded to Jefferson eight days later. He wrote that Jefferson's understanding of the word "necessary" was too narrow. Hamilton said the word necessary could mean just "useful." Since a national bank would be useful for exercising Congress's specific powers, it was permitted by the Constitution. Hamilton won the argument, and Congress opened the Bank of the United States with branches throughout the country.

The controversy, however, was not over. Thanks to a poor economy and conflict with state banks, the Bank of the United

Changes in the Legislative Branch

In 1791, Secretary of State Thomas Jefferson (right) told President George Washington that he believed Congress did not have the power to establish a national bank.

States became unpopular in areas in the south and west where commerce was not as important as in the north and east. Conflicts involved efforts by the Bank of the United States to restrict the volume of loans made by private banks chartered by the states. Some people saw such regulation as a violation of states' rights. Eventually, some states in these regions tried to get rid of the national bank's branches in their borders, either by outlawing them or by taxing them heavily. Maryland chose the latter strategy, laying a heavy tax on the Baltimore branch in 1818.

When the Baltimore branch violated the tax law, Maryland sued the branch manager, James W. McCulloch, in county court. The case, called *McCulloch v. Maryland,* went all the way to the U.S. Supreme Court. There, the Court had to decide whether Congress had the power to open a national bank.

On March 6, 1819, Chief Justice John Marshall (1755–1835) announced the Court's decision. He said Congress had implied power under the Necessary and Proper Clause to open a national bank, even though it did not have specific power to do so. Marshall said that "necessary and proper" did not mean "absolutely indispensable." Instead, when Congress has a specific power under the Constitution, the Necessary and Proper Clause lets it do anything that is "appropriate" for exercising that power. Marshall's written decision echoed Hamilton's opinion to Washington of twenty-eight years earlier. Every associate justice on the Supreme Court agreed with the decision, which strengthened Congress's powers of legislation.

The Interstate Commerce Clause

Commerce means the transportation and sale of goods and services. Interstate commerce is commerce between two or more states, and foreign commerce is commerce with foreign states or nations. When the constitutional convention met in 1787, Congress did not have the power to regulate interstate or foreign commerce. Instead, the thirteen American states each had their own commercial laws. To raise money, states often passed laws to tax goods brought from other states. At the same time, Great Britain passed laws banning many American products from that empire, which hurt producers of those goods in America.

The men who wrote the Constitution wanted to give Congress the power to deal with such situations. They did so with the Commerce Clause in Article I, Section 8: "The Congress shall have power ... to regulate commerce with foreign nations, and among the several states, and with the Indian tribes."

The portion of this clause relating to commerce among the several states is called the Interstate Commerce Clause. For the first century after the foundation of the new government in 1789, Congress used this power mostly to prevent the states from restricting interstate commerce.

Changes in the Legislative Branch

John Marshall, chief justice of the U.S. Supreme Court from 1801 to 1835.

By the late 1800s, commerce in America had grown greatly thanks to the Industrial Revolution. This was a period in which machines, steam power, electricity, and oil replaced human skill and animal power in the production of goods. The industrial boom led to greater regulation of commerce by Congress, which resulted in an increase in the number of cases requiring the U.S. Supreme Court to interpret Congress's power under the Interstate Commerce Clause.

In an 1824 case called *Gibbons v. Ogden,* Chief Justice Marshall said the Interstate Commerce Clause gave Congress complete power over commerce that "concerns more than one state," but probably not over commerce that concerns "the completely interior traffic of a state."

In the first half of the 1900s, the U.S. Supreme Court changed this interpretation, greatly expanding Congress's power under the Interstate Commerce Clause. The Court said that if a particular business activity can have a substantial effect on interstate commerce, Congress may regulate it, even if the activity itself is not part of interstate commerce. This meant, for example, that Congress could regulate the price of train trips inside a state (*Houston, E. & W. Tex. Ry. v. United States*), or the production of wheat that would be used entirely on the producing farm instead of sold in interstate commerce (*Wickard v. Filburn*).

Congress's power under this expanded interpretation of the Interstate Commerce Clause has allowed it to pass laws that do not deal strictly with commerce. Environmental laws, such as the Clean Air Act, are based on the power to regulate businesses in interstate commerce. Most federal criminal laws are based upon either the effect a crime has on interstate commerce, or upon the use of tools or "instrumentalities" of interstate commerce, such as the post offices, telephone companies, and interstate highways, for committing a crime.

Civil rights legislation Even civil rights legislation is based on the Interstate Commerce Clause. Civil rights are the basic rights a citizen has in society. Some civil rights laws are written to prevent discrimination against, or unfair treatment of, people on the basis of their race, color, gender, or other features.

Congress first tried to prevent race discrimination after the states in 1868 adopted the Fourteenth Amendment, which made discrimination by the states illegal. Congress used the Fourteenth Amendment to pass the Civil Rights Act of 1875. The Act made discrimination illegal in places of public accommodation, such as inns and theaters. The U.S. Supreme Court, however, struck down the Act in 1883. It said the Fourteenth Amendment only prohibited discrimination by states, not by private persons in their businesses.

In 1964, Congress passed the Civil Rights Act. This Act also made discrimination illegal in public places, such as motels and restaurants. Congress, however, said it passed the Act using its power under the Interstate Commerce Clause. That year in *Heart of Atlanta Motel v. United States* and *Katzenbach v. McClung*, the U.S. Supreme Court ruled that the Civil Rights Act of 1964 was lawful under the Constitution. It

Changes in the Legislative Branch

Heart of Atlanta motel owner Morton Rolleston, who refused to rent rooms to African Americans in 1964, and challenged the Civil Rights Act of 1964, arguing that it violated his Fifth and Thirteenth Amendment rights. The U.S. Supreme Court ruled in favor of the U.S. government in a lawsuit against Heart of Atlanta. © Bettmann/Corbis.

said discrimination at motels and restaurants affects interstate commerce, because motels give rooms to people who travel from state to state, and restaurants serve food that comes from other states. So Congress can outlaw such private discrimination under its power to regulate interstate commerce, but not under the equal rights provisions of the Fourteenth Amendment.

Two justices, William O. Douglas (1898–1980) and Arthur J. Goldberg (1908–1990), expressed some disappointment with the Court's decisions. They agreed that the Civil Rights Act of 1964 was lawful. But they felt it should be lawful as an exercise of congressional power under the Fourteenth Amendment, not just under the Interstate Commerce Clause. Justice Goldberg expressed his belief that "the Fourteenth Amendment guarantees to all Americans the constitutional right

Changes in the Legislative Branch

Lester Maddox, owner of the Pickrick Motel in Atlanta, Georgia, pickets outside the Atlantic City Convention Hall, where the Democratic Party was holding its convention in August 1964. Maddox was against the Civil Rights Bill of 1964.
© Bettmann/Corbis.

'to be treated as equal members of the community with respect to public accommodations....'"

Income tax: the Sixteenth Amendment

Income tax is a tax collected out of the money that a person or business earns in a year. Income tax has become the federal government's primary source of funds for its operations. When the government began to operate under the Constitution in 1789, however, it did not collect any income tax. Into the early

Changes in the Legislative Branch

1900s, its largest source of tax revenue was a tax on goods imported to America from other countries.

During the American Civil War (1861–65), Congress passed an income tax to help pay for the war. The tax was unpopular and so it was allowed to expire in 1872. In 1881, the U.S. Supreme Court had to decide a case that challenged whether the income tax had been lawful under the Constitution. The Court decided that the tax had been lawful under Article I, Section 8, of the Constitution, which gives Congress the power "to lay and collect taxes."

In 1894, Congress was controlled by the Democratic Party, a political party that tended to find support in the laborers and less wealthy classes of society. Because the economy was not doing well, people were not buying as many imported goods as they had in good times, so the federal government was not collecting as much money as it needed from its import taxes. At the same time, the Industrial Revolution had produced a class of Americans getting wealthy on money earned from various industries.

These factors led Congress to enact an income tax as part of the Wilson-Gorman Tariff Act of 1894. The law imposed a tax of 2 percent on a person's income. It also contained an exemption so that people who earned less than $4,000 a year would not have to pay any income tax.

The following year, the U.S. Supreme Court heard two cases challenging the income tax portions of the Act. Lawyers for the challenging party argued that the income tax violated the Constitution. Under Article I, Section 9, Congress is forbidden to pass direct taxes that are not in proportion to the population of the states. The delegates to the Constitutional Convention never defined what such a tax would be, but the lawyers arguing the case before the Supreme Court, Joseph Choate (1832–1917) and George Edmunds (1828–1919), said an income tax on rents earned from land violated the restriction. According to *The American Constitution,* Edmunds also argued that allowing poor people to use Congress to tax rich people would lead to "communism, anarchy, and then, the ever following despotism [tyranny]."

Going against its decision from 1881, the U.S. Supreme Court ruled that the entire income tax portion of the Act violated the Constitution. Justice Stephen J. Field (1816–1899) wrote an opinion concurring (agreeing) with the Court's decision. In it, he said, "The present assault on capital [money] is but the beginning. It will be but the stepping stone to others, larger and more sweeping, till our political contests will become a war of the poor against the rich; a war constantly growing in intensity and bitterness."

Interest in a federal income tax did not go away, and the issue came up again in Congress in 1909. In April that year, the Senate was considering the country's tariff rates, taxes on imports. U.S. senator Joseph W. Bailey (1862–1929) of Texas proposed to add to the tariff law another income tax law like the one from 1894. Bailey believed the Supreme Court's decision that the 1894 tariff act was illegal was wrong, and he wanted the Court to have another chance to consider the question.

Senators who were opposed to an income tax, including Nelson W. Aldrich (1841–1915) of Rhode Island, held meetings with President William Howard Taft (1857–1930; served 1909–13) to develop a strategy. The plan they came up with was to have President Taft ask Congress to propose a constitutional amendment for making income taxes lawful. To succeed, a constitutional amendment would have to be ratified by three-fourths of the state legislatures. Taft and Aldrich did not think the legislatures would ratify such an amendment, so the proposal was really a clever plan for killing the idea of passing a federal income tax. If the amendment failed to be ratified, Congress would not dare pass an income tax law.

The plan failed. After Congress proposed the Sixteenth Amendment in July, state legislatures began to approve it. By February 25, 1913, thirty-eight states had ratified it, officially making it part of the Constitution. The Amendment says, "The Congress shall have power to lay and collect taxes on incomes, from whatever source derived, without apportionment among the several States, and without regard to any census or enumeration."

Popular election to the Senate: the Seventeenth Amendment

Democracy is a form of government in which the power of government rests with the people. According to Kelly and Harbison, "the men who drafted the Constitution had known little and believed less of the dogma [principle] of democracy."

Changes in the Legislative Branch

Most of the Founding Fathers believed, instead, that white men with property should control government. To accomplish this, they wrote the Constitution of 1787 to enable the election of members of Congress in two ways: Members of the House of Representatives would be elected by people who had the right to participate in state elections, and members of the Senate would be selected by state legislatures. In general, state laws said that only free white men who owned a certain amount of property could participate in state elections and be elected to state legislatures. This meant that the men choosing the members of both the House and the Senate would come primarily from that social class. (See chapter 3, "Constitutional Role of the Legislative Branch.")

Beginning in 1789, the people of France overthrew that nation's monarchy, a government under which power is held by someone who inherits power by birth or takes it by force, such as a king or queen. Although the revolution was violent and deadly, it spread ideas of democracy to other European nations and America.

The spirit of democracy grew in America during the 1800s. Evidence of this came between 1816 and 1821, when the new states of Alabama, Illinois, Indiana, Mississippi, and Missouri adopted constitutions that gave every free white man the right to vote and to be elected to state government, regardless of property. By the time of the Civil War, most free white men in the country enjoyed suffrage, the right to vote. Adoption of the Fifteenth Amendment in 1870 extended the right to vote to all American men regardless of race or color. While many states continued to use poll, or property, taxes to prevent poor men (especially African Americans) from voting, the movement toward democracy continued.

The growth of democracy led to interest in amending the Constitution to provide for popular election of the Senate instead of selection by the state legislatures. The House of Representatives proposed such a constitutional amendment as early as 1828, and did so again in 1893, 1894, 1898, 1900, and 1902. Fearful of losing their power, the members of the Senate did not support the proposals.

Frustrated with the Senate, many states passed laws at the beginning of the 1900s to hold primary elections for choosing senators. Under these laws, state legislatures were pressured to select the senators who had been chosen by the voters during the primaries. This led both chambers of Congress to propose the Seventeenth Amendment in May 1912. The Amendment says senators are to be elected "by the people," and it became effective May 1913 after thirty-six states ratified it.

Election of senators became even more democratic after the adoption of the Nineteenth, Twenty-fourth, and Twenty-sixth Amendments. The Nineteenth and Twenty-sixth Amendments extended suffrage to women and to young people at least eighteen years old. The Twenty-fourth Amendment made it illegal for the United States or any state to charge a poll tax for participating in presidential and congressional elections.

The Twenty-seventh Amendment

The Twenty-seventh Amendment says that if Congress passes a law changing the salaries for senators or representatives, the law cannot take effect until after at least one House election passes. The purpose of the amendment is to prevent representatives from giving themselves pay raises while in office. It became part of the Constitution in May 1992.

The amendment is not very important in the overall scheme of the Constitution, but the story of its adoption is, because it was one of the original twelve amendments crafted by James Madison and proposed by Congress in 1789. By 1791, the states had ratified only ten of the twelve. Those ten came to be known as the Bill of Rights.

Six out of the fourteen American states had approved the congressional pay amendment by 1791, but it needed eleven states (three-fourths of fourteen) to become law. So the country assumed the amendment was dead. Ohio, however, ratified it in 1873. Then in the 1980s, a congressional aide to a Texas legislator discovered the amendment, which led to a campaign for its adoption. By May 1992, over three-fourths of America's fifty states had approved it, which officially made it part of the Constitution as the Twenty-seventh Amendment.

The Amendment caused a controversy in the field of constitutional law. Some scholars said that an amendment proposed by Congress in 1789 should not be capable of ratification over two hundred years later. The Constitution, however, sets no time limit for ratification of an amendment. If an amendment as

Changes in the Legislative Branch

Eighteenth Amendment: Prohibition

Prohibition refers to laws making it a crime to produce or sell alcoholic beverages. A movement for Prohibition began in America in the 1820s. The Anti-Saloon League worked for Prohibition state-by-state in the early 1900s.

In 1917, during World War I, Congress passed the Lever Act. This law adopted Prohibition nationwide for the remainder of the war in order to save grain, from which alcohol is made, for use as food.

In December of the same year, Congress proposed a constitutional amendment to make the manufacture, sale, and transportation of alcoholic beverages illegal all the time, war or no war. Enough state legislatures ratified the proposal to make it the Eighteenth Amendment to the Constitution in January 1919.

The Eighteenth Amendment gave Congress the power to enforce Prohibition with legislation. Congress did so with the National Prohibition Act of 1919, also called the Volstead Act after U.S. representative Andrew J. Volstead (1860–1947) of Minnesota. States also had the power under the amendment to pass enforcement legislation.

Americans disagreed strongly over Prohibition from the beginning, and Prohibition became more unpopular as time passed. In the 1920s, bootlegging (the illegal manufacture and sale of alcoholic beverages) led to violence and other crimes by rival gangs. By 1932, the Great Depression (1929–41), the American economy's lowest period in history, had caused unemployment, or joblessness, for one out of every four Americans. Needing money, many American workers, farmers, and manufacturers wanted to end Prohibition to revive the jobs and income generated by the alcoholic beverages industry. In *Good Spirits*, Gene Logsdon wrote that during Prohibition, the federal government lost $11 billion of revenue that would have come from taxes on beverages. Meanwhile, law enforcement agencies nationwide spent $300 million on mostly unsuccessful enforcement efforts.

In 1932, presidential candidate Franklin D. Roosevelt (1882–1945; served 1933–45) and the Democratic Party favored the repeal of Prohibition. When Roosevelt defeated incumbent Herbert Hoover (1874–1964; served 1929–33) to win the election, Congress proposed the Twenty-first Amendment before Roosevelt even took office. Ratified the following year, the Twenty-first Amendment ended nationwide prohibition by repealing the Eighteenth Amendment.

proposed by Congress or the state legislatures does not have a time limit in it, it may be able to last forever until finally adopted.

The future

Individual senators and representatives propose many constitutional amendments each year. For an amendment to become law, it must first pass both chambers of Congress by a two-thirds vote or be proposed by two-thirds of the state legislatures. It then must be ratified by three-fourths of the states, either in their legislatures or in state conventions. (Congress gets to decide whether ratification is by legislature or convention.)

Changes in the Legislative Branch

Federal agents pour whiskey into a sewer during Prohibition. © Bettmann/Corbis.

Amendments that individual senators and representatives propose rarely pass one chamber of Congress, and almost never pass both chambers to be presented to the states for consideration. Similarly, amendments almost never get the two-thirds support needed from state legislatures to be *proposed* for consideration by the people.

Americans have expressed interest in a number of amendments relating to the powers of Congress. Two of the more popular proposals are for limiting how long a person can serve in Congress, and for requiring Congress to balance the federal budget each year.

Checks and **Balances** *The Three Branches of the American Government*

Changes in the Legislative Branch

Term limits Under the Twenty-second Amendment, a person cannot be elected president more than twice. The Constitution does not, however, contain term limits for senators and representatives. J. Strom Thurmond (1902–2003), who served as a senator from South Carolina for forty-eight years, holds the record for longest service in Congress as of 2004. Thurmond retired from the Senate in January 2003 at age 100 and died that June.

Some Americans think term limits are unfair, because people should be able to elect whomever they want to office. Many Americans, however, want a constitutional amendment to

President George W. Bush (left) sits with U.S. senator J. Strom Thurmond of South Carolina in October 2002. As a result of no term limits for U.S. senators, Thurmond was able to serve as a senator for forty-eight years before retiring in January 2003 at the age of 100. He died five months later. © Reuters/Corbis.

limit how long a person can serve in Congress. Organizations such as U.S. Term Limits and Citizens for Term Limits are working for such change. The homepage of the Web site for U.S. Term Limits captures the spirit of this movement with the saying, "Citizen Legislators, *Not* Career Politicians."

In 1994, many Republicans running for the House of Representatives used a campaign strategy that they called the "Contract with America." It was a list of promises to try to change government if they won their elections. One of their promises was to propose a constitutional amendment for imposing term limits on members of Congress. Although Republicans took control of the House with heavy wins in the November 1994 elections, the House failed to pass a term limits amendment.

Twenty state legislatures took matters into their own hands by passing state laws imposing term limits on federal senators and representatives from their states. In 1995, however, the U.S. Supreme Court struck down these laws. In *U.S. Term Limits, Inc. v. Thornton,* the Court said states lack power under the Constitution to impose term limits on federal legislators. Instead, the nation will have to adopt a constitutional amendment if it wants congressional term limits. (In the meantime, many states have imposed term limits on state legislators, which the states clearly have power to do.)

Balanced budget amendment A budget is a plan for how the federal government will raise and spend money each year. When the government raises more money than it spends, it is operating at a surplus. When it spends more money than it raises, it is operating at a deficit.

Under the Constitution, Congress is the branch with the power to raise money and distribute it for spending. This means that Congress has the ultimate authority to make the federal budget.

A topic that arises periodically in Congress is the balanced budget amendment. This is an amendment that would require Congress to balance the budget each year to eliminate federal deficits. In other words, the federal government would have to operate each year under a budget with a surplus or at least without a deficit.

Changes in the Legislative Branch

People who support a balanced budget amendment, such as members of the Concord Coalition, a nonpartisan, grassroots organization in favor of fiscal responsibility, say it would reduce wasteful spending by the federal government and make Americans more prosperous. People who oppose such an amendment, such as members of the Center on Budget and Policy Priorities, a group that works at the federal and state levels on fiscal policy and public programs that affect citizens with low and moderate incomes, say it would prevent the government from helping the American economy improve during bad times.

A proposed balanced budget amendment passed in the House in 1995, and was just one vote short of passing in the Senate in 1997. In February 2003, U.S. representative Ernest Istook (1950–) of Oklahoma, a Republican, introduced another balanced budget amendment. At the time, the federal government was expecting deficits of $304 billion for 2003 and another $307 billion for 2004. As of 2005, however, the amendment has not been passed for presentation to the states for ratification.

For More Information

BOOKS

Beard, Charles A. *American Government and Politics.* 10th ed. New York: Macmillan Co., 1949.

Burnham, James. *Congress and the American Tradition.* New Brunswick, NJ: Transaction Publishers, 2003.

Kelly, Alfred H., and Winfred A. Harbison. *The American Constitution: Its Origins and Development.* 5th ed. New York: W. W. Norton & Co., 1976.

Kurland, Philip B., and Ralph Lerner. *The Founders' Constitution.* 5 vols. Indianapolis: Liberty Fund, 1987.

Levy, Leonard W. *Original Intent and the Framers' Constitution.* New York: Macmillan, 1988.

Logsdon, Gene. *Good Spirits: A New Look at Ol' Demon Alcohol.* White River Junction, VT: Chelsea Green Pub., 1999.

Roelofs, H. Mark. *The Poverty of American Politics.* 2nd ed. Philadelphia: Temple University Press, 1998.

Volkomer, Walter E. *American Government.* 8th ed. Upper Saddle River, NJ: Prentice Hall, 1998.

Wolfensberger, Donald R. *Congress and the People.* Washington, DC, and Baltimore: Woodrow Wilson Center Press and Johns Hopkins University Press, 2000.

Zinn, Howard. *A People's History of the United States.* New York: HarperCollins, 2003.

PERIODICALS

Dewar, Helen. "On Term-Limits Amendment, Republican Divisions Are Widening." *Washington Post* (November 30, 1994). Also available at *washingtonpost.com.* http://www.washingtonpost.com/wp-srv/politics/special/termlimits/stories/113094.htm (accessed on March 10, 2005).

CASES

Gibbons v. Ogden, 22 U.S. 1 (1824).

Heart of Atlanta Motel v. United States, 379 U.S. 241 (1964).

Houston, E. & W. Tex. Ry. v. United States, 234 U.S. 342 (1914).

Katzenbach v. McClung, 379 U.S. 294 (1964).

McCulloch v. Maryland, 17 U.S. 316 (1819).

Pollock v. Farmers' Loan and Trust Co., 157 U.S. 429 (1895).

Pollock v. Farmers' Loan and Trust Co., 158 U.S. 601 (1895).

U.S. Term Limits, Inc. v. Thornton, 514 U.S. 779 (1995).

Wickard v. Filburn, 317 U.S. 111 (1942).

WEB SITES

"Amend Our Constitution to Require a Balanced Federal Budget." *Concord Coalition.* http://www.concordcoalition.org/news/bba_drop.html (accessed on March 10, 2005).

Center on Budget and Policy Priorities. http://www.cbpp.org/ (accessed on March 11, 2005).

Greenstein, Robert. "The Balanced Budget Constitutional Amendment: An Overview." *Center on Budget and Policy Priorities.* http://www.cbpp.org/Bbaovrvw.htm (accessed on March 10, 2005).

Harris Poll. "More Than Two-Thirds of Americans Continue to Support the Death Penalty." *Harris Interactive.* http://www.harrisinteractive.com/harris_poll/index.asp?PID=431 (accessed on March 14, 2005).

"House Members Introduce Balanced Budget Amendment." *CNN.com.* http://www.cnn.com/2003/ALLPOLITICS/02/13/budget.amendment.ap/ (accessed on March 10, 2005).

"State Legislative Term Limits." *U.S. Term Limits.* http://www.termlimits.org/Current_Info/State_TL/ (accessed on March 10, 2005).

Changes in the Legislative Branch

"U.S. Constitution: Twenty-Seventh Amendment." *Findlaw.com.* http://caselaw.lp.findlaw.com/data/constitution/amendment27/ (accessed on March 10, 2005).

U.S. Term Limits. http://www.termlimits.org/ (accessed on March 11, 2005).

Key Positions in the Legislative Branch

Congress is the legislative branch of the U.S. government, the branch that passes laws. It has two chambers, the House of Representatives and the Senate. When Congress votes on a bill, or proposed law, each representative, or member, in the House and each senator in the Senate gets one vote. A bill must pass both chambers by a simple majority to go to the president of the United States for consideration. If the president signs it, it becomes law. If the president vetoes, or rejects, a bill, Congress can still make it a law if two-thirds of the representatives and two-thirds of the senators vote to override the president's veto.

House of Representatives

The House of Representatives has 435 members. The fifty states in the United States are divided into 435 congressional districts, and one member is elected for each district. Besides the job of representative, key positions and organizations in the House include Speaker of the House, majority leader, minority leader, whips, the Democratic Caucus, the Republican Conference, and congressional staff.

Representative Article I, Section 2, of the U.S. Constitution governs the election of representatives to the House. The Constitution requires that people who want to be elected to the House be at least twenty-five years old, live in the state from which they are elected, and be a citizen of the United States for at least seven years.

Key Positions in the Legislative Branch

Words to Know

bicameralism: The practice of dividing the legislative, or lawmaking, power of government into two chambers.

casework: Work that a member of Congress does to help a voter with a personal governmental problem.

checks and balances: The specific powers in one branch of government that allow it to limit the powers of the other branches.

Congress: The legislative, or lawmaking, branch of the federal government. Congress has two chambers, the Senate and the House of Representatives.

Constitution of the United States of America: The document written in 1787 that established the federal government under which the United States of America has operated since 1789. Article I covers the legislative branch.

lobbying: Meeting with members of Congress to convince them to pass laws that will benefit businesses, citizens' groups, or other organizations.

republic: A government under which power is held by the people, who elect public servants to represent them in the bodies of government.

separation of powers: Division of the powers of government into different branches to prevent one branch from having too much power.

Elections to the House take place once every two years, including the year of presidential elections (held once every four years) and two years after that. Elections are held on the first Tuesday after the first Monday in November.

After being elected in November, a representative joins the House when it begins its next session the following January. The most visible work a representative does includes voting on bills to determine whether they become laws. Many laws concern how to raise money through taxes and how to spend it on government programs, such as Social Security for retired people. Other laws create rules on matters of national concern, such as controlling airline traffic, constructing interstate highways, regulating radio and television broadcasting, and preventing racial discrimination. Criminal laws define illegal behavior and the punishment for those who break them.

Voting on bills, however, is only a small part of a member's work. Committee work is a larger part of what a member does. Committees are smaller groups of representatives that handle specific government topics, such as agriculture, the federal budget, or national security. As of 2005, the House has nineteen permanent

Proportional Representation

The United States uses a winner-takes-all system for elections to the House of Representatives. Under this system, the states are carved into 435 legislative districts. At election time, the person who gets the most votes in a district gets to represent the entire district in the House.

The Ninth Congressional District for Pennsylvania, for example, had a special election in May 2001. Four people were candidates to serve the Ninth District: William Shuster from the Republican Party, Scott Conklin from the Democratic Party, Alanna Hartzok from the Green Party, and John Kensinger II from the Reform Party. On Election Day, Shuster got 52 percent of the votes, Conklin got 44 percent, and Hartzok got 4 percent. This gave Shuster the privilege of representing everyone in the Ninth District.

Many Americans believe a winner-takes-all system is unfair. Some say it prevents the people who vote for losing candidates from having someone represent their interests in Congress. It even makes it possible for someone who gets less than half the votes to win. The winner-takes-all system makes it almost impossible for people to be elected unless they are members of the two major political parties, the Republicans or Democrats. It also makes it harder for women and people from racial minorities to get elected.

Proportional representation is an alternative to the winner-takes-all system. Under proportional representation, states would be carved in fewer, larger districts, and each district would get a certain number of representatives. At election time, the seats in each district would be divided in proportion to the number of votes each political party received in that district.

For example, imagine that the Ninth Congressional District was a larger district that got ten representatives in the House. In the election above, the Republicans would have won 52 percent of the seats, or five of them, and the Democrats would have won the other half. If the Green Party had received 10 percent of the votes instead of just 4 percent, it would have won one of the ten seats. With proportional representation, more political parties, and hence more Americans, would be represented in Congress.

Many democratic countries use proportional representation instead of the winner-takes-all system in their elections. The United States, Canada, and Great Britain are major countries that rely solely on a winner-takes-all system. Because proportional representation would allow so-called third parties to take legislative seats away from Democrats and Republicans, it is unlikely that the United States will ever adopt such a system for Congress, given the power of the current two-party structure.

committees, called standing committees, plus many other committees and subcommittees. Working in committees is how members prepare most of the bills to be voted on in Congress.

Members also spend much of their time on casework. This is personal work to help voters from the member's district with particular problems, such as getting veteran's benefits or a tax refund. Members also spend time meeting with voters who want certain bills to become law. Generating goodwill by helping voters is an important part of getting reelected.

Key Positions in the Legislative Branch

Opening ceremonies of the second session of the 59th Congress in 1905. Joseph G. Cannon of Illinois was the Speaker of the House.
Photograph by Frances Benjamin Johnson. Library of Congress.

Two other parts of a member's day-to-day work are important to reelection. The first is meeting with lobbyists. Lobbyists are people who represent businesses or organizations that want Congress to pass certain laws. The U.S. Chamber of Commerce, for example, lobbies Congress for laws helpful to American businesses. The National Rifle Association lobbies Congress for laws protecting the right for individuals to own guns and other weapons. The people and groups who lobbyists represent donate money to help members get elected, so members make lots of time to hear their wishes.

The second task important to reelection is campaigning. Representatives face reelection every two years. This means they must begin working on a reelection campaign, or strategy, soon after getting into office. Once in, however, it is much easier to win an election. Statistics show that a representative in office, called the incumbent, has a 90 percent chance of beating an outsider who runs for the same position at election time.

Key Positions in the Legislative Branch

Actor and National Rifle Association (NRA) president Charlton Heston testifies before the House Government Reform subcommittee in November 1999 on the merits of Project Exile, a zero-tolerance policy for gun crimes. The NRA is a high-profile lobbying group. © Reuters/Corbis.

Speaker of the House The Speaker of the House is the only House leadership position specifically mentioned in the Constitution. The Constitution says, "The House of Representatives shall chuse their Speaker and other officers." The House makes this choice at the beginning of every two-year term after the Democratic Caucus and the Republican Conference each nominate one person for the position. (The Democratic Caucus and Republican Conference are House organizations for members of those political parties.) Since the whole House selects the Speaker from the two choices, the

Key Positions in the Legislative Branch

Joseph G. Cannon of Illinois, who served in the U.S. House of Representatives from 1873 to 1890 and 1893 to 1922, and was the powerful Speaker of the House from 1903 to 1910. Library of Congress.

Speaker is always a member of the majority party, the political party that has the most members in the House.

The position of Speaker was very powerful until 1910, which marked the end of the Speakership for the combative Joseph G. Cannon (1836–1926), a Republican from Illinois who became Speaker in 1903. Until 1910, the Speaker got to decide which members served on and chaired, or headed, the House's various committees. The Speaker was allowed to be chair of the House Rules Committee, which makes the rules for how the House operates. This allowed the Speaker to control which bills made it from House committees to the floor for a vote.

Cannon used his power to the fullest during his term as Speaker. This upset many members who had trouble bringing their desired bills to a vote. According to Congressional Quarterly's *Guide to the Congress of the United States,* if a representative would get up to speak on the House floor before checking with Cannon, Cannon would ask, "For what purpose does the gentleman rise?" Cannon used his power to prevent people from speaking if he did not want them to.

In 1910, House Democrats joined with unhappy House Republicans to force the House to change the rules for the Speaker. Since then, the Speaker is not allowed to serve on the House Rules Committee, and the whole House makes appointments to its various committees.

The Speaker, however, still has special powers. The Speaker presides over House sessions, recognizing members who want to speak and interpreting House rules. The Speaker assigns new bills to committees, which can often affect whether a bill makes it back out of the committee for a vote on the floor. The Speaker also gets to appoint members to special committees, including joint committees with the Senate for resolving differences between bills in the two chambers. In these cases, the Speaker often appoints people recommended by the chair, or head, of the House committee that wrote the bill.

House majority leader With 435 members, the House is too large for one person to run alone. As Neil MacNeil wrote in *Forge of Democracy,* "The House has been from the beginning such a sprawling, discordant [disagreeing] mass of men that the Speaker has had to depend on lieutenants to guide and oversee its multiple operations in its committees and on its floor, and to ensure the orderly flow of responsible legislation."

After the Speaker of the House, the House majority leader is the next most powerful person in the House. Until 1911, the Speaker of the House selected the majority leader. Since the revolt against Cannon, the majority party as a whole has appointed the majority leader. This means the Democratic Caucus appoints the majority leader when it controls the House, and the Republican Conference does so when it controls the House.

The majority leader's main job is to help the Speaker and other party leaders plan and carry out legislative strategy. In other words, they must decide what bills they want to pass and make sure those bills get into and out of the proper committees for a vote on the House floor.

For bills where the vote might be close, the majority leader works to convince undecided members to pass bills that the party likes. The job requires strong people skills and the ability to bargain. Often an undecided member will agree to vote for (or against) a particular bill in exchange for promised support on another bill. When the time comes for the House to debate, or discuss, a particular bill, the majority leader lets the Speaker know which members should be heard by the House.

House minority leader Just as the party in charge appoints a majority leader, the party with the second most members appoints a minority leader. This happens through either the Republican Conference or the Democratic Caucus, depending on which party is the minority party. The minority leader usually ends up being the person that the minority party nominated to be Speaker of the House.

The minority party has little hope of passing bills that the majority party does not want. This means the minority party usually does not develop a legislative program of its own. Instead, led by the minority leader, the minority party develops a strategy for changing or defeating the majority party bills it does not like. The minority leader may arrange meetings with undecided members to convince them to defeat unwanted bills when the vote is going to be close.

Since the minority party loses most close votes in the House, the position of minority leader is very difficult. A 1967 study by Randall B. Ripley in *Party Leaders in the House of Representatives* found that out of thirteen minority leaders from 1900 to 1967, five had left the job and three had been dismissed by their party. In comparison, out of twelve majority leaders, only two had left the job and none had been dismissed. Since 1967, five representatives have served as minority leader; three left the job (one, Gerald Ford, to become vice president), one retired, and one is still serving as of 2005. Eight have served as majority leader since 1967; four became Speaker of the House, one became minority leader, one died, one retired, and one is still serving as of 2005.

Newt Gingrich (1943–) and the Contract with America

Newt Gingrich, a Republican from Georgia, was Speaker of the House from 1995 to 1999. Gingrich was a key player in the Republican Revolution of 1994 and the Contract with America.

As of 1994, the Republican Party had not been the majority party in the House for forty years. At that time, Democrats controlled both chambers of Congress and had President Bill Clinton (1946–; served 1993–2001) in office. At a meeting in Salisbury, Maryland, in February 1994, House Republicans hatched a plan. They called it the Contract with America. It was a set of changes that House Republicans promised to strive for in government if they gained control of the House in the upcoming November elections.

On September 27, 1994, more than three hundred Republicans running for Congress gathered in front of the Capitol building in Washington, D.C. There they revealed the Contract with America to the public. The Contract covered ten major areas of change. These included a constitutional amendment to require a balanced federal budget, term limits for members of Congress, and a line-item veto. The line-item veto would give the president of the United States power to veto, or reject, portions of spending bills instead of having to veto whole bills to get rid of unwanted portions.

Led by Gingrich, the Republicans enjoyed heavy victories in the November 1994 elections, putting them in control of both the House and the Senate at the start of the 104th Congress in January 1995. Gingrich, as a result, won election as Speaker of the House in December 1994.

Gingrich delivered on the Contract with America by bringing each of its proposals to a vote in the House within the first hundred days of the 104th Congress. Most of the proposals passed in the House, with few Republicans voting no. Some that passed died in the Senate or were vetoed by President Clinton, but others became law. The line-item veto became law, the balanced budget amendment failed to pass in the Senate, and term limits for members of Congress did not even pass in the House.

Gingrich's popularity began to decline in 1996, the same year President Clinton won reelection to a second term. Although Gingrich was reelected to office that year, too, and remained Speaker of the House, he decided to resign from Congress before the new term began in January 1999. He retired from public office after twenty years as a U.S. representative.

Key Positions in the Legislative Branch

Whips Just as the Speaker gets help from the majority leader, the majority and minority leaders get help from the whips. According to *Guide to the U.S. Congress of the United States,* the term "whip" comes from the fox-hunting term "whipper-in," the person in charge of keeping the hounds together as they chase the fox. The British Parliament, Great Britain's legislative body, first used the term "whip" around 1770. The U.S. House of Representatives got its first official whip in 1899.

Chief, or head, whips are elected by the Democratic Caucus and the Republican Conference. In turn, the chief whips choose many assistant whips to help them with the job. The main job of

Newt Gingrich, leader of the Republican Party's Contract with America plan, addresses Republican congressional candidates in September 1994, four months before he became Speaker of the House. A P / W i d e   W o r l d   P h o t o s .

Key Positions in the Legislative Branch

Congressional leaders speak with the media following a meeting with President George W. Bush in March 2003: (left to right) House majority leader Tom DeLay of Texas, Speaker of the House Dennis Hastert of Illinois, and House minority leader Nancy Pelosi of California. © Ron Sachs/Corbis.

the whips is to encourage members to appear for votes, count how votes are likely to go, and help convince undecided or unfavorable members to change their minds and vote the party line. If the majority leader or minority leader cannot be on the House floor for some reason, the majority or minority whip temporarily serves as acting party leader.

Democratic Caucus and Republican Conference Republican and Democratic members of the House meet privately and separately in either the Republican Conference or the Democratic Caucus. The Democratic Caucus is the older of the two organizations. According to its Web site, a forerunner of the Caucus formed in April 1792 to oppose a treaty with Great Britain that it felt was bad for American sailors.

274 Checks and Balances *The Three Branches of the American Government*

The Caucus is a forum for developing party strategy, nominating party leadership, and approving the assignment of Democrats to House committees. In the hierarchy of House leadership for the Democrats, the chair and vice chair of the Democratic Caucus come after the chief Democratic whip.

The Republican Conference serves the same function as the Democratic Caucus. Over their histories, both the Conference and the Caucus have varied in how active they have been as organized units.

Since the nineteenth century, almost all members of the House have been Democrats or Republicans. Occasionally, however, someone from a so-called third party gets elected to the House. In the twentieth century, the Progressive Party, the Prohibition Party, and the Socialist Party all succeeded in winning seats in Congress. Also, people called Independents, who are not affiliated with any political party, sometimes reach the House. As of 2005, the only Independent in the House is U.S. representative Bernard Sanders of Vermont, who was first elected to the House in 1990. Members from third parties might seek to meet with either the Republican Conference or the Democratic Caucus, depending on which party most closely resembles their own political views. The Caucus or Conference, however, may say no to such a request.

Congressional staff Each member of Congress gets to hire staffers. Staffers help the members run their offices, both in Washington, D.C., and in their home districts. Staffers meet with lobbyists and constituents, or voters, because members do not have time for everyone who wants to see them. Staffers also research how a member's constituents, lobbyists, and other supporters feel about specific bills to help the member decide how to vote. Finally, staffers do a lot of the work that is involved in casework for constituents.

Members are restricted to a specific number of staffers, and have additional staffers working for them in the various House committees. The total cost of congressional staff throughout Congress is large. According to Mark Roelofs in *The Poverty of American Politics,* the cost of paying for Senate and congressional staffs, committee and subcommittee staffs, staffs of the Congressional Research Service of the Library of Congress and the Congressional Budget Office, staff of the offices of the

Key Positions in the Legislative Branch

sergeant-at-arms and the parliamentarian, and staff at the shops, discount stores, gymnasiums, TV/video facilities, restaurants, and cafeterias for Congress is over one billion dollars each year.

Senate

The Constitution says that each state gets two senators in the Senate. When Hawaii became the fiftieth state in 1959, the Senate arrived at a total of one hundred senators. Besides the job of senator, key positions and organizations in the Senate include president of the Senate, president *pro tempore,* majority leader, minority leader, whips, the Democratic and Republican Conferences, and staff.

Senator Article I, Section 3, of the Constitution governs the election of senators. To be a senator, a person must be at least thirty years old, a citizen of the United States for nine years, and a resident of the state to be represented.

The Constitution requires each senator's seat to be up for election every six years. To accomplish this, all the seats in the Senate are divided into three groups. Every year that the House is up for election, about one-third of the senatorial seats are up for election. Two years later, when the whole House faces election again, the second group of senatorial seats faces election. Two years later, again during an election for the entire House, the third group of senatorial seats faces election.

Senators, like representatives, begin service in Congress the January after their November elections. Also like representatives, senators spend much of their time working in Senate committees to draft bills. Then they meet on the Senate floor to debate and vote on bills that get that far.

If both the Senate and the House pass a bill by simple majorities, the bill goes to the president of the United States for consideration. If the Senate and House pass different versions of the same bill, they form a conference committee with members from both chambers to try to work out their differences. If the committee agrees upon one version of the bill, both chambers vote on that version to pass or reject it. If passed, the joint version goes to the president for consideration.

Like representatives, senators spend much time meeting with lobbyists and doing casework for constituents. Because they face reelection just every six years, senators do not have to spend as much time campaigning as representatives do.

Senators have special duties under the Constitution that representatives do not have. Under Article II, Section 2, the president of the United States may make treaties, or formal agreements, with other nations if two-thirds of the senators concur, or agree. When the president proposes a treaty, the Senate Foreign Relations Committee holds special hearings to consider the issue and then votes on whether to recommend approval by the Senate. Two-thirds of the Senate must vote for a treaty for it to become part of American law.

The same part of the Constitution says the president may appoint ambassadors (diplomats assigned to foreign countries who represent the United States), judges of the Supreme Court, and other officers of the United States "with the advice and consent of the senate." When the president nominates a person to serve on the U.S. Supreme Court or one of the lower federal courts, the Senate Judiciary Committee holds hearings to consider the nomination. The committee then makes a recommendation to the Senate, which votes as a whole on the nomination. A simple majority of senators must vote in favor to approve a president's nomination to the Supreme Court or other federal office.

President of the Senate The Constitution says, "The Vice-President of the United States shall be President of the senate, but shall have no vote, unless they be equally divided." The job sounds like it would be powerful. The Founding Fathers imagined that the president of the Senate would preside over all sessions of the Senate, recognizing members who wanted to speak and interpreting Senate rules. As the first vice president, however, John Adams (1735–1826) set an example of being a neutral participant in Senate affairs except when a tie-breaking vote was required.

From 1789 until 1952, presiding over the Senate was the vice president's main job. During this time, the vice president had an office in the Capitol building and hired staff with funds from Congress. In 1953, Vice President Richard Nixon (1913–1994) moved the office of the vice president from the Capitol to the White House. Nixon attended Senate sessions only at critical times, such as to cast a tie-breaking vote.

Key Positions in the Legislative Branch

Vice President Richard Nixon makes a speech on November 2, 1960, several days before he lost the presidential election to John F. Kennedy. Nixon was the first vice president to have an office in the White House, rather than in the Capitol. © Bettmann/Corbis.

Vice presidents since Nixon have followed his example. Normally tie votes that need to be broken concern bills. They also can involve appointments of Senate officers and committees. According to the Web site of the Senate, as of early 2005, vice presidents had cast tie-breaking votes 242 times in the nation's history. The first vice president, John Adams, holds the record with twenty-nine such votes. Twelve vice presidents never had to cast a tie-breaking vote. The president of the Senate does not get to participate in floor debate on bills, even if a tie-breaking vote might be required.

President *pro tempore* The Constitution requires the Senate to select a president *pro tempore*, a Latin term that means "for the time being." The constitutional duty of the president pro tempore, or pro tem, is to preside over the Senate when the president of the Senate cannot be there. Under a law passed in 1947, the president pro tem is in line after the vice president and Speaker of the House to replace the president of the United States if the president dies, leaves office, or is removed by impeachment.

The whole Senate elects the pro tem. Since 1945, the Senate has tended to elect the person from the majority party with the most years of continuous senatorial service. By law, once

Key Positions in the Legislative Branch

Outgoing vice president Al Gore and his wife, Tipper, greet Vice President-Elect Dick Cheney at the White House on Inauguration Day, on January 20, 2001. As president of the Senate, the primary constitutional requirement of the vice president is to break tie votes in the Senate.
© Reuters/Corbis.

elected, the pro tem serves until leaving the Senate or until the Senate elects a different pro tem, which it can do at any time.

Like the position of president of the Senate, the position of president pro tem is not very powerful. The pro tem rarely presides over the Senate, even when the president of the Senate is not there, which is most of the time. Instead, other members of the Senate appointed by the pro tem share the job of presiding over sessions. The pro tem often appoints young members who need to learn the rules of the Senate. This makes the position of pro tem largely one of honor and prestige. Unlike the president of the Senate, however, the pro tem, as an elected member, may speak in debate and vote on all bills under consideration.

Senate majority leader With fewer members than the House of Representatives, the Senate tends to operate with less official

Key Positions in the Legislative Branch

leadership than the House. In *Congressional Government* in 1885, then-future president Woodrow Wilson (1856–1924) wrote, "No one is *the* Senator. No one may speak for his party as well as for himself; no one exercises the special trust of acknowledged leadership. The Senate is merely a body of individual critics."

In the 1920s, the Senate began to elect official majority and minority leaders. The majority party elects the Senate majority leader. This is the most powerful position in the Senate, more powerful than the president of the Senate and the president pro tem. It tends, however, to be less important than the position of Speaker of the House of Representatives.

The Senate majority leader has two main duties. The first is to organize the flow of bills from Senate committees onto the Senate floor for debate and consideration. The second is to meet with the Senate minority leader to arrive at unanimous consent concerning debate over bills. Unanimous consent is an agreement on how much time the Senate will spend debating a bill, and how much of that time each of the two major political parties gets.

If many people want to speak about a bill, the president of the Senate (if present) or the pro tem gives the majority leader the first chance to speak. This means the majority leader is the first person who can offer amendments, or proposed changes, to bills being considered. According to the Senate's Web site, U.S. senator Robert C. Byrd (1917–) of West Virginia, who has had stints as both majority leader (1977–80; 1987–88) and minority leader (1981–86), called the right to speak first "the most potent weapon in the majority leader's arsenal."

The Senate majority leader also has other responsibilities. He helps develop the majority party's strategy for getting bills passed and opposing unwanted bills. This involves meeting and cutting deals with other senators, which requires strong people skills. The majority leader is the majority party's official spokesperson on legislative issues in the Senate. He also serves as the official spokesperson for the whole Senate, greeting foreign officials who visit the Senate.

Senate minority leader The minority party in the Senate elects the Senate minority leader. Like the minority leader in the

House, the Senate minority leader's main job is to plan an attack on the majority party's legislative plan. Like the majority leader, the minority leader spends lots of time meeting with other senators, cutting deals to get enough votes to prevent unwanted bills from passing. When many people want to speak about a particular bill, the minority leader gets to speak second, after the majority leader.

Whips The Republican and Democratic senators both elect whips for their parties. The main job of the whips is to count heads to see how a vote on a bill might go and to gather party members when it is time to vote. Because the Senate is smaller than the House, Senate whips tend to be less influential than House whips. History even has instances of strong disagreements between party leaders and whips. Majority leader Mike Mansfield (1903–2001) of Montana, for example, clashed much with majority whip Russell B. Long (1918–2003) of Louisiana from 1966 until 1969, when Edward M. Kennedy (1932–) of Massachusetts replaced Long as whip.

Democratic and Republican Conferences

As they do in the House, Republicans and Democrats in the Senate meet separately in groups called the Republican Conference and the Democratic Conference. The Conferences are where the parties elect their Senate leaders and whips, select senators for serving on Senate committees, and make their legislative plans and strategies. According to the Senate Web site, as of 2005, the party leader for the Democrats also serves as chair of the Democratic Conference. The Republicans elect a senator different from their floor leader to serve as chair of the Republican Conference.

Senatorial staff Senators, like representatives, hire staffers to help them do their jobs, both as individual senators and as members of Senate committees. Because senators represent entire states instead of just districts, they get to hire more staffers than representatives do. Senators from larger states also get to hire more staffers than do senators from smaller states.

For More Information

BOOKS

Beard, Charles A. *American Government and Politics.* 10th ed. New York: Macmillan Co., 1949.

Burnham, James. *Congress and the American Tradition.* New Brunswick, NJ: Transaction Publishers, 2003.

Congressional Quarterly Inc. *Guide to the Congress of the United States.* 1st ed. Washington, DC: Congressional Quarterly Service, 1971.

Janda, Kenneth, Jeffrey M. Berry, and Jerry Goldman. *The Challenge of Democracy.* 5th ed. Boston: Houghton Mifflin Company, 1997.

MacNeil, Neil. *Forge of Democracy: The House of Representatives.* New York: David MacKay Co., 1963.

McClenaghan, William A. *Magruder's American Government 2003.* Needham, MA: Prentice Hall School Group, 2002.

Ripley, Randall B. *Party Leaders in the House of Representatives.* Washington, DC: Brookings Institution, 1967.

Shelley, Mack C., II. *American Government and Politics Today.* 2004–2005 ed. Belmont, CA: Wadsworth Publishing, 2003.

Volkomer, Walter E. *American Government.* 8th ed. Upper Saddle River, NJ: Prentice Hall, 1998.

Wilson, Woodrow. *Congressional Government.* Houghton Mifflin Co., 1885. Reprint, New Brunswick, NJ: Transaction Publishers, 2002.

Wolfensberger, Donald R. *Congress and the People.* Washington, DC, and Baltimore: Woodrow Wilson Center Press and Johns Hopkins University Press, 2000.

WEB SITES

Amy, Douglas. "The Most Needed Political Reform." *FairVote: The Center for Voting and Democracy.* http://www.fairvote.org/op_eds/tompaineamy.htm (accessed on March 14, 2005).

United States House of Representatives. http://www.house.gov (accessed on March 14, 2005).

United States Senate. http://www.senate.gov (accessed on March 14, 2005).

"Unofficial Returns for the Special Election Held on May 15, 2001." *Pennsylvania Department of State.* http://www.dos.state.pa.us/bcel/cwp/view.asp?A=1099&Q=431861&pp=3 (accessed on March 14, 2005).

Daily Operations of the Legislative Branch

Congress is the legislative branch of the government of the United States of America. The legislature is the branch that makes the laws. Congress has two chambers, the House of Representatives and the Senate. The House has 435 representatives, one from each of 435 districts in the United States. The Senate has one hundred senators, two from each of America's fifty states.

Making laws is one of the things that representatives and senators do daily, but it is not the only thing. Members of Congress meet with lobbyists, people working for businesses or interest groups that want Congress to pass certain laws. They also work on the national budget, America's plan for raising money through taxes and spending it on governmental programs. Members of Congress do casework, helping voters from their districts or states with governmental problems. They also spend time campaigning for reelection. Finally, Congress operates miscellaneous offices, such as the Library of Congress, that perform services for the government.

Lobbying

Before Congress can propose a law, the idea for the law needs to come from somewhere. Sometimes the legislators in Congress propose the idea, and other times the president of the United States does. The legislators and the president often get their ideas from business leaders, lobbyists, and private interest groups.

Lobbyists are people who work for private interests to get favorable legislation passed in Congress. Private interests can be

Words to Know

bicameralism: The practice of dividing the legislative, or lawmaking, power of government into two chambers.

casework: Work that a member of Congress does to help a voter with a personal governmental problem.

checks and balances: The specific powers in one branch of government that allow it to limit the powers of the other branches.

cloture rule: A rule that allows senators to end a filibuster, or prolonged speech, by a vote of three-fifths of the Senate.

Congress: The legislative, or lawmaking, branch of the federal government. Congress has two chambers, the Senate and the House of Representatives.

constituents: The voters who are in a representative's district or a senator's state.

Constitution of the United States of America: The document written in 1787 that established the federal government under which the United States of America has operated since 1789. Article I covers the legislative branch.

filibuster: A tactic used by one or more senators who speak for a prolonged period of time so that the time for considering a bill runs out before a vote can be taken on the Senate floor.

iron triangle: The three-way relationship between congressional committees, executive agencies, and private interest groups that all specialize in the same area of government.

lobbying: Meeting with members of Congress to convince them to pass laws that will benefit businesses, citizens' groups, or other organizations.

republic: A government under which power is held by the people, who elect public servants to represent them in the bodies of government.

separation of powers: Division of the powers of government into different branches to prevent one branch from having too much power.

single entities, such as a defense contractor, or an organization that represents many people or groups, such as People For the American Way, a group that advocates a diverse democratic society. The word "lobbyist" comes from the fact that they spend a great deal of time in the halls and lobbies of Congress, meeting with members and congressional staffers. According to Walter E. Volkomer in *American Government,* the term was first used in Great Britain to describe journalists waiting to meet with legislators in the lobbies of the House of Commons, a chamber of the British legislature.

Many of the lobbyists in Washington, D.C., represent business interests. According to Michael Parenti in *Democracy*

Daily Operations of the Legislative Branch

John Rother, chief lobbyist for the American Association for Retired Persons (AARP), a powerful lobbying group (1997 photo).
AP/Wide World Photos.

for the Few, President Woodrow Wilson (1856–1924; served 1913–21) once said:

> Suppose you go to Washington and try to get at your Government. You will always find that while you are politely listened to, the men really consulted are the men who have the big stake—the big bankers, the big manufacturers, and the big masters of commerce.... The masters of the Government of the United States are the combined capitalists and manufacturers of the United States.

Lobbyists help members of Congress analyze how their votes on particular bills will affect their chances to be reelected. They also analyze the chances that different bills, or proposed laws, have of passing Congress. Lobbyists supply members of

Congress with information concerning the subject matter of congressional bills. When congressional committees hold hearings, lobbyists testify, or speak, before the committees in an effort to influence the passing of a law their clients want.

Washington, District of Columbia

Article I, Section 8, of the Constitution gives Congress control over the seat of government of the United States of America. Since 1801 that seat has been the city of Washington, District of Columbia.

Throughout the capital city's history, Congress has created the laws for the District of Columbia through committees. As of 2005, this responsibility rests in the House Government Reform Committee, the Senate Governmental Affairs Committee, and the District of Columbia Appropriations Subcommittees of both the House and Senate Appropriations Committees.

The residents of the District of Columbia pay taxes to the federal government. They do not, however, have voting members in Congress. Over the years, this "taxation without representation" has resulted in movements for giving the District of Columbia voting representation in Congress.

In 1871, Congress passed a law giving the District of Columbia a nonvoting delegate to the House of Representatives. This delegate, Norton P. Chipman (1834–1924), was allowed to represent the District's interests in House committees and on the House floor, but was not allowed to vote on any bills or other issues before Congress. The delegate position lasted only four years, until 1875, when Congress changed the form of government in the District of Columbia and ended the delegate position.

In 1970, Congress passed a law to revive the position of nonvoting delegate in the House. The residents of the District of Columbia get to elect the delegate. Walter E. Fauntroy (1933–) held this position from 1971 to 1991. He was succeeded by Eleanor Holmes Norton (1937–), who, as of 2005, remained in the seat. In 2001, 2003, and 2005, Norton introduced a bill called the "No Taxation Without Representation Act." (U.S. senator Joseph Lieberman [1942–] of Connecticut did the same on the Senate side.) If passed, the bill would give the District of Columbia voting members in both the House and the Senate. According to a national poll in 2005, 82 percent of Americans support voting rights in Congress for the District of Columbia.

Opposition to "taxation without representation" is not the only reason some people want the District of Columbia to have voting representatives in Congress. Since the Constitution gives Congress the power to make the laws for the capital city, voting representation would give the residents more say in the city's laws and daily government affairs. This is called the "home rule" issue, because it concerns whether the residents of the capital city have control over their local government.

In 1802, Congress passed a law for the District of Columbia to be governed by a mayor appointed by the president of the United States. From 1802 to 1967, the ability of the residents of the capital city to elect their local officials varied with different congressional laws. According to Congressional Quarterly's *Guide to the Congress of the United States*, many members of Congress, particularly from the south, did not want to give home rule to the District because most of its residents were African Americans.

Daily Operations of the Legislative Branch

According to Parenti, "Lobbyists make themselves so helpful that members of Congress sometimes rely on them to perform tasks normally done by congressional staffs. Lobbyists will draft legislation, write speeches, and

In 1967, Congress passed yet another law. This one provided for the District to be governed by a mayor and council composed of nine people. In 1973, Congress expanded the council to thirteen members and gave the residents the right to elect both the mayor and council members.

As of 2005, the mayor, council, and many local agencies do most of the day-to-day work of governing the city. Congress, however, still has the power to approve the city's annual budget and to pass, change, or abolish any laws it wants for the District. Meanwhile, capital city residents still have no voting power in Congress. Since adoption of the Twenty-third Amendment to the Constitution in 1961, however, citizens of the District of Columbia have been allowed to vote in presidential elections.

A view of the National Mall in Washington, D.C., shows (left to right) the Lincoln Memorial, the Washington Monument, and the U.S. Capitol. Washington, D.C., Convention & Visitors Association.

Checks and **Balances** *The Three Branches of the American Government*

plant stories in the press on behalf of cooperative lawmakers."

Lobbyists also help members of Congress through campaign contributions from the interest groups the lobbyists represent. Businesspeople regularly donate money to individual legislators and political parties who work for favorable legislation. Because it is illegal for corporations to donate money directly to a congressional campaign, businesses create political action committees, called PACs. Corporations use the PACs to raise money from corporate executives and other contributors for donation to members of Congress. Labor unions, which represent workers, use PACs to raise money for politicians, too.

There are many nonbusiness interest groups that hire lobbyists. Environmental, religious, and other organizations hire lobbyists to represent their general interests. Many single-issue organizations hire lobbyists, too, such as groups that support or oppose abortion and reproductive rights.

According to Jack Anderson in "Lobbyists: The Unelected Lawmakers in Washington," Speaker of the House Tip O'Neill (1912–1994) once said, "The grab of special interests is staggering. It will destroy the legislative process." Many Americans, like O'Neill, believe PACs allow financial contributors to have too much control over congressional policy. Others believe PACs allow people and businesses to avoid campaign finance restrictions by using complicated financial maneuvers. For example, in early 2005, U.S. representative Tom DeLay of Texas faced charges that he ran corporate contributions through the Republican Party's national organization and then back to individual races for the state House of Representatives in Texas. Under Texas law, it was illegal for corporate contributions to help state legislative candidates.

Supporters of PACs say the First Amendment freedom of speech protects the right to influence government by supporting politicians and political causes with financial contributions.

Enacting legislation

On September 29, 1789, President George Washington (1732–1799; served 1789–97) signed the first appropriations law for the United States of America. An appropriations law gives money to a particular government program. The law President Washington signed that September was only a few lines long. It provided $568,000 for government salaries, the Department of War, the Department of the Treasury, and pensions.

The lawmaking process has grown more complicated and specialized since then. It begins when a representative or senator introduces a bill in either the House or the Senate. From there, the bill is assigned to a House or Senate committee for consideration. If the committee sends the bill back to the House or Senate, the representatives or senators debate, or discuss, the bill and then vote on it.

If a bill passes both the House and the Senate by simple majorities, it goes to the president of the United States for consideration. If the president signs it, the bill becomes law. If the president vetoes, or rejects, the bill, it does not become law unless two-thirds of both chambers of Congress vote to override the president's veto.

Introduction of a bill A bill is a draft of a proposed law. Any senator or representative can introduce a bill into his or her chamber of Congress. Senators introduce bills in the Senate by sending them to the Senate desk on the Senate floor. Representatives introduce bills by putting them in a hopper, a mahogany box, on the House floor.

The president of the United States cannot introduce bills into Congress. The president, however, is the source of many bills introduced by senators and representatives. Every year in January, the president delivers a State of the Union address to Congress. The president is required to give the address under Article II, Section 3, of the Constitution. Part of the address describes what laws the president would like Congress to enact in the upcoming year. People who work for the president in the executive branch draft many bills for these proposed laws, and members of Congress who favor the president's proposals introduce the bills into the House or Senate.

Each year, of the thousands of bills introduced in the House and the Senate, only hundreds make it through the legislative process to become laws.

Daily Operations of the Legislative Branch

Committee consideration President Woodrow Wilson once said, "Congress in session is Congress on exhibition, whilst Congress in its committee-rooms is Congress at work," according to the authors of *The Challenge of Democracy*. The most important committees in both chambers of Congress are called standing committees, or permanent committees. Standing committees cover the major areas of government. Examples include the Armed Services, Foreign Relations, and Judiciary Committees in the Senate, and the Agriculture, Science, and Small Business Committees in the House. As of 2005, the Senate had sixteen standing committees, and the House had nineteen. Most standing committees have subcommittees that handle specific portions of the committee's area of concern.

President Woodrow Wilson on his League of Nations tour in St. Louis, Missouri, in September 1919. Wilson worked hard to convince Congress of the merits of his League of Nations plan, but failed. © Bettmann/Corbis.

Committees are like miniature chambers of Congress. Each senator and representative gets to serve on a small number of committees and subcommittees. The majority party, the political party with the most members in the House or Senate, gets to have the most members on each committee and subcommittee. The chair, or head, of each committee is always from the majority party. The minority party, the party with the second most members in each chamber, is allotted fewer members on each committee than the majority party. This way, the majority party controls each committee just as it controls the entire House or Senate.

After a bill is introduced into Congress, the next step is for it to be sent to a committee for consideration. The majority party in each chamber gets to decide which committees get which bills. Sometimes a bill is sent to more than one committee.

When a bill reaches a committee, the committee first decides whether it wants to consider it. The vast majority of bills get tabled, or set aside, dying without consideration. The rest of the bills are studied, usually by a subcommittee.

When a subcommittee gets a bill, it uses its staff to study and research the bill to decide whether Congress should enact it. If the bill is particularly important, the subcommittee might hold hearings on it. Hearings allow the subcommittee to collect testimony on whether and why Congress should enact the bill,

Standing Committees in the House and Senate, 108th Congress (2003–5)

House Committees: Agriculture; Appropriations; Armed Services; Budget; Education and the Workforce; Energy and Commerce; Financial Services; Government Reform; House Administration; International Relations; Judiciary; Resources; Rules; Science; Small Business; Standards of Official Conduct; Transportation and Infrastructure; Veterans Affairs; and Ways and Means

Senate Committees: Agriculture, Nutrition, and Forestry; Appropriations; Armed Services; Banking, Housing, and Urban Affairs; Budget; Commerce, Science, and Transportation; Energy and Natural Resources; Environment and Public Works; Finance; Foreign Relations; Governmental Affairs; Health, Education, Labor, and Pensions; Judiciary; Rules and Administration; Small Business and Entrepreneurship; and Veterans Affairs

what the bill should accomplish, and how the bill should be written. Hearings feature testimony by experts, officials from federal agencies, lobbyists, and other people interested in the legislation. The subcommittee can rewrite the bill and decide whether to report it, or send it, to the main committee for a vote.

When the main committee gets a bill back, it can conduct research and hold hearings just like the subcommittee did. Committee hearings used to be closed to the public, but are

Iron Triangles

Members of Congress do much of their legislative work in committees. Each committee is devoted to one or more areas of government, such as commerce or the military. A committee usually has many subcommittees, which are smaller committees devoted to a specific area of government for which the committee is generally responsible.

Starting in the 1950s, congressional committee work depended largely on relationships called iron triangles. An iron triangle was a relationship between a specific congressional committee or subcommittee, an agency in the executive branch of government, and private interest groups, all of which specialized in a particular area of government. Burdett A. Loomis described an iron triangle for sugar in *The Contemporary Congress:*

> In the 1950s, ... sugar interests worked with the appropriate Agriculture Committee subcommittees in the House and the Senate and the relevant U.S. Department of Agriculture officials to maintain domestic sugar prices that were consistently several times higher than those in world markets. By the 1960s, various interests began to challenge the tidy, profitable sugar subsystem. Consumer and environmental groups, among others, began to influence agricultural policies. In 1974, the sugar triangle broke apart, as the subcommittee could not maintain control over the price support policies. Subsequently, however, sugar interests succeeded in lobbying a broad mix of legislators to reconstruct a similar marketing that continues to fix U.S. prices at a considerably higher level than elsewhere in the world.

The number of private interest groups working through lobbyists in Washington, D.C., has grown tremendously since the 1950s. According to Kenneth Janda, Jeffrey Berry, and Jerry Goldman in *The Challenge of Democracy* in 1997, "The explosion in the number of interest groups and the growth of government and overlapping jurisdictions [areas of responsibility] put an end to iron triangles." These authors explain that iron triangles have been replaced by issue networks—large, informal groups made up of members of Congress, committee staffers, agency officials, lobbyists, and others who specialize in specific government issues. Because the growing numbers of interest groups and agency regulators are competing for a fixed amount of government dollars, these authors say issue networks have much more conflict than iron triangles had.

now usually open since the House changed its rules in the 1990s. A committee considers a bill line-by-line and creates a report on why the bill is important. Committee members opposed to the bill can include their concerns in the report. Then the committee votes on the bill. If the vote is against the bill, it dies in the committee. If the vote is in favor of the bill, it goes back to the House or Senate.

Calendar If a Senate committee votes in favor of a bill, the bill goes to the full Senate, where it is placed on a calendar. The Senate considers most bills in the order in which they appear on the calendar. The leaders of the parties in the Senate, called the majority leader and minority leader, work together to arrange a time for debating the bill. They also set limitations on what kinds of amendments, or changes, senators can offer for the bill on the Senate floor. Their agreement on debate and amendments is called unanimous consent, because the entire Senate must approve it.

If a House committee votes in favor of a bill, the bill goes to the full House, where it is placed on one of various House calendars. If the bill is an appropriations bill, the House Appropriations Committee works with the Speaker of the House and the House majority leader to set the time for debate. If the bill is not an appropriations bill, the House Rules Committee gets to set the time for debate and to decide what kinds of amendments representatives can offer on the floor. The House has complicated rules for determining the order in which it considers bills from its various calendars.

Floor procedure Debate is a chance for members of Congress to show their supporters, both voters and private interest groups, how hard they are working for them. When it is time to debate a bill, the House follows the arrangement worked out by the House Rules Committee. The House has strict rules governing who may speak on a bill and for how much time.

Debate in the Senate is not restricted as much as in the House. In fact, a senator can normally speak for as long as desired about a particular bill. This occasionally results in a filibuster, which happens when one or more senators speak for a long time so that the time for considering a bill runs out before a vote is taken. A successful filibuster kills a bill before

Daily Operations of the Legislative Branch

(From left to right) Harry Reid of Nevada, minority leader Tom Daschle of South Dakota, Colombian president Alvaro Uribe, and majority leader Bill Frist of Tennessee meet in March 2004. Less than a year later, following Daschle's defeat in the November election, Reid replaced him as minority leader. © Yuri Gripas/Reuters/Corbis.

the full Senate gets to vote on it. The longest filibuster on record was by U.S. senator Strom Thurmond of South Carolina, who spoke against civil rights legislation for 24 hours, 18 minutes, on August 28–29, 1957.

Beginning in 1917, the Senate adopted a cloture rule, which is a way to end a filibuster. (The word comes from the alteration of a French word meaning "closure.") Under the cloture rule as of 2005, three-fifths of the Senate, or sixty senators, can bring a filibuster to an end by voting for cloture.

When debate has ended in either the House or the Senate, the senators and representatives who are present vote on the bill under consideration. To pass one chamber, the bill must receive a simple majority of votes. This means that in the House, at least 218 of the 435 representatives must vote in favor of a bill to pass it. In the Senate, fifty-one senators (or fifty senators and the vice president of the United States) must vote in favor of a bill to pass it. When the Senate is split 50-50, the vice president of the United States gets to cast the tie-breaking vote as president of the Senate under Article I, Section 2, of the Constitution.

If only one chamber of Congress passes a bill, it dies there. If both chambers pass identical versions of the same bill, it goes to the president of the United States for consideration. If the House and Senate pass different versions of the same bill, the two bills go to a congressional conference committee.

Conference committees When the House and Senate have different versions of the same bill, they usually work out the differences informally. Often the chairs, or heads, of the committees that wrote the bills meet to agree on a single, identical version.

If the bill is very important or controversial, meaning there is a lot of disagreement, the two chambers may pass their own versions and then send them to a conference committee. About 20 percent of all bills that pass Congress go through conference committees.

Conference committees have members from both the House and Senate, usually between three and nine altogether. The Speaker of the House and the majority leader of the Senate appoint the conference committee members with advice from the chairs of the committees that wrote the bills. The Speaker and Senate majority leader normally appoint members from the very committees that wrote the bills being sent to conference.

Members of a conference committee meet to work out the differences in the House and Senate bills. If a majority of the committee can agree on a single version of the bill, that version goes to the House and Senate with a conference report. The report explains the version that the committee agreed upon. The House and Senate then vote on that version. They are not allowed to make any changes to it.

Daily Operations of the Legislative Branch

President Bill Clinton vetoes a Republican-backed $792 billion tax cut plan in September 1999. Under the Constitution, Congress may override a president's veto by a two-thirds vote of both the House and Senate. © Reuters/Corbis.

If both chambers pass the conference committee's bill by simple majorities, it goes to the president of the United States for consideration. If the bill fails to pass in both chambers, it either dies or can be sent back to the conference committee for further work.

Presidential consideration When both chambers of Congress pass a bill, it is signed by the president of the Senate (the vice president of the United States) and by the Speaker of the House. The bill then goes to the president of the United States for consideration. If the president signs the bill, it becomes law.

The president, however, can veto, or reject, a bill by sending it back to Congress with reasons for the veto. This is called a return veto. If the president vetoes a bill, it does not become law unless Congress votes to override the president's veto. For a bill to become law despite a president's veto, two-thirds of both the

House and Senate must vote for the bill in the override vote. According to a study in 2004, prior to 1969, Congress overrode one out of every eighteen return vetoes. Since 1969, Congress has overridden one out of every five return vetoes. As of 2005, the most recent override happened in February 1998, when Congress overrode a veto from President Bill Clinton (1946–; served 1993–2001) of a bill for funding thirty-eight military construction projects.

Committee work

Drafting legislation is not the only work members of Congress do in committees. Standing committees do oversight work, select committees investigate specific issues, and joint committees handle matters that require action by both chambers of Congress.

Legislative oversight Many congressional laws concern the operation of federal departments and agencies. Departments and agencies are offices that administer programs for a specific area of government. The Department of Agriculture, for example, administers federal programs for American agribusinesses and farmers. The Central Intelligence Agency collects intelligence (information) concerning national security, or safety.

Most departments and agencies function in the executive branch of the federal government, under the president of the United States. Congress and its standing committees, however, are responsible for the legislation concerning these departments and agencies. To make sure the departments and agencies are working properly, the standing committees of Congress engage in oversight work.

Oversight work can take many forms. Committee members and their staffs often meet informally with agency officials to learn how things are going and to discuss specific problems. A committee might require a department to provide a report about an area of concern. If a department or agency is having a major problem, the committee can hold formal hearings to investigate the situation.

Oversight work can lead to correction of a problem by the department or agency. It also can result in new legislation to change the way a department or agency works or is funded.

Daily Operations of the Legislative Branch

Lt. Col. Oliver North is sworn in before his testimony before a congressional committee investigating the Iran-Contra scandal in July 1987. Special committees are frequently formed to investigate governmental problems. AP/Wide World Photos.

Select committees Select committees, also called special committees, are committees that the House and Senate create, individually, to investigate specific issues. Select committees are usually temporary instead of permanent.

Select committees can investigate governmental problems. In 1987, for example, both chambers of Congress created select committees to investigate the administration of President Ronald Reagan (1911–2004; served 1981–89), which sold weapons to Iran and used the money illegally to provide weapons to rebels fighting the government in Nicaragua. After the terrorist attacks in America on September 11, 2001, the House created the Select

Committee on Homeland Security to develop government policies regarding homeland safety in America and to oversee homeland safety activities in the executive branch. It became a standing committee in January 2005.

The chambers of Congress also use select committees to investigate new areas of legislation. Usually, however, select committees cannot receive bills that are introduced into Congress for consideration or send bills to Congress for a vote.

Joint committees Joint committees are committees that both chambers of Congress create together. These committees usually conduct research and provide Congress with information. The Joint Economic Committee, for example, studies and provides information on the nation's economy. The Joint Committee on Taxation studies and provides information on the tax effects of America's laws and policies. As with select committees, joint committees usually cannot receive bills from Congress for consideration or send bills to Congress for a vote.

The national budget

The national budget is the plan for how America is going to raise and spend money each year. The Constitution gives Congress the power to raise money through taxes and debt, or borrowing, and to decide how to spend it. Under this authority, Congress had primary responsibility for preparing the national budget each year until 1921.

In 1921, Congress passed the Budgeting and Accounting Act, or BAA. The BAA gave the president of the United States the job of preparing an initial budget plan each year. It also created the Bureau of the Budget, a governmental office for helping the president prepare the annual budget. (In 1970, the Bureau of the Budget was renamed the Office of Management and Budget, or OMB.)

Even after 1921, Congress retained the constitutional power to pass the final budget each year in tax and spending laws. The president's power under the BAA, however, made it hard for Congress to change the president's annual budget plan very much. So in 1974, Congress passed another law, called the Budget and Impoundment Control Act, or BICA. This act created standing budget committees in both chambers of

Daily Operations of the Legislative Branch

Preparing the federal budget is a critical responsibility that both the executive and legislative branches have a hand in. Here, President Ronald Reagan (left) offers budget director David Stockman some jelly beans during a budget meeting in the 1980s.
© Bettmann/Corbis.

Congress. It also created the Congressional Budget Office (CBO). CBO helps Congress with the budget process just as OMB helps the president.

To give Congress more control over the federal budget, BICA established a schedule for the process. It made the government's official budget planning year, or fiscal year, the period that runs from October 1 through the following September 30. Each year by the first Monday in February, the president must present the administration's proposed budget for the upcoming October through September cycle. With assistance from OMB, the president prepares the proposal with budget requests from the various government departments and agencies.

In February, the budget committees of both chambers of Congress begin studying the president's proposal with assistance from the CBO. By spring, the budget committees prepare their own proposal for overall government revenue, debt, and spending

Daily Operations of the Legislative Branch

levels for the upcoming fiscal year. Congress's standing committees then work on budgets for their areas of concern using the budget committees's spring resolutions as a guide.

For the revenue side of the budget, the House Ways and Means Committee and the Senate Finance Committee work on laws pertaining to taxes and other sources of income.

Authorization committees in the various standing committees prepare bills for appropriating, or giving, money to mandatory government programs. A mandatory program is one that must be funded under the law. As of 2005, mandatory spending covers about two-thirds of the annual federal budget.

Finally, the Appropriations Committees in the House and Senate work on thirteen bills assigning discretionary money to the various government departments and agencies. Discretionary money covers programs that are not mandatory, or required, but that Congress chooses to fund. For example, Congress might decide to give money to the Department of Defense for new bomber aircraft. The thirteen bills drafted by the Appropriations Committees cover thirteen broad areas of government.

During the whole process, members of Congress and their staffs meet with the president and the president's staff to negotiate deals on how the final budget will look. If all goes according to plan, which it usually does not, Congress passes the budget in the form of the mandatory appropriations bills and the thirteen discretionary appropriations bills by October 1. If some of the bills are not passed by then, Congress has to pass temporary laws to provide money to keep the government running until all the appropriations bills pass.

Casework

Members of Congress and their staffs spend lots of time on casework, helping constituents with personal governmental problems. Constituents are the people whom a member of Congress represents. A senator's constituents are the residents of the senator's entire state. A representative's constituents are the residents of the congressional district for which the representative was elected. Each congressional district has an average of about six hundred thousand residents.

Constituents ask members of Congress for help with a variety of governmental issues. Some might be having trouble getting a refund from the Internal Revenue Service, which

Gerrymandering

Representatives are elected to the House from districts, or sections, that are created in each state. Districts are supposed to be formed fairly so that they do not give any political party an advantage in elections. History, however, includes many examples of districts that were shaped unfairly to crowd voters from a state's weaker political party into fewer districts.

One of the most popular examples of such an occurrence is named for Governor Elbridge Gerry (1744–1814) of Massachusetts. In 1812, Gerry signed a law creating new districts in Massachusetts for election to the state senate. The law shaped the districts so that Elbridge's party, the Democratic-Republicans, would control most of the districts, while the Federalist Party would control fewer.

Crowding Federalist Party voters into fewer districts had a curious result. On a map, the outline of one of the districts looked like the shape of a lizard. The shape reminded cartoonist Elkanah Tisdale of a salamander. In a political cartoon in the Boston Gazette, Tisdale called the district a "Gerry-mander."

"Gerrymandering" became a term for the strategy of shaping election districts for political advantage. America's most infamous example of gerrymandering may be the "shoestring" district in Mississippi. This district crowded African American voters into a district that looped like a lazy shoestring, stretching 300 miles long and only 20 miles wide.

Gerrymandering took an interesting turn after the census of 1990, which counted and assessed the makeup of the population of America. States used the census to create new district boundaries, an issue they reconsider each decade after the new federal census comes out. Many of the new districts specifically gave African Americans and Latino Americans a majority of votes to allow them to elect members to Congress. The result was that fifty-eight minorities won election to the House in 1992, up from thirty-eight in 1990.

The new districts, however, faced challenges in the federal court system. Ultimately, the U.S. Supreme Court ruled that gerrymandering done to favor racial groups violates the Constitution. Political gerrymandering continues, however, because it is possible to create districts that look fair but still give major parties a political advantage.

Elkanah Tisdale cartoon shows an electoral district in Massachusetts, twisted in what Tisdale thought of as a salamander. A friend of his suggested it was a "Gerry-mander," in "honor" of Massachusetts governor Elbridge Gerry, who agreed with the districting plan. © Bettmann/Corbis.

collects federal income taxes. Others might be having trouble getting a passport from the Department of State for traveling to foreign countries. Senators and representatives help constituents by talking to people in the appropriate government offices to try to resolve such problems. According to Mark Roelofs in *The Poverty of American Politics,* one estimate says members of Congress spend 80 percent of their time on casework.

Doing casework for constituents is part of building support for reelection. When Congress is in session, the members are usually in committee meetings and on the floor of Congress from Tuesday through Thursday. The rest of the week they fly back to their home states or districts to make public appearances, meet with constituents, campaign for reelection, and pay attention to casework. According to Walter E. Volkomer in *American Government,* when U.S. representative Gary Ackerman (1942–) of New York was asked how important casework is, he said, "About second to breathing."

Campaigning

Campaigning is not technically part of the job for senators and representatives. They are paid to make laws, not to run for reelection. Campaigning, however, consumes a lot of time for members of Congress.

Under the U.S. Constitution, the entire House of Representatives is up for election every two years. This means representatives who want to serve more than one term have to begin working on reelection campaigns soon after taking office. Representatives who make careers out of working in the House have reelection campaigns working all the time.

Senators face reelection every six years. This means they do not have to spend quite as much time on reelection campaigns as representatives do. The Senate seats are divided into three groups for election purposes. Every two years, when the entire House is up for election, one group of Senate seats faces reelection, so there are always some members of the Senate working on reelection.

The first thing members of Congress must do to get reelected is raise lots of money. In 2000, winning candidates in the House spent an average of about $636,000 on their campaigns. Winning senators spent an average of $5.6 million.

Daily Operations of the Legislative Branch

First lady Hillary Rodham Clinton listens to Hezekiah Walker of the Love Fellowship Tabernacle in Brooklyn, New York, during a U.S. Senate campaign appearance on November 5, 2000. Two days later, she was victorious. Getty Images.

The money for campaigns comes from many sources. Candidates can spend as much of their own money as they want to get elected, which means that wealthy people often have an advantage over candidates who are not as financially endowed. The rest of the money raised during campaigns comes from donations, mostly from political action committees (PACs) and individual citizens.

PACs are organizations that businesses and other groups form for collecting money for donation to political candidates. Members of Congress usually get more donations from PACs than their challengers get. This is because members of Congress can already pass laws favorable to the businesses and organizations that make PAC donations.

In addition to raising money, campaigning involves making public appearances, visiting with voters, creating media

Daily Operations of the Legislative Branch

advertising campaigns, debating challengers, and appearing on the evening news whenever possible. Name recognition goes a long way toward winning an election.

Statistics show that members of the House who run for reelection win about 90 percent of the time. Senators who run for reelection win most of the time too, but less frequently than members of the House. This is because senators have to win support from an entire state. Representatives only have to win support from a district of about six hundred thousand people, and these districts are usually drawn to favor one of the major political parties, the Republicans or the Democrats.

Miscellaneous offices

Congress has miscellaneous offices that support the lawmaking process or serve another governmental function. One of the most well known is the Library of Congress. President John Adams (1735–1826; served 1797–1801) and Congress created the Library by law in 1800. In 1801, it received its first collection of materials, 740 books and 3 maps ordered from London.

In 1814, during the War of 1812 (1812–14), Great Britain burned many government offices in Washington, D.C., including the 3,000-volume Library of Congress. The next year, former president Thomas Jefferson (1743–1826; served 1801–9) restocked the library by selling his personal collection of 6,487 books to Congress for $23,940. As of 2005, the Library has 29 million books and 99 million other items on 530 miles of shelving. According to the Library's Web site, its mission is "to make its resources available and useful to the Congress and the American people and preserve a universal collection of knowledge and creativity for future generations."

Other congressional offices include the Architect of the Capitol, which develops, operates, and maintains the Capitol and congressional office buildings, Library of Congress buildings, Supreme Court building, U.S. Botanic Garden, Capital power plant, and other facilities. The U.S. Botanic Garden operates indoor greenhouses and outdoor gardens for plants from the United States and around the world. The Government Printing Office, created in 1860 to serve as a printer for Congress, collects and publishes information about the federal government for all three of its branches: executive, legislative, and judicial.

For More Information

BOOKS

Beard, Charles A. *American Government and Politics.* 10th ed. New York: Macmillan Co., 1949.

Burnham, James. *Congress and the American Tradition.* New Brunswick, NJ: Transaction Publishers, 2003.

Congressional Quarterly Inc. *Guide to the Congress of the United States.* 1st ed. Washington, DC: Congressional Quarterly Service, 1971.

Green, Mark. *Who Runs Congress?* 3rd ed. New York: The Viking Press, 1979.

Janda, Kenneth, Jeffrey M. Berry, and Jerry Goldman. *The Challenge of Democracy.* 5th ed. Boston: Houghton Mifflin Company, 1997.

Loomis, Burdett A. *The Contemporary Congress.* 3rd ed. Boston: Bedford/St. Martin's, 2000.

McClenaghan, William A. *Magruder's American Government 2003.* Needham, MA: Prentice Hall School Group, 2002.

Parenti, Michael. *Democracy for the Few.* 6th ed. New York: St. Martin's Press, 1995.

Roelofs, H. Mark. *The Poverty of American Politics.* 2nd ed. Philadelphia: Temple University Press, 1998.

Shelley, Mack C., II. *American Government and Politics Today.* 2004–2005 ed. Belmont, CA: Wadsworth Publishing, 2003.

Volkomer, Walter E. *American Government.* 8th ed. Upper Saddle River, NJ: Prentice Hall, 1998.

Wolfensberger, Donald R. *Congress and the People.* Washington, DC, and Baltimore: Woodrow Wilson Center Press and Johns Hopkins University Press, 2000.

PERIODICALS

Anderson, Jack. "Lobbyists: The Unelected Lawmakers in Washington." *Parade* (March 16, 1980).

Wolman, David, and Heather Wax. "Fighting City Hall: Corporations 1, Citizens 0." *UU World* (May/June 2003). Also available at http://www.uuworld.org/2003/03/Feature1b.html (accessed on May 4, 2005).

WEB SITES

Davis, Tom, et al. "Strong Nationwide Support for D.C. Voting Rights across all Groups of Americans." http://www.norton.house.gov/pdf/Dear%20Colleague-voting%20rights%203-07-05.pdf (accessed on March 16, 2005).

Library of Congress. http://www.loc.gov (accessed on March 15, 2005).

"Money Wins Big in 2000 Elections." *Center for Responsive Politics.* http://www.opensecrets.org/pressreleases/Post-Election2000.htm (accessed on March 15, 2005).

Sollenberger, Mitchell A. "Congressional Overrides of Presidential Vetoes." http://www.house.gov/rules/98-157.pdf (accessed on March 16, 2005).

"TRMPAC for Dummies: Understanding the Tom DeLay Fundraising Scandal." http://www.democrats.org/specialreports/trmpac/index.html (accessed on March 16, 2005).

United States House of Representatives. http://www.house.gov (accessed on March 15, 2005).

United States Senate. http://www.senate.gov (accessed on March 15, 2005).

Legislative-Executive Checks and Balances

The U.S. Constitution divides the powers of government into three branches: legislative, executive, and judicial. Generally speaking, the legislative branch, Congress, makes the nation's laws. The executive branch enforces the laws through the president and various executive offices. The judicial branch, made up of the Supreme Court and lower federal courts, decides cases that arise under the laws.

This division of government is called the separation of powers. The purpose of the separation of powers is to prevent tyranny, which is arbitrary (random) or unfair government action that can result when one person has all the power to make, enforce, and interpret the laws.

In addition to the broad separation of powers into three branches, the Constitution keeps the legislative and executive branches separate with various specific provisions. Article I, Section 6, prevents members of Congress from serving as officers of the government in the executive branch. Article I, Section 5, says each chamber of Congress, namely the House of Representatives and the Senate, is the sole judge of who wins congressional elections and who is qualified to serve there. The same part of the Constitution gives the House and Senate sole authority to make their rules of operation.

Article I, Section 6, is known as the Speech and Debate Clause and says representatives and senators cannot be punished for speeches made in Congress. Neither can they be arrested while in office, except for treason, felony, and breach of the peace. (Treason is defined as levying war against America or giving aid

Words to Know

appropriations bill: A bill, or law, that assigns money to a government department or agency.

bicameralism: The practice of dividing the legislative, or lawmaking, power of government into two chambers.

checks and balances: The specific powers in one branch of government that allow it to limit the powers of the other branches.

Congress: The legislative, or lawmaking, branch of the federal government. Congress has two chambers, the Senate and the House of Representatives.

Constitution of the United States of America: The document written in 1787 that established the federal government under which the United States of America has operated since 1789. Article I covers the legislative branch and Article II covers the executive branch.

impoundment: The presidential practice of refusing to spend money that Congress appropriates for an executive department, agency, or program.

personnel floor: A congressional minimum on the number of employees a governmental department, agency, or program must employ.

president: The highest officer in the executive branch of the federal government, with primary responsibility for enforcing the nation's laws.

quorum: The number of members of Congress who must be present for Congress to conduct business, such as voting on bills. The U.S. Constitution says a chamber has a quorum when a simple majority of its members are present.

reprogramming: The practice of using money that Congress appropriates to one governmental program for a different program.

separation of powers: Division of the powers of government into different branches to prevent one branch from having too much power.

veto: Rejection of a bill, or proposed law, by the president of the United States. If the president vetoes a bill, it does not become law unless two-thirds of both chambers of Congress vote to override the veto.

and comfort to its enemies. A felony is the most serious kind of crime, usually punishable by imprisonment for more than a year. Breach of the peace refers to disorderly conduct.)

Article II, Section 1, says the president must get a salary, which Congress sets, but that Congress may not raise or lower the salary while the president is in office. The same provision prevents the president from getting any compensation other than the salary set before the president entered office.

Checks and balances

The men who wrote the Constitution in 1787 wanted each branch's power to be separate, but not absolute. They considered

Legislative-Executive Checks and Balances

President Andrew Jackson was dubbed "King Andrew" by political and media enemies after he attempted to dismantle the federal banking system and deposit funds into various state banks. He was soon censured by both the U.S. House of Representatives and Senate, a powerful example of the legislative branch using checks and balances with the president.
Library of Congress.

absolute power, even over just a portion of the government, to be dangerous. They were especially fearful of giving too much power to the president, who might come to resemble an uncontrollable king. They were also fearful of giving too much power to the House of Representatives, which they saw as the chamber of Congress that would represent the popular will of America. The men who wrote the Constitution wanted to protect the wealthy class of society from the passions of popular democracy.

To prevent the power of any one branch from being absolute, the Founding Fathers wrote the Constitution to contain a system of checks and balances. These are powers that each branch has for limiting the power of the other branches. Some scholars say

Legislative-Executive Checks and Balances

the system of checks and balances actually creates a government of shared powers instead of one with separated powers.

The checks and balances between Congress and the president are many. The most important are the president's power to

Chambers of Congress

The term "checks and balances" usually refers to the power that one branch of government has to limit the powers of the other branches. For example, the president checks the power of Congress with the ability to veto laws that Congress passes.

Congress, however, has an internal system of checks and balances. Its two chambers, the House of Representatives and the Senate, check each other, because a law cannot pass Congress unless both chambers approve it by simple majorities.

This internal check was important to the Founding Fathers, the men who wrote the Constitution in 1787. Many of them saw the Senate as the voice of wealthy Americans, and the House as the popular voice of free Americans (primarily whites) generally. As described by Philip Kurland and Ralph Lerner in *The Founders' Constitution:*

> The first or lower chamber could then be viewed as an embodiment of the popular will of the day, an assemblage of representatives who come close to being reflexes of the people at large. Across the range of republican opinion, it was agreed that such a body was the necessary foundation of popular government resting on consent. But where the people at large can be arbitrary, tyrannical, and passionate, so too can their faithful mouthpieces [the representatives in the House]. Or, partaking of the failings to which any unchecked body is exposed, a single assembly may be improperly influenced or self-serving or foolish with none to call it to its senses. Such a people, such an assembly, require a check [the Senate] to save them from themselves. Alternatively, one could argue that it is precisely in a regime grounded on popular sovereignty [authority] and devoid of any class vested with hereditary prerogatives [privileges] that a second chamber [the Senate], free to veto "the *united will* of the *whole community,* is not only *absurd* and *ridiculous,* but *highly dangerous.*"

Most of the Founding Fathers agreed that a unicameral, or single-chamber, legislature would be highly dangerous. Many of them feared that the House, if unchecked, would make laws unfavorable to the wealthy class of society. According to Burdett Loomis in *The Contemporary Congress,* Virginia delegate James Madison (1751–1836) felt it was safer "to divide the legislature into different branches; and to render them, by different modes of election, and different principles of action, as little connected with each other, as the nature of their common functions and their common dependence on society, will admit."

Under the Constitution of 1787, representatives were chosen by Americans with voting rights, while senators were chosen by state legislatures. This was supposed to give the chambers different compositions. The House would represent free Americans, and the Senate would represent the states. Under the Seventeenth Amendment in 1913, however, the Constitution changed to provide for popular

Legislative-Executive Checks and Balances

veto, or reject, laws that Congress passes, and Congress's power to override a presidential veto. Other legislative-executive checks and balances are the executive recommendation power, the legislative appropriations power, senatorial advice and consent, the

election of senators, too. Some political scientists believe this weakened the checks and balances between the two chambers, since they both came to be elected the same way, by the people of America.

The rise of the two-party system of Republicans and Democrats in America in the late 1800s also changed the way checks and balances works in Congress. When one party controls the House and the other controls the Senate, Congress can be a battleground for the two parties. Some citizens and scholars, however, believe that the private interest groups that contribute money to the political parties control both of them. Moreover, when one party controls both chambers, there is much less competition between the chambers. Many citizens, historians, and political scientists, therefore, wonder if the chambers of Congress effectively check each other as they originally were supposed to do.

A bird's-eye view of President Bill Clinton delivering the State of the Union Address to members of Congress and to U.S. Supreme Court justices in the U.S. Capitol on February 4, 1997. © Wally McNamee/Corbis.

Legislative-Executive Checks and Balances

division of powers concerning war, congressional oversight work, and removal of the president and other executive officers by impeachment.

Veto power and override

The U.S. Constitution gives the president the power to veto laws passed by Congress. It also gives Congress the power to override a presidential veto. This gives both the executive and legislative branches a role in making America's laws.

Presidential veto To pass Congress, a bill must receive a simple majority of votes in both chambers. This means at least 218 of the 435 representatives in the House must vote in favor of a bill for it to pass. In the Senate, either 51 of the 100 senators or else 50 senators plus the vice president of the United States must vote in favor of a bill to pass it. When the Senate is split 50-50, the vice president gets to cast the tie-breaking vote as president of the Senate under Article I, Section 2, of the Constitution.

Article I, Section 7, of the Constitution says:

Every bill which shall have passed the house of representatives and the senate, shall, before it become a law, be presented to the president of the United States; if he approve he shall sign it, but if not he shall return it, with his objections to that house in which it shall have originated.... If any bill shall not be returned by the president within ten days (Sundays excepted) after it shall have been presented to him, the same shall be a law, in like manner as if he had signed it, unless the Congress by their adjournment prevent its return, in which case it shall not be a law.

Under this procedure, there are four things that can happen to a bill when Congress passes it and presents it to the president for consideration. Two are ways the bill can become a law. If the president signs the bill within ten days, not counting Sunday, it becomes a law. The president can also choose to do nothing with the bill. If ten days pass, not counting Sunday, and Congress is still in session when the president has not acted on it, the bill becomes a law as if the president had signed it.

After Congress passes a bill, the president has the power to veto it. The usual way to do this is to send the bill back to

Legislative-Executive Checks and Balances

Congress with a veto message within ten days of receiving it. The veto message explains to Congress and the nation why the president is rejecting a bill. This is called a return veto.

The other way to veto a bill happens when Congress adjourns, or takes an official break, before the president has had the bill for ten days. Because such an adjournment prevents the president from having a full ten days for a return veto, the Constitution provides that bills do not become laws in such situations. This kind of veto is called a pocket veto, for it is as if the president simply puts the bill in his pocket, waiting for Congress to adjourn.

Generally speaking, members of Congress believe that pocket vetoes can happen only at the end of each official two-year term of Congress. (Congress's two-year terms begin the January after every November election for the House of Representatives.) Presidents, however, use the pocket veto when Congress breaks between the first and second one-year sessions of its terms, and even during congressional recesses, or breaks, in the middle of a session. The Supreme Court has declined to decide the issue of when the president may use a pocket veto. The Supreme Court prefers to stay out of disputes between the executive and legislative branches of government.

The presidential veto is powerful. Obviously, it allows presidents to reject bills of which they disapprove. The mere threat of a veto can discourage Congress from considering or passing a bill in the first place. A veto threat also gives the president the power to encourage Congress to change a bill to the president's liking before passing it.

According to a study by the Congressional Research Service in April 2004, presidents used the return veto 1,484 times and the pocket veto 1,065 times up to that point in history. The number of pocket vetoes is high because Congress often passes many bills in a flurry of activity less then ten days before it adjourns. Many of these die from pocket vetoes.

As of 2005, Franklin D. Roosevelt (1882–1945; served 1933–45) holds the record for the president with the most vetoes—635. As of 2005, eight presidents never used the veto power. George W. Bush (1946– ; served 2001–) did not use his veto power during his first term in office. Prior to Bush, the last president not to use the veto power was James A. Garfield

Line Item Veto

The U.S. Constitution gives the president the power to veto bills passed by Congress. To exercise the veto power, the president must reject an entire bill. The veto power does not include the power to veto portions of a bill.

The governors of most states have a power called the line item veto. This allows them to veto portions of appropriations bills of which they disapprove. The line item veto is supposed to allow governors to cut down on excessive government spending.

Presidents, especially Ronald Reagan (1911–2004), have asked Congress to give them a line item veto power, too. According to Louis Fisher in *The Politics of Shared Power*, Reagan said to Congress in his 1986 State of the Union address, "Tonight I ask you to give me what forty-three governors have: Give me a line-item veto this year. Give me the authority to veto waste, and I'll take the responsibility, I'll make the cuts, I'll take the heat." President Bill Clinton (1946–) echoed the request in his State of the Union address in 1995.

In 1996, Congress surprised the nation by passing the Line Item Veto Act. The Act allowed the president to strike specific dollar amounts and tax benefits from appropriations bills passed by Congress. Congress could override the line item veto only by passing another bill containing the portions the president had stricken. The new bill would be subject to the normal veto and veto override provisions of the Constitution.

The Line Item Veto Act was a surprise because it shifted power over the annual federal budget from Congress to the president. According to the authors of *The Challenge of Democracy*, U.S. senator Dan Coats of Indiana said of the Act, "It's Congress's way of saying, 'We've lost control of the spending process.'"

The line item veto, however, did not last long. In the case of *Clinton v. City of New York* in 1998, the U.S. Supreme Court struck down the act. The Court said the act violated the Constitution because under the Constitution, the only way for a president to use the veto power is to veto an entire bill. In order to give the president line item veto power, the nation would have to adopt a constitutional amendment. Many scholars, including Louis Fisher, believe the line item veto would give presidents too much power over government spending compared with the power of Congress.

(1831–1881), who served for only a short time in 1881 before dying after being shot by an assassin.

Congressional override When the president vetoes a bill by returning it to Congress while Congress is still in session, the Constitution allows Congress to try to override the veto. It says that if the president vetoes a bill:

> he shall return it, with his objections to that house in which it shall have originated, who shall enter the objections at large on their journal, and proceed to

Legislative-Executive Checks and Balances

Former president Ronald Reagan (left) greets President-elect Bill Clinton at his office in November 1992. Both were supporters of the line item veto. © Gary Hershorn/Reuters/Corbis.

reconsider it. If after such reconsideration two-thirds of that house shall agree to pass the bill, it shall be sent, together with the objections, to the other house, by which it shall likewise be reconsidered, and if approved by two-thirds of that house, it shall become a law.

Under this provision, Congress can override a return veto when two-thirds of both chambers vote in favor of a bill after the veto.

Legislative-Executive Checks and Balances

President George W. Bush did not use his veto power during his first term in office. The White House.

The language of the Constitution makes it sound like Congress must vote on whether to override every return veto. In practice, however, the chamber that first gets the bill back from the president holds an override vote only if there is a chance that two-thirds of its members will vote in favor of the bill (as opposed to the simple majority required to pass the bill in the first place). Through practice, Congress also has established that only two-thirds of the members present for an override vote, not two-thirds of the entire membership, must vote for a bill to override the veto. To hold an override vote or conduct any other business, however, a chamber must have a quorum of members in attendance. A quorum exists when a majority of the chamber's members are present.

If the president pocket vetoes a bill, Congress does not get a chance to override the veto. This is because a pocket veto happens when Congress adjourns before the president has the bill for ten days. Adjournment prevents Congress from reconsidering the bill and holding an override vote.

It is very hard, politically, to override a return veto. Normally, neither of the two major parties, the Republicans and Democrats, has two-thirds of the seats in the House or Senate. Members of the president's political party rarely vote to override a veto. According to a Congressional Research Service study in April 2004, Congress had overturned only 106, or 7.1 percent, of the 1,484 return vetoes to that point in history. As of 2005, the president whose vetoes were overruled the most times was Andrew Johnson (1808–1875). Congress voted to override fifteen of Johnson's twenty-nine return vetoes. This was the period of Reconstruction, in which Congress was trying to help bring the South back into the Union after the American Civil War (1861–65). Johnson disagreed with Congress's Reconstruction policies. The disagreement fueled the House's 1868 impeachment of Johnson for violation of a federal law. The Senate came one vote short of convicting Johnson and removing him from office.

Legislative veto The Constitution contains a veto power only for the president. Congress, however, created a veto power for itself. In 1932, for example, it passed a law giving the president the power to reorganize the offices of the executive branch without first getting congressional approval. Either chamber of Congress, however, could reject a reorganization by passing a simple resolution against it within sixty days of the president's action. (A resolution is a statement of congressional will or opinion.) This process gave each chamber of Congress the power to veto presidential action on reorganization.

Legislative vetoes have many forms. They can be simple resolutions by one chamber of Congress, concurrent resolutions by both chambers, and even resolutions by a single committee of Congress.

Congress has used its veto power to strengthen its control of the departments and agencies of the executive branch. Many laws, for example, have given Congress the power to disapprove a department or agency's spending decisions. Other laws have given Congress the power to disapprove department or agency action.

The legislative veto power has been challenged in court many times. In 1983, in *INS v. Chadha,* the U.S. Supreme Court decided that the legislative veto violates the Constitution. The Constitution says the only way Congress can pass a bill or resolution is when both chambers approve it and present it to the president for executive veto consideration. Legislative vetoes violate this by giving either one or both chambers of Congress the power to take official action that the president cannot veto.

Despite the Supreme Court's ruling, Congress continues to include the legislative veto power in the nation's laws. According to Louis Fisher in *The Politics of Shared Power,* Congress enacted four hundred legislative vetoes between the time of the decision in *INS v. Chadha* and the end of 1987. Congress also gets around the Supreme Court's decision by using informal arrangements with agencies. Through such arrangements, agencies agree to give Congress unofficial legislative veto power over agency spending or action. Agency officials make such arrangements to appease Congress in order to get the funding and programs they want.

Executive recommendation power

Article II, Section 3, of the Constitution says the president "shall from time to time give the Congress information of the state of the union, and recommend to their consideration such measures as he shall judge necessary and expedient [proper]." Every year in January, the president carries out this duty by giving a State of the Union address to Congress and the nation. The address outlines what the president would like to see Congress do in the upcoming year. The president conveys such information to Congress in reports during the year, too.

The power to recommend action to Congress serves as a check on Congress's power to pass laws. Congress is not required to do what the president asks. There can be political pressure, however, to do much of what a popular president recommends. For example, after Republican president Ronald Reagan (1911–2004; served 1981–89) won a landslide reelection to a second term in 1984, he was able to get large tax cut bills through Congress even though the Democrats controlled the House of Representatives.

Legislative appropriations power

The Constitution gives the House of Representatives the power to write, and both chambers of Congress the power to pass, bills for raising revenue through taxes and other methods. By tradition, the House also writes appropriations bills. An appropriations bill, also called a spending bill, is one that gives money to a government department or agency. Under Article I, Section 9, of the Constitution, "No money shall be drawn from the Treasury, but in consequence of appropriations made by law."

The appropriations power is supposed to serve as a check on the president. It restricts the president and the various executive departments and agencies to spending only the money Congress appropriates. The power, however, has led to conflict between the legislative and executive branches. Three of those conflicts involve impoundment, reprogramming, and personnel ceilings and floors.

Impoundment Impoundment happens when the president refuses to spend money Congress has appropriated to a specific department, agency, or program. Presidents and executive agencies use impoundment to control government spending. They also use it to prevent the government from spending tax dollars on projects of which the president's administration does not approve.

The administration of President Richard Nixon (1913–1994; served 1969–74) used the impoundment power a lot from 1969 to 1974. Many in Congress felt this violated the Constitution, an opinion shared by prior members of Congress when presidents used impoundment. When Congress passes an appropriations bill, the

Legislative-Executive Checks and Balances

only way for the president to strike it is by using the veto power under the Constitution. By signing appropriations bills but impounding money for specific programs, the president was creating a sort of line item veto, the power to strike only portions of a spending bill. In other words, impoundment was giving the president greater control over spending and violating the will of Congress concerning government funding.

To fix the situation, Congress passed the Budget and Impoundment Control Act of 1974. In addition to changing the whole federal budget process, the act changed the impoundment power. It requires the president to submit reports to

'DON'T PUT UP ANY RESISTANCE! JUST KEEP IN STEP'

Cartoon shows a small man, labeled "Congress," being hustled away from the Capitol by three men resembling President Richard Nixon. Labels on each of the Nixons are "executive privilege," "impounding of funds," and "veto power." Many in Congress believed the president abused his impoundment power. Illustration by Edmund S. Valtman. Library of Congress.

Legislative-Executive Checks and Balances

Congress when the president impounds funds. If an impoundment is temporary, either chamber of Congress can disapprove it. If an impoundment is permanent, both chambers have to approve it before it takes effect.

Congressional power to disapprove impoundments is a form of legislative veto. As noted earlier, the Supreme Court declared legislative vetoes illegal under the Constitution in the 1983 case of *INS v. Chadha*. However, the executive and legislative branches continue to use the impoundment procedures in the Act of 1974 to guide the exercise of the impoundment power.

Reprogramming Each year the federal government sets a budget for spending for the period October 1 through September 30. The overall budget is based on detailed budget requests that the various departments and agencies submit to the president and Congress. Budget requests specifically identify the programs the departments and agencies want to fund.

Congress gets to set the final annual budget in its appropriations bills. These bills, however, do not contain specifics concerning the programs being funded. Instead, the bills appropriate lump sums of money to the various departments and agencies, such as the Central Intelligence Agency (CIA) or the U.S. Army. The details on the amount being appropriated for specific government programs appear in the reports of the congressional committees that write the appropriations bills.

Reprogramming happens when a department or agency takes money appropriated for one program and spends it on a different program. Reprogramming, like impoundment, can frustrate Congress. This is particularly true when an agency uses reprogramming to fund a project that Congress specifically decided not to fund in its appropriations bills. For example, in July 2002, President George W. Bush had $700 million transferred from unidentified programs into programs for planning an invasion of Iraq. Bush made the transfer without notifying Congress, as he was required by law to do. According to the Center for American Progress, White House allies in Congress told *USA Today* that Bush's move was acceptable because the amount was small compared to overall spending bills.

During the latter half of the twentieth century, Congress tried to gain control over reprogramming. It began by requiring some departments or agencies to advise Congress when reprogramming occurred. Next, some congressional committees required departments and agencies to ask permission for certain reprogramming. In 1974, the appropriations bill for the Department of Defense specifically made it illegal for the Pentagon to use reprogramming to fund projects rejected by Congress. Future defense appropriations bills have repeated this restriction.

Many scholars and government officials believe that requiring committee approval of reprogramming is a legislative veto that is illegal after *INS v. Chadha*. Departments and agencies, however, live with such procedures to appease the committees that are responsible for funding their projects. In addition, the federal government is so large that it is impossible for Congress to catch and correct every instance of reprogramming.

Personnel ceilings and floors Another way presidents have tried to control spending is through personnel ceilings. A personnel ceiling is a limit on the total number of employees a department or agency may hire.

Presidents, through the Office of Management and Budget (OMB), use personnel ceilings to prevent agencies from spending all the money appropriated by Congress for specific projects. In other words, if an agency cannot hire the people it needs for a particular project, the project goes nowhere and the money appropriated for it is saved or spent elsewhere.

Just as Congress tries to control impoundment and reprogramming, it also tries to control personnel ceilings. Its tactic for doing so is called personnel floors. A personnel floor is a minimum number of employees that a department or agency must hire. Congressional committees often write personnel floors into the reports supporting appropriations bills. Congress occasionally includes a personnel floor in an actual bill, making the floor a mandatory part of the law. Floors in committee reports are not absolute, but departments and agencies might follow them to appease their funding committees.

Senatorial advice and consent

There are two powers in the Constitution that the president shares with the Senate alone. One is the appointment of executive officers, judges, and other important positions in the federal government. The other is the making of treaties, or formal agreements, with other nations.

Executive appointments and removals Article II, Section 2, of the Constitution says the president "shall nominate, and by and with the advice and consent of the senate, shall appoint ambassadors, other public ministers and consuls, judges of the supreme court, and all other officers of the United States, whose appointments are not herein otherwise provided for, and which shall be established by law."

Under this provision, when Congress creates important positions in the federal government, the president gets to nominate, or recommend, people for those positions. The Senate then gets to consider and either approve or disapprove the nominations.

There are thousands of positions that the president gets to appoint under the nomination power. With support from trusted advisors, the president personally works on the most important nominations. These include the heads of the executive departments, called secretaries (except for the head of the Department of Justice, who is called the attorney general). The president also works personally to nominate the heads of important agencies (such as the Central Intelligence Agency), Supreme Court justices, and commissioners on the independent regulatory commissions (IRCs). IRCs are governmental bodies, such as the Federal Communications Commission (FCC), that regulate specific areas of the national economy.

Before making an important nomination, the president often checks with key members of the Senate to see if the Senate will approve the nomination. This helps the president eliminate people who have no chance of being appointed. Sometimes a person who is nominated, called a nominee, withdraws his or her name from consideration if it looks like the nomination will fail. For example, in December 2004, President George W. Bush nominated former New York City police commissioner Bernard Kerik (1955–) to be secretary of the Department of Homeland Security (DHS). The DHS is a department that Congress created after the terrorist attacks of September 11, 2001, to coordinate protection of the American homeland. One of the DHS's duties is to enforce immigration laws concerning illegal aliens. Illegal aliens are people from other

Legislative-Executive Checks and Balances

countries who live and work in America without complying with immigration laws. One week after being nominated to lead the DHS, Kerik withdrew his name because he once employed a housekeeper and nanny who was an illegal alien, and he had failed to pay taxes on some of her wages. This information probably would have led the Senate to vote against Kerik for the DHS post.

When the president makes a nomination, the appropriate Senate committee holds hearings to consider the matter. For example, the Senate Judiciary Committee holds hearings to consider nominations to the U.S. Supreme Court and lower federal courts. Upon recommendation from its committees, the Senate usually approves the president's nominations, but occasionally rejects them, requiring the president to make another nomination. If enough senators oppose a nominee, they can prevent the nomination from coming to a vote by using a procedure called a filibuster. A filibuster is a way to use up all of the time assigned to a particular issue without allowing the issue to come to a vote in the Senate. During the first term of Republican president George W. Bush, a minority of Democratic senators used the filibuster to block the Senate from voting on some of Bush's nominations of federal judges. The conflict led some senators to call for revising their filibuster rules to make it harder for a minority of senators to block Senate votes.

There are thousands of positions to fill that the president does not have time to handle personally. The president's cabinet and staff handle the details of these nominations. For less important positions located in a particular state, the president's staff usually checks with senators from that state who are also in the president's political party. If the president fails to extend this courtesy to senators for such appointments, the Senate might reject a nomination. The effect of this practice, called "senatorial courtesy," is to encourage presidents to check with senators before nominating people to positions located in a particular state.

The Constitution refers only to the power to make and approve appointments to federal offices. It does not address who has the power to remove people from important executive positions. Through case law, the Supreme Court has established that except in cases of impeachment, the president has the sole

Legislative-Executive Checks and Balances

Robert Bork was nominated by Ronald Reagan in 1987 to be a U.S. Supreme Court justice but was voted down by the U.S. Senate.

authority to remove people from purely executive positions, such as the heads of the executive departments. The president can remove such people at any time for any reason, because these positions must be held by people in which the president has complete confidence.

To remove commissioners from IRCs, the president must follow the guidelines set by Congress in the laws governing the commissions. Commissioners are supposed to be independent of the executive branch, so the president does not have the right to remove them at will.

Under the Constitution, justices of the Supreme Court and judges of the lower federal courts cannot be removed "during good behavior." Instead, they can only be removed by impeachment and conviction for "treason, bribery, or other high crimes and misdemeanors." Congress has the sole authority to remove judges through the impeachment process. As of 2005, Congress has removed just seven judges from office through impeachment.

Treaties A treaty is a formal agreement with another nation. The Constitution gives the president the power to make treaties "provided two-thirds of the senators present concur [agree]." When the president signs a treaty, the Senate Foreign Relations Committee studies it before submitting it to the entire Senate for a vote. Presidents starting with George Washington (1732–1799; served 1789–97) have involved the Senate in the process of negotiating treaties. This way a treaty has a greater likelihood of being approved by the Senate.

The Senate usually approves treaties signed by the president. One of the most famous exceptions was the Treaty of Versailles, which ended World War I (1914–18). The Treaty of Versailles created the League of Nations, an international organization that was the forerunner of the United Nations. President Woodrow Wilson (1856–1924; served 1913–21) negotiated this important treaty without Senate involvement, and the Senate refused to approve it.

The House plays no role in the process of negotiating and approving treaties. If a treaty program requires federal money, however, the House can determine whether the program gets money through its role in passing appropriations bills.

The Constitution does not say who has the power to cancel treaties. According to Louis Fisher in *The Politics of Shared Power,* treaties have been cancelled by congressional laws, Senate resolutions, new treaties, and presidential action. The Supreme Court has not resolved the issue. Generally speaking, the Supreme Court prefers to have Congress and the president work together to determine who has the power to cancel treaties.

Legislative-Executive Checks and Balances

Officials from many allied countries draft the Versailles Treaty in December 1918. President Woodrow Wilson was involved in the treaty's negotiations, without U.S. Senate involvement. © Bettmann/Corbis.

In addition to treaties, presidents often sign executive agreements with the heads of other nations. Executive agreements are not officially treaties, so they do not require the consent of the Senate. The U.S. Supreme Court, however, has ruled that executive agreements are part of the supreme law of the land, just like treaties.

Presidents typically use treaties for the most important issues and executive agreements for less important issues. Sometimes, however, presidents use an executive agreement for an important issue. Presidents Franklin D. Roosevelt and Harry S. Truman (1884–1972; served 1945–53), for example, used executive agreements at meetings in Yalta and Potsdam to end World War II (1939–45). Using an executive agreement instead of a treaty is significant, because the Senate can require a president to change a treaty before the Senate will approve it.

War powers

The Constitution divides the nation's war powers between Congress and the president. Congress has the power to create an army and navy, and to make rules and appropriate money for their operation. Congress also has the sole power to declare war. The president is "commander in chief of the army and navy." This means the president ultimately controls the operations of the military forces.

This separation of war powers was important to the men who wrote the Constitution in 1787. According to Louis Fisher in *The Politics of Shared Power,* convention delegate James Madison (1751–1836) wrote:

> Those who are to conduct a war cannot in the nature of things, be proper or safe judges, whether a war ought to be commenced [begun], continued, or concluded. They are barred from the latter functions by a great principle in free government, analogous [comparable] to that which separated the sword from the purse, or the power of executing from the power of enacting laws.

Hence, the men who wrote the Constitution generally felt that the president would be able to use military forces without congressional approval only to defend against an attack. To wage an offensive attack would require a declaration of war by Congress.

Presidents have generally ignored this constitutional separation of powers. America has fought in several hundred military actions since the adoption of the Constitution in 1788. As of 2005, Congress has declared war only eleven times for five wars: the War of 1812 (1812–14), the Mexican-American War (1846–48), the Spanish-American War (1898), World War I (1914–18), and World War II.

During the Vietnam War (1954–75), Presidents Lyndon B. Johnson (1908–1973; served 1963–69) and Richard Nixon sent more than five hundred thousand American soldiers to fight without a congressional declaration of war. Over fifty-eight thousand of them died. When the war became politically unpopular, Congress passed the War Powers Resolution of 1973.

The War Powers Resolution requires the president to report to Congress "in every possible instance" within forty-eight

Legislative-Executive Checks and Balances

President Richard Nixon greets Vietnam soldiers as a presidential candidate in 1968. © Corbis.

hours after sending troops into hostile situations. The president is then supposed to withdraw the troops unless Congress declares war or otherwise authorizes the military action within sixty days. Presidents, however, have routinely ignored the requirements of the War Powers Resolution, taking for themselves absolute authority over America's military decisions, offensive and otherwise. Some members of Congress occasionally object when the president violates the War Powers Resolution. For example, in October 1983, President Ronald Reagan sent nineteen hundred troops to the Caribbean island of Grenada to take control away from communist Bernard Coard (1944–), who had taken control of Grenada in a military coup. Eleven members of Congress filed a lawsuit, saying Reagan's invasion violated the U.S. Constitution, which gives Congress sole power to declare war. A federal court of appeals dismissed the case because the invasion was over.

Legislative oversight

To make sure the government is operating as Congress wants it to operate, Congress engages in legislative oversight. This is the process of reviewing the work of government departments and agencies and investigating specific problems. Congress has the power to engage in oversight by virtue of its power to make the laws and appropriate money for governmental operations.

Committees of Congress handle oversight of the departments and agencies for which they write laws and appropriate money. Oversight can take many forms. Much is informal, as when members of a congressional committee meet with federal bureaucrats to see how a program is working. Congress often takes the more formal step of asking an agency to submit an official report of its operations or a specific problem. If a problem is serious, a committee can hold hearings to investigate the situation. Oversight work can lead to informal correction of a problem by a department or agency or to official correction through new laws or different appropriations.

Congressional oversight often leads to conflict with the executive branch. Sometimes the president or executive agencies withhold information from Congress to protect national security, or safety. Other times they withhold information that has nothing to do with national safety, but that they do not want to share with Congress or the nation for some other reason. In the case of *United States v. Nixon* in 1974, the Supreme Court ruled that the executive branch can withhold information relating to "confidential executive deliberations," or discussions, unless there is a compelling, or strong, governmental interest for forcing the executive branch to release the information. Struggles between Congress and the president over withholding information often end up being resolved in federal court.

Legislative-Executive Checks and Balances

Impeachment

The Constitution says, "The president, vice-president and all civil officers of the United States, shall be removed from office on impeachment for, and conviction of, treason, bribery, or other high crimes and misdemeanors." This is called the impeachment process. It is the only way to remove the president, vice president, and federal judges from office.

Congress alone has the power to impeach and remove federal officers. The process has two parts. Under the first part, the House of Representatives holds hearings and votes on whether to impeach an officer. Impeachment is a formal charge that an officer has committed treason, bribery, or other high crimes or misdemeanors. To impeach someone, the House must vote for impeachment by a simple majority.

If an officer is impeached in the House, the second part of the process is an impeachment trial in the Senate. The Senate conducts the trial much like a courtroom trial, but there is no judge or jury apart from the Senate. (An exception to this is impeachment trials of presidents, over which the U.S. Constitution requires the chief justice of the Supreme Court to preside. Even then, however, the chief justice simply enforces the Senate's rules for the trial. He does not question witnesses or vote on whether to convict the president, as the senators do, because the Constitution limits his role to presiding over the trial.) At the end of the trial, the Senate votes on whether to convict the officer of the charges made by the House. Two-thirds of the senators present must vote in favor of conviction to convict an officer. If the Senate convicts an officer, the officer is removed from office. The Senate can also prevent a convicted officer from serving in another federal office in the future.

The Constitution says that when the House impeaches the president of the United States, the chief justice of the United States presides over the impeachment trial in the Senate. The chief justice is the head of the U.S. Supreme Court. Normally the vice president of the United States has the right to preside over Senate activities, but that would be inappropriate in a presidential impeachment trial because the vice president stands to get the president's job if the president is removed from office.

When presiding over a presidential impeachment trial, the chief justice gets to rule on what evidence may and may not be presented to the Senate for consideration. Under its own rules, however, the Senate may overrule any ruling that the chief justice makes. The chief justice, moreover, does not get to vote on whether to convict the accused president. The chief justice's main role is to see that the process runs smoothly.

As noted, impeachment can happen when a federal officer commits treason, bribery, or other high crimes and misdemeanors. The Constitution defines treason as levying war against America or giving aid and comfort to its enemies. Bribery is when someone gives a government officer money or something else of value to influence the officer's official conduct.

The Constitution does not define "high crimes and misdemeanors." Some scholars think it means a serious violation of a criminal law. Others think it means what Alexander Hamilton (1757–1804) called it in *The Federalist,* No. 65, "a violation of public trust." In practice, the House and Senate get to define the term themselves in the impeachment process. For example, in 1998, the House impeached President Bill Clinton (1946–; served 1993–2001) for lying under oath regarding whether he had an affair with White House intern Monica Lewinsky (1973–). The case generated much debate over whether lying under oath is a "high crime or misdemeanor" under the constitutional requirements for impeachment.

Although the Supreme Court has not addressed the issue as of 2005, members of Congress probably cannot be removed from office by impeachment. The House of Representatives impeached a U.S. senator once, William Blount of Tennessee in 1797. Blount was accused of conspiring to conduct military activities for the king of England. The Senate, however, voted not to conduct an impeachment trial, reasoning that it did not have power under the Constitution to conduct an impeachment trial of a senator. No senator or representative has been impeached since then.

Under Article I, Section 5, of the Constitution, however, each chamber of Congress gets to make its own rules for how to expel its members for misconduct. Under that provision, a two-thirds vote is necessary to expel a member from either the House or Senate. Although declining to hold an impeachment trial, the Senate expelled Senator Blount in 1797.

For More Information

BOOKS

Beard, Charles A. *American Government and Politics.* 10th ed. New York: Macmillan Co., 1949.

Burnham, James. *Congress and the American Tradition.* New Brunswick, NJ: Transaction Publishers, 2003.

Fisher, Louis. *Constitutional Conflicts between Congress and the President.* 3rd ed., rev. Lawrence: University Press of Kansas, 1991.

Fisher, Louis. *The Politics of Shared Power: Congress and the Executive.* 4th ed. College Station: Texas A&M University Press, 1998.

Janda, Kenneth, Jeffrey M. Berry, and Jerry Goldman. *The Challenge of Democracy.* 5th ed. Boston: Houghton Mifflin Company, 1997.

Kurland, Philip B., and Ralph Lerner. *The Founders' Constitution.* 5 vols. Indianapolis: Liberty Fund, 1987.

Loomis, Burdett A. *The Contemporary Congress.* 3rd ed. Boston: Bedford/St. Martin's, 2000.

McClenaghan, William A. *Magruder's American Government 2003.* Needham, MA: Prentice Hall School Group, 2002.

Roelofs, H. Mark. *The Poverty of American Politics.* 2nd ed. Philadelphia: Temple University Press, 1998.

Shelley, Mack C., II. *American Government and Politics Today.* 2004–2005 ed. Belmont, CA: Wadsworth Publishing, 2003.

Volkomer, Walter E. *American Government.* 8th ed. Upper Saddle River, NJ: Prentice Hall, 1998.

Wolfensberger, Donald R. *Congress and the People.* Washington, DC, and Baltimore: Woodrow Wilson Center Press and Johns Hopkins University Press, 2000.

CASES

Clinton v. City of New York, 524 U.S. 417 (1998).

INS v. Chadha, 462 U.S. 919 (1983).

United States v. Nixon, 418 U.S. 683 (1974).

WEB SITES

Center for American Progress. "Bush's Legal Obligation to Tell Congress about $700M for Iraq." http://www.american progress.org/site/pp.asp?c=biJRJ8OVF&b=46962 (accessed on February 24, 2005).

CNN.com. "Homeland Security Nominee Withdraws." http://www.cnn.com/2004/ALLPOLITICS/12/10/kerik.withdraws/ (accessed on February 24, 2005).

CRS Report for Congress. "The War Powers Resolution: Thirty Years Later." http://www.fas.org/man/crs/RL32267.html (accessed on February 24, 2005).

Griffin, Pat. "Mandate for Leadership: Working with Congress to Enact an Agenda." *The Heritage Foundation.* http://www.heritage.org/Research/Features/Mandate/keys_chapter6.cfm (accessed on February 24, 2005).

Grossman, Joel B. "Impeach Gary Condit?" *FindLaw.com.* http://writ.news.findlaw.com/commentary/20010910_grossman.html (accessed on February 17, 2005).

"Judicial Nominations." *Federalist Society.* http://www.fed-soc.org/judicialnominations.htm (accessed on February 24, 2005).

Sollenberger, Mitchel A. "Congressional Overrides of Presidential Vetoes." CRS Report for Congress, April 7, 2004. *United States House of Representatives.* http://www.senate.gov/reference/resources/pdf/98-157.pdf (accessed on February 14, 2005).

Sollenberger, Mitchel A. "The Presidential Veto and Congressional Procedure." CRS Report for Congress, February 27, 2004. *United States House of Representatives.* http://www.senate.gov/reference/resources/pdf/RS21750.pdf (accessed on February 14, 2005).

United States House of Representatives. http://www.house.gov (accessed on March 14, 2005).

United States Senate. http://www.senate.gov (accessed on March 14, 2005).

The White House. http://www.whitehouse.gov (accessed on February 16, 2005).

Legislative-Judicial Checks and Balances

*T*he U.S. Constitution divides the powers of government into three branches: legislative, executive, and judicial. Generally speaking, the legislative branch, Congress, makes the nation's laws. The executive branch enforces the laws through the president and various executive offices. The judicial branch, made up of the Supreme Court and lower federal courts, decides cases that arise under the laws.

This division of government is called the separation of powers. The separation of powers is supposed to prevent tyranny. Tyranny is random or unfair government action that can result when one person has all the power to make, enforce, and interpret the laws.

In addition to the broad separation of powers into three branches, the Constitution keeps the legislative and judicial branches separate with various specific provisions. Article I, Section 5, says the chambers of Congress, namely the House of Representatives and the Senate, are the sole judge of who wins congressional elections and who is qualified to serve there. The same part of the Constitution gives the House and Senate sole authority to make their rules of operation.

Article I, Section 6, the so-called Speech and Debate Clause, says representatives and senators cannot be punished for speeches made in Congress, and cannot be arrested while in office, except for treason, felony, and breach of the peace. (Treason is defined as levying war against America or giving aid and comfort to its enemies. A felony is the most serious kind of crime, usually punishable by imprisonment for more than a year.)

Legislative-Judicial Checks and Balances

Words to Know

bicameralism: The practice of dividing the legislative, or lawmaking, power of government into two chambers.

checks and balances: The specific powers in one branch of government that allow it to limit the powers of the other branches.

circuit court of appeals: A court in the federal judicial system that handles appeals from the trial courts, called federal district courts. The United States is divided into twelve geographic areas called circuits, and each circuit has one court of appeals that handles appeals from the federal district courts in its circuit. A party who loses in a circuit court of appeals may ask the Supreme Court to review the case.

Congress: The legislative, or lawmaking, branch of the federal government. Congress has two chambers, the Senate and the House of Representatives.

Constitution of the United States of America: The document written in 1787 that established the federal government under which the United States of America has operated since 1789. Article I covers the legislative branch and Article III covers the judicial branch.

federal district courts: The courts in the federal judicial system that handle trials in civil and criminal cases. Each state is divided into one or more federal judicial districts, and each district has one or more federal district courts. A party who loses in a federal district court may appeal to have the case reviewed by a circuit court of appeals.

judicial review: The process by which federal courts review laws to determine whether they violate the U.S. Constitution. If a court finds that a law violates the Constitution, it declares the law unconstitutional, which means the executive branch is not supposed to enforce it anymore. Congress can correct such a defect by passing a new law that does not violate the Constitution.

judiciary: The branch of the federal government that decides cases that arise under the nation's law. The federal judiciary includes the Supreme Court of the United States, circuit courts of appeals, and federal district courts.

separation of powers: Division of the powers of government into different branches to prevent one branch from having too much power.

Supreme Court: The highest court in the federal judiciary. The judiciary is the branch of government responsible for resolving legal disputes and interpreting laws on a case-by-case basis.

Article III, Section 1, of the Constitution says judges of the Supreme Court and lower courts "shall hold their offices during good behavior." This means they cannot be removed from office except by impeachment and conviction for treason, bribery, or other high crimes and misdemeanors under Article II, Section 4. Article III, Section 1, says judges must receive a salary for their services, which Congress sets. Congress cannot lower a judge's salary during the judge's service on the court.

Checks and balances

The men who wrote the Constitution in 1787 wanted each branch's power to be separate, but not absolute. They considered absolute power, even over just a portion of the government, to be dangerous.

To prevent the power of any one branch from being absolute, the Founding Fathers wrote the Constitution to contain a system of checks and balances. These are powers that each branch has for limiting the power of the other branches. Some scholars say the system of checks and balances actually creates a government of shared powers instead of one with separated powers.

The judiciary's main powers over Congress are judicial review and judicial interpretation. Judicial review is the power to review congressional laws to determine if they violate the Constitution. Judicial interpretation is the power to decide what congressional laws mean and how they apply in specific cases.

Congress's main checks on the judiciary include the power to amend the Constitution, pass new laws, approve the president's appointment of judges, control the number of justices on the Supreme Court, and impeach judges guilty of treason, bribery, or high crimes and misdemeanors.

Judicial review

The Constitution says "the judicial power of the United States, shall be vested in one supreme court, and in such inferior courts as the Congress may from time to time ordain and establish." The Constitution defines the kinds of cases to which the "judicial power" applies, including cases arising under the Constitution, laws, and treaties of the United States. Beyond hearing and deciding such cases, however, the Constitution does not define what the "judicial power" is.

Constitutionality of judicial review Scholars have debated whether the federal judicial power includes the power of judicial review. Judicial review means reviewing congressional laws (and executive action) to determine if they are valid under the Constitution.

Legislative-Judicial Checks and Balances

The Constitution does not specifically give the federal judiciary the power of judicial review. Instead, the Supremacy Clause of Article VI says, "This constitution, and the laws of the United States which shall be made in pursuance thereof; and all treaties made, or which shall be made, under the authority of the United States, shall be the supreme law of the land."

Some scholars believe that only the judicial branch can determine, on a case-by-case basis, whether congressional laws have been "made in pursuance" of, or in carrying out, the Constitution. Others believe that Congress and the president are responsible for deciding if their own actions are constitutional. Still others believe that the people of America, who elect Congress and, indirectly, the president, are ultimately responsible for deciding what is lawful under the Constitution and what is not.

Although the Constitution is unclear on judicial review, many of the men who wrote it in 1787 generally believed the judiciary would have this power. Foremost among them was Alexander Hamilton (1757–1804), who in 1789 became the first secretary of the treasury under President George Washington (1732–1799; served 1789–97). According to Joan Biskupic and Elder Witt in *The Supreme Court & the Powers of the American Government*, Hamilton wrote in No. 78 of *The Federalist Papers* in 1788:

> Limitations [on Congress] ... can be preserved in no other way than through the medium of courts of justice, whose duty it must be to declare all acts contrary to the manifest tenor of the Constitution void. Without this, all the reservations of particular rights or privileges would amount to nothing.... No legislative act, therefore, contrary to the Constitution, can be valid.... The interpretation of the laws is the proper and peculiar province of the courts. A constitution is, in fact, and must be regarded by the judges as, a fundamental law. It therefore belongs to them to ascertain [determine] its meaning as well as the meaning of any particular act proceeding from the legislative body. If there should happen to be an irreconcilable [conflicting] variance between the two, that which has the superior obligation and validity ought, of course, to be preferred; or, in other words, the Constitution ought to be preferred to the statute, the intention of the people to the intention of their agents [in Congress].

Legislative-Judicial Checks and Balances

Chief Justice John Marshall was the leading Federalist in deciding the Marbury v. Madison *case that addressed the issue of judicial review.* National Portrait Gallery/Smithsonian Institution.

Marbury v. Madison In 1803, fifteen years after adoption of the Constitution, the Supreme Court officially answered the question of whether the federal judiciary has the power of judicial review. It did so in the famous case of *Marbury v. Madison*. The case was part of a political battle between Federalists, led by Chief Justice John Marshall (1755–1835), and Democratic-Republicans, led by President Thomas Jefferson (1743–1826; served 1801–9) and Secretary of State James Madison (1751–1836).

Legislative-Judicial Checks and Balances

In the election of 1800, the Federalists lost control of both Congress and the presidency to the Democratic-Republicans. Before leaving office, Congress created sixteen new federal judgeships and authorized Federalist president John Adams (1735–1826; served 1797–1801) to name as many justices of the peace in the District of Columbia as he wished. Adams, in turn, named Federalists to fill the sixteen new federal judgeships plus forty-two justice of the peace positions. He also appointed Marshall, then serving as his secretary of state, to be the chief justice of the Supreme Court. (The chief justice is the head of the Supreme Court.)

One of Marshall's last duties before leaving office as secretary of state was to deliver the commissions, or official orders, to the people appointed to be justices of the peace in the District of Columbia. Somehow he failed to deliver four of them, including one to an attorney named William Marbury. When President Jefferson took office in March 1801, Marbury asked Jefferson's secretary of state, Madison, to give him the commission. Under orders from Jefferson, Madison refused to give the commission to Marbury.

Marbury decided to sue Madison in the Supreme Court. The Judiciary Act of 1789 gave the Supreme Court power to issue writs of mandamus. A writ of mandamus is an official court order for a government official to do his or her job. Marbury asked the Supreme Court to issue a writ of mandamus to Madison, ordering him to deliver the commission to Marbury.

Marshall, the very man who had failed to deliver the commission in the first place, helped to decide the case in 1803 as chief justice of the Supreme Court. Writing the Court's official opinion in the case, Marshall agreed that Marbury should get the commission. He also agreed that a writ of mandamus was the proper tool for forcing Madison to deliver the commission. Marshall surprised everyone, however, by concluding that the Supreme Court did not have the power to issue a writ of mandamus. His reason was that the Judiciary Act of 1789, which gave the Supreme Court power to issue the writ, violated the Constitution. The Constitution did not give the Supreme Court power to issue writs in such cases, so a congressional law trying to give the Supreme Court that power was in violation of the Constitution.

Legislative-Judicial Checks and Balances

William Marbury, the plaintiff in the U.S. Supreme Court case **Marbury v. Madison.** The Granger Collection.

In the course of his written opinion, Marshall announced that the judiciary has the power of judicial review:

> It is a proposition too plain to be contested, that the constitution controls any legislative act repugnant [offensive] to it.... It is, emphatically, the province and duty of the judicial department to say what the law is. Those who apply the rule to particular cases, must of necessity expound [explain] and interpret that rule. If two laws conflict with each other, the courts must decide on the operations of each.... If then the courts are to regard the constitution, and the constitution is superior to any ordinary act of the legislature, the constitution, and not such

ordinary act, must govern the case to which they both apply.

The case was a political victory for Marshall and the Federalists. Although he declared the Court incapable of giving Marbury the commission, Marshall assumed the greater power to review, in cases before the Court, laws passed by the Democratic-Republican controlled Congress.

Marshall's opinion on judicial review still stands, and federal courts routinely review congressional laws in the cases before them. Americans would probably have to enact a constitutional amendment to strip the federal judiciary of the power of judicial review.

As of 2005, the Supreme Court has struck down only around 125 federal laws and executive orders as unconstitutional. The mere existence of judicial review, however, can affect the laws that Congress passes.

Judicial interpretation

Deciding whether a law violates the constitution is a part of the judiciary's job. Federal courts, however, do not engage in judicial view as often as they engage in judicial interpretation. This is the process of deciding what a law means and how it applies in a specific case.

Judicial interpretation becomes necessary for many reasons. Sometimes a situation arises that Congress did not envision when it wrote a law. Other times a law is written in a poor or confusing fashion. And in some instances, Congress purposefully writes a law in general terms, leaving it to the courts to apply the law to specific cases.

The judiciary has been called the least dangerous branch of the federal government in terms of how much power it has compared to the president and Congress. Judicial interpretation, however, can be very powerful. For example, in 1890 Congress passed the Sherman Antitrust Act. The act was meant to prevent business monopolies from dominating areas of commerce, or the economy. It declared that every contract, combination, or conspiracy that restrains trade is illegal. (A restraint of trade is something that interferes with the free operation of the economy.)

In 1920, the U.S. Supreme Court heard a case that required interpretation of the Sherman Antitrust Act. The Court decided that the act does not prohibit every restraint of trade, but only "unreasonable" restraints of trade. Deciding what is reasonable and what is unreasonable gives the federal courts great discretion in Sherman Act cases. Engaging in judicial interpretation, the Supreme Court has also used the Sherman Act to defeat activity by labor unions trying to protect the rights of workers, even though Congress passed the act to prevent unfair business activity.

Some scholars and citizens believe judicial interpretation gives the courts too much power, allowing them to make policies that Congress should make instead. For instance, in 1866, Congress proposed, and in 1868 America adopted, the Fourteenth Amendment of the Constitution. The amendment says all Americans are entitled to equal protection of the laws. One purpose of the amendment was to prevent unequal treatment of African Americans, who had been freed from slavery in 1865 under the Thirteenth Amendment.

In the 1896 case *Plessy v. Ferguson,* however, the Supreme Court decided that the Fourteenth Amendment did not prevent states from requiring whites and blacks to use separate railway cars. The Court ruled that "separate but equal" facilities satisfied the "equal protection" requirements of the Fourteenth Amendment. This rule stood until 1954, when the Supreme Court unanimously decided in *Brown v. Board of Education of Topeka* that separate public services are not equal under the Fourteenth Amendment. The Fourteenth Amendment, however, did not change between 1896 and 1954; the Supreme Court's *interpretation* of it changed. Hence, it is sometimes hard to distinguish between the power of judicial interpretation and the power to make the laws.

Limitations on judicial review and interpretation

While judicial review and interpretation are powerful, they have limits. The strongest limit is the constitutional requirement that the Supreme Court decide only cases and controversies. Other limits have been created by the judiciary itself, which does not always abide by them.

Legislative-Judicial Checks and Balances

Cases and controversies Article III, Section 2, of the Constitution contains a list of the "cases" and "controversies" to which the judicial power extends, or applies. It includes:

- ★ cases arising under the Constitution, laws, and treaties of the United States
- ★ cases affecting ambassadors and other public ministers
- ★ cases concerning the use of navigable, or crossable, waters
- ★ controversies in which the United States is a party
- ★ controversies between two or more states, between citizens of different states, and between citizens of the same state claiming lands under grants from different states
- ★ controversies between a state (or its citizens) and a foreign state or nation (or its citizens or subjects)

The Supreme Court and lower federal courts have the power to resolve only those "cases" and "controversies" listed in the Constitution. This means that if someone files a federal lawsuit that does not come from this list of cases and controversies, the court cannot hear the case. It also means that if Congress passes a law of which the Supreme Court disapproves, the Court cannot strike down the law on its own. Instead, it must wait until someone files an appropriate "case" or "controversy" to challenge the law. Likewise, the Court cannot express an official opinion on a question from another branch of the government. It can only speak through the opinions it issues in real cases or controversies.

Friendly suits and test cases Sometimes people who want to challenge a law or governmental action will create a lawsuit even though they do not have a real problem between them. The judiciary calls such lawsuits friendly suits or test cases.

Federal courts generally will not hear friendly suits or test cases. The reason is that such cases are not real "cases" or "controversies" under the Constitution. The Supreme Court and lower courts, however, occasionally break this rule, hearing friendly suits and test cases when the issues are important. This happened in the 1895 case of *Pollock v. Farmers' Loan and Trust Co.* In this lawsuit, a shareholder of a corporation sued the corporation to prevent it from paying an income tax passed by Congress. (A shareholder is a person who owns a portion of a corporation. An income tax is a tax on earnings.) The corporation and the shareholders both did not want to pay the tax, so there was no true dispute between them. The purpose of the lawsuit was to give the Supreme Court a chance to rule whether the income tax was lawful under the Constitution. The Supreme Court considered the case important enough to decide even though the lawsuit was really a friendly suit or test case. The Supreme Court declared the tax law unconstitutional, eliminating federal income taxes until the nation amended the Constitution to allow income taxes under the Sixteenth Amendment in 1913.

Ripeness and mootness Ripeness and mootness are doctrines the judiciary uses to limit the kinds of cases it will consider. Under the ripeness doctrine, a court will not hear a case until the law that applies to the case has been enforced. The reason is that the way in which an enforcement agency enforces or interprets a law might affect the way a court decides a case. Until then, the case is not ripe, or ready, for consideration.

Under the mootness doctrine, a court will not hear a case when the problem that resulted in the case has disappeared or has otherwise been resolved by the parties. Courts prefer to decide cases only when there is a problem to resolve. If the problem has been resolved, the case is considered moot, or dead.

Despite these doctrines, courts sometimes hear and decide cases that are moot or not ripe if the case is important enough to the judges or justices in charge.

Avoiding constitutional issues If a federal court can decide a case without interpreting the Constitution, it generally will do so. This is because courts usually prefer to save constitutional interpretation for cases that cannot be resolved any other way. The practice is supposed to protect the Constitution from being interpreted in an unnecessary fashion. This can be frustrating for parties and other citizens who want the courts to answer constitutional questions.

Political question doctrine Under the political question doctrine, a court will not review government action that is committed to the discretion, or sound judgment, of another branch. The political question doctrine comes from the

Legislative-Judicial Checks and Balances

separation of powers. The judicial branch usually believes that the separation of powers prevents it from reviewing discretionary action by the legislative and executive branches. An example of discretionary action in the executive branch is the decision to file or drop criminal charges against a suspected criminal. An example of discretionary action in the legislative branch is the decision to expel a senator or representative for misconduct.

Congressional power over the courts

Congress checks the power of the judiciary mainly through its power to propose constitutional amendments and pass new laws. Congress also has the power to confirm the president's appointments to the federal bench, change the number of justices on the Supreme Court, and impeach and convict judges who commit treason, bribery, or other high crimes and misdemeanors.

Proposed constitutional amendments Congress is the only branch that can officially propose a constitutional amendment. An amendment is a change to the Constitution. As of 2005, the Constitution has been amended twenty-seven times since it was adopted in 1788.

To propose an amendment under Article V of the Constitution, either two-thirds of both chambers of Congress or two-thirds of the state legislatures must vote in favor of the proposal. A proposed amendment becomes part of the Constitution only if ratified, or approved, by either three-fourths of the state legislatures or three-fourths of the state constitutional conventions called to consider the amendment. Congress gets to determine whether ratification is by state legislatures or conventions.

The power to propose constitutional amendments can check the power of the judiciary when America ratifies an amendment that overturns a Supreme Court decision. As of 2005, America has ratified five constitutional amendments to overturn decisions of the U.S. Supreme Court. The Eleventh Amendment, adopted in 1798, overturned a Supreme Court decision that citizens of domestic and foreign states could sue state governments in federal court. The Fourteenth Amendment, adopted in 1868, overturned decisions that African Americans were not citizens and that Congress could not protect their civil rights. The Sixteenth Amendment, adopted

Legislative-Judicial Checks and Balances

in 1913, overturned a decision that Congress could not enact income tax laws. The Nineteenth Amendment, adopted in 1920, overturned a decision that women had no right to vote in elections. Finally, the Twenty-sixth Amendment, adopted in 1971, overturned a decision that Congress could not lower the voting age for state elections to eighteen. Previously, Congress had the power to require states to allow eighteen-year-olds to vote in national elections. A congressional law in the 1960s required states to register 18-year-olds for both federal and state elections. Oregon challenged the law, and the U.S. Supreme Court decided that Congress could not control the voting age for state elections. The Twenty-sixth Amendment reversed that.

Members of Congress frequently propose constitutional amendments, but such proposals rarely come to a vote in one chamber and even more rarely get passed by both chambers. This means the power to propose amendments is not a very useful tool for checking the power of the judiciary.

Legislative power If the Supreme Court makes an error when it interprets a law, or simply interprets a law in a manner with which Congress disagrees, Congress can pass a new law with language that corrects the Court's interpretation. The ability to do this comes from Congress's basic lawmaking power under Article I, Section 8, of the Constitution. The power to pass a new law to change a judicial interpretation is very useful. Congress uses this power much more than it uses the power to propose a constitutional amendment.

Confirmation power The president of the United States has the power to nominate, or appoint, people to serve as judges on the Supreme Court and lower federal courts. This power comes from Article II, Section 2, of the Constitution. The same provision gives the Senate the power to either confirm or reject the president's nominations. A simple majority of senators must vote for a president's nomination to confirm it.

Confirmation or rejection of a Supreme Court nominee can affect the result the Court reaches in future cases, because the Court decides cases by a simple majority vote of the nine justices who serve on it. As of March 2005, the Senate has rejected 28 of the 148 people presidents have nominated to serve on the Supreme Court since 1789.

Clement Haynesworth Jr. was one of two judges nominated to the U.S. Supreme Court in 1969–70 by President Richard Nixon who were rejected by the U.S. Senate. AP/Wide World Photos.

Legislative-Judicial Checks and Balances

The Senate also gets to confirm appointments to the lower federal courts. The process is guided by an informal practice called senatorial courtesy. Under this practice, the president checks with senators from the president's own political party before nominating a federal judge to serve on a federal court in the senators' state. Failure to employ senatorial courtesy reduces the chances of a president's nominee being accepted. In practice, the Senate rejects nominations to the lower federal courts less frequently than it rejects nominations to the Supreme Court.

Income Tax

Every year by April 15, Americans pay an income tax to the federal government. Income tax is a tax on the money or other income a person or business makes each year. The story of the beginning of the federal income tax illustrates the checks and balances between Congress and the Supreme Court.

Americans did not pay an income tax for almost a century after the birth of the nation. Congress first enacted an income tax in 1862, during the American Civil War (1861–65). This tax lasted until only 1872.

In 1893, the American economy went through a depression. This reduced the amount of money people spent on goods imported into the country, which reduced the amount of taxes the federal government collected on imports. To raise more money for the government, Congress enacted another income tax law. The law charged a 2 percent tax on annual income that exceeded $4,000. Congress passed the law under its power "to lay and collect taxes" under Article I, Section 8, of the Constitution.

Charles Pollock, a stockholder in a bank called the Farmers' Loan and Trust Company, sued the bank to prevent it from paying the income tax. Pollock's lawyers argued that the tax violated Article I, Section 9, of the Constitution, which prohibits Congress from imposing certain direct taxes on Americans. A direct tax is a tax on property based on the value of the property.

The case, *Pollock v. Farmers' Loan and Trust Co.*, went all the way to the U.S. Supreme Court. Using the power of judicial review when deciding the case, the Supreme Court struck down the income tax law. It said the tax was a direct tax prohibited by the Constitution, as Pollock's lawyers had argued. That meant the bank did not have to pay the tax.

Congress continued to want an income tax to pay for government. Many farmers and laborers wanted the men getting rich through industry and business to pay an income tax. In 1909, Congress considered passing another income tax law to give the Supreme Court a chance to reverse its decision from the *Pollock* case.

Later that year, Congress voted instead to propose a constitutional amendment to make income taxes specifically legal under the Constitution. Congress made this suggestion with its power to propose amendments under Article V of the Constitution.

Legislative-Judicial Checks and Balances

Number of Supreme Court justices The Constitution created a Supreme Court but did not specify the number of justices to serve on it. Instead, Congress sets the number by law under its power to make all laws necessary for the government to function.

In the Judiciary Act of 1789, Congress set the number of Supreme Court justices at six. Between then and 1869, Congress raised or lowered the number seven times, finally settling on nine justices in 1869. Lowering the number of justices is a way to prevent a president in office from getting to appoint new justices when old ones die or retire. Raising the number is a way to allow

The Sixteenth Amendment became part of the Constitution after thirty-eight states ratified it between 1909 and February 1913. Americans have paid an income tax ever since.

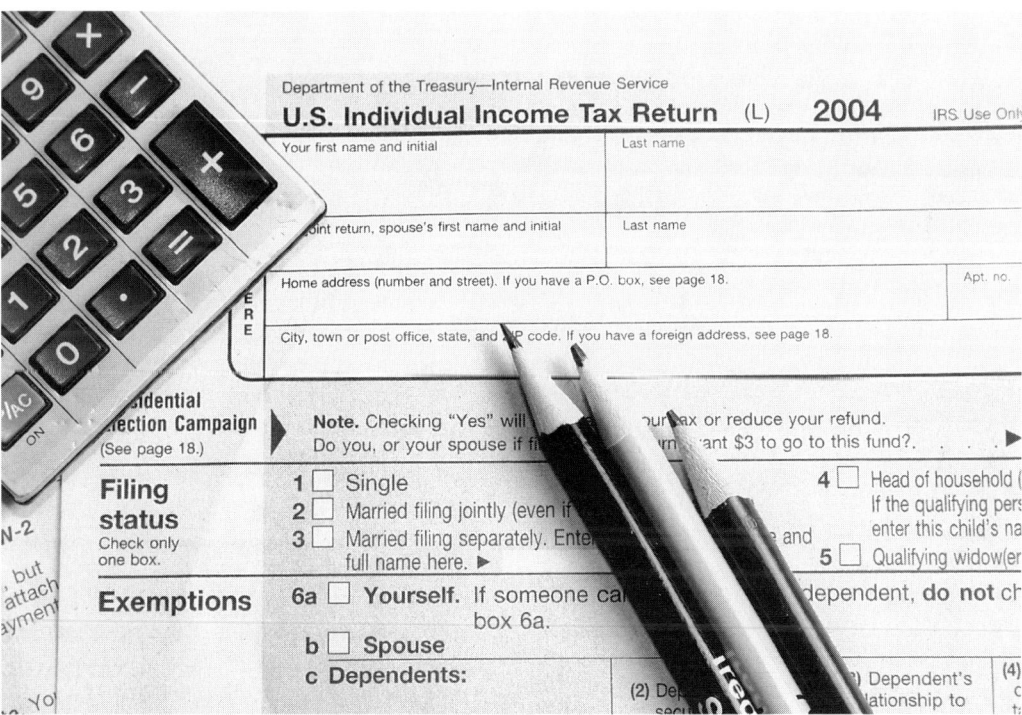

Individual income tax return form for 2004. © Nell Redmond/ZUMA/Corbis.

a president to fill the Court with justices who agree with the administration's philosophy of government.

Supreme Court justices decide cases by a simple majority vote. Congress has occasionally considered changing this practice to require either greater majorities or even unanimous votes for Court action. None of these proposals has come close to passing in Congress.

Supreme Court Confirmations

The president of the United States has the power to nominate, or appoint, judges to the Supreme Court and lower federal courts under Article II, Section 2, of the Constitution. The Senate, however, must approve the president's nominations by a simple majority.

When the Supreme Court has a vacancy and the president nominates someone to fill the position, the Senate Judiciary Committee holds confirmation hearings to consider the nomination. (The Judiciary Committee is composed of a small group of senators.) After the hearings, the committee recommends whether the Senate should confirm or reject the nomination. Fifty-one senators, or fifty senators plus the vice president of the United States, must vote in favor of a nominee to confirm, or approve, the appointment. (When the Senate is split 50-50, the vice president gets to break the tie as president of the Senate under the Constitution.)

Senate confirmation hearings and votes can be controversial, because justices on the Supreme Court have enormous power to shape American law. When the president is a member of a different political party than a majority of the Senate, the vote on Supreme Court nominations can be close. As of 2005, the Senate has rejected 28 of the 148 Supreme Court nominations presidents have made.

In 1987, for example, President Ronald Reagan (1911–2004; served 1981–89) nominated Robert H. Bork (1927–) to replace Supreme Court justice Lewis F. Powell Jr. (1907–1998), who was retiring. Bork, a judge on the federal court of appeals in the District of Columbia, had strong political views. Opponents of Bork said he was an enemy of civil rights. Supporters said he was a fair-minded judge who favored strict interpretation of the Constitution. The Senate Judiciary Committee recommended rejecting the nomination, which the Senate did when the confirmation vote was defeated, 58–42.

Sometimes a nominee withdraws his or her name from consideration after controversy arises. After Bork was defeated, President Reagan nominated Douglas H. Ginsburg (1946–) to replace Powell. It soon became known, however, that Ginsburg used marijuana, an illegal drug, as a college student in the 1960s and as a Harvard Law School professor in the 1970s. Ginsburg withdrew himself from consideration during the controversy.

In 1991, President George Bush (1924–; served 1989–93) nominated Clarence Thomas (1948–) to replace the retiring Justice Thurgood Marshall (1908–1993), the Supreme Court's first African American justice. Shortly before the Senate was to vote on the nomination, the media reported that Anita F. Hill (1956–), a professor and attorney who used to work with Thomas, accused him of sexually harassing her. The Senate sent the nomination back to its Judiciary Comzmittee, which held more hearings.

Legislative-Judicial Checks and Balances

Impeachment Judges on the Supreme Court and lower federal courts are appointed for life. Under Article II, Section 4, of the Constitution, the only way to remove a judge from office is by impeachment and conviction for treason, bribery, or other high crimes and misdemeanors.

The Constitution defines treason as levying war against America or giving aid and comfort to its enemies. Bribery is the

During the hearings, Hill accused Thomas of making unwelcome sexual advances to her while they worked at the Department of Education and the Equal Employment Opportunity Commission in the early 1980s. In the televised, high-profile hearings, Thomas vehemently denied the accusations. Despite the controversy, in October 1991, the Senate confirmed his nomination by a vote of 52-48.

As President Ronald Reagan (left) watches, Douglas Ginsburg addresses the audience after being nominated to be a Supreme Court associate justice in October 1987. Ginsburg soon withdrew from consideration after it was divulged that he had used marijuana in the 1960s and 1970s. © Bettmann/Corbis.

Legislative-Judicial Checks and Balances

Samuel Chase was the only U.S. Supreme Court justice to be impeached. The Senate voted not to convict Chase in 1804, however, and he remained on the Court until his death in 1811. Independence National Historical Park Collection.

act of giving money or something else of value to influence government conduct. The Constitution does not define the phrase "high crimes and misdemeanors." This essentially gives Congress the power to impeach judges and other federal officers for political reasons, even if an officer has not committed a true crime.

The Constitution gives the House of Representatives the sole power to impeach a federal judge (or any other federal officer). Impeachment is a formal accusation that a judge has committed an impeachable offense. Once impeached, a judge faces trial in the Senate, which has the sole power to convict a judge (or any other federal officer) who has been charged by the House with an impeachable offense. Conviction by the Senate results in removal from office, and can result in being banned from serving in federal office in the future.

The House has impeached only one Supreme Court justice, Samuel Chase (1741–1811), in 1804. The Senate, however, voted not to convict Chase. As of 2005, the House has impeached only twelve lower court judges, and the Senate convicted just seven of them. The three most recent convictions were of Nevada federal district court judge Harry Claiborne (1917–2004) in 1986, Florida federal district court judge Alcee L. Hastings (1936–) in 1989, and Mississippi federal district court judge Walter L. Nixon Jr. in 1989.

Constitutional limitations on congressional power

The Constitution contains provisions that specifically limit Congress's power to check the judiciary. They include the preservation of writs of habeas corpus, prohibition of bills of attainder, and protection of the right to jury trials.

Writ of habeas corpus "Habeas corpus" is a Latin term meaning "to have the body." Habeas corpus procedures allow a prisoner to ask a court to investigate whether the prisoner is being held illegally. If so, the court can issue an order, a writ of habeas corpus, that the prisoner be released.

Article I, Section 9, of the Constitution says, "The privilege of the writ of habeas corpus shall not be suspended, unless when in cases of rebellion or invasion the public safety may require it." This means Congress cannot deprive the federal judiciary of its power to issue writs of habeas corpus, except during rebellions or invasions. As of 2005, the habeas corpus procedure has been suspended officially only four times: during the American Civil War (1861–65); in South Carolina during Reconstruction (1865–77) after the Civil War; in the Philippines in 1905 during American occupation of the nation subsequent to the Spanish-American War (1898); and in Hawaii during World War II (1939–45).

Bills of attainder Article I, Section 9, of the Constitution also prohibits Congress from passing bills of attainder. A bill of attainder is a law that inflicts punishment on someone without a trial. This provision checks Congress by protecting the right to jury trials in federal courts.

Jury trials and location Besides the prohibition of bills of attainder, other provisions in the Constitution protect the right to jury trials in federal courts. Article III, Section 2, says, "The trial of all crimes, except in cases of impeachment, shall be by jury; and such trial shall be held in the state where the said crimes shall have been committed." This provision is reinforced by the Sixth Amendment, which says, "In all criminal prosecutions, the accused shall enjoy the right to a speedy and public trial, by an impartial jury of the State and district wherein the crime shall have been committed." These provisions prevent Congress from eliminating jury trials in criminal cases.

The Seventh Amendment protects the right to jury trials in civil cases, which are cases between private citizens, businesses, or organizations. It says, "Where the value in controversy shall exceed twenty dollars, the right of trial by jury shall be preserved." As of 2005, however, Congress has passed a law that prevents parties with state law claims from suing in federal court unless the amount in controversy exceeds $75,000. Parties with federal law claims generally do not have to satisfy this requirement to sue in federal court.

For More Information

BOOKS

Beard, Charles A. *American Government and Politics*. 10th ed. New York: Macmillan Co., 1949.

Biskupic, Joan, and Elder Witt. *The Supreme Court & the Powers of the American Government*. Washington, DC: Congressional Quarterly Inc., 1997.

Dougherty, J. Hampden. *Power of Federal Judiciary over Legislation.* New York: Putnam's Sons, 1912. Reprint, Clark, NJ: Lawbook Exchange, 2004.

Janda, Kenneth, Jeffrey M. Berry, and Jerry Goldman. *The Challenge of Democracy.* 5th ed. Boston: Houghton Mifflin Company, 1997.

Loomis, Burdett A. *The Contemporary Congress.* 3rd ed. Boston: Bedford/St. Martin's, 2000.

McClenaghan, William A. *Magruder's American Government 2003.* Needham, MA: Prentice Hall School Group, 2002.

Parenti, Michael. *Democracy for the Few.* 6th ed. New York: St. Martin's Press, 1995.

Roelofs, H. Mark. *The Poverty of American Politics.* 2nd ed. Philadelphia: Temple University Press, 1998.

Shelley, Mack C., II. *American Government and Politics Today.* 2004–2005 ed. Belmont, CA: Wadsworth Publishing, 2003.

Volkomer, Walter E. *American Government.* 8th ed. Upper Saddle River, NJ: Prentice Hall, 1998.

Wolfensberger, Donald R. *Congress and the People.* Washington, DC, and Baltimore: Woodrow Wilson Center Press and Johns Hopkins University Press, 2000.

CD-ROM

21st Century Complete Guide to U.S. Courts. Progressive Management, 2003.

CASES

Brown v. Board of Education of Topeka, 347 U.S. 483 (1954).

Marbury v. Madison, 1 Cranch 137 (1803).

Plessy v. Ferguson, 163 U.S. 537 (1896).

Pollock v. Farmers' Loan and Trust Co. 158 U.S. 601 (1895).

Scott v. Sandford, 19 How. 393 (1857).

WEB SITES

Federal Judiciary. http://www.uscourts.gov (accessed on February 18, 2005).

"Judge Douglas Ginsburg's Marijuana Use—1987." *Washington Post.* http://www.washingtonpost.com/wp-srv/politics/special/clinton/frenzy/ginsburg.htm (accessed on March 18, 2005).

Supreme Court of the United States. http://www.supremecourtus.gov (accessed on February 18, 2005).

United States House of Representatives. http://www.house.gov (accessed on March 14, 2005).

United States Senate. http://www.senate.gov (accessed on March 14, 2005).

Appendix

THE CONSTITUTION OF THE UNITED STATES OF AMERICA

We the People of the United States, in Order to form a more perfect Union, establish Justice, insure domestic Tranquility, provide for the common defence, promote the general Welfare, and secure the Blessings of Liberty to ourselves and our Posterity, do ordain and establish this Constitution for the United States of America.

Article I.

SECTION 1. All legislative Powers herein granted shall be vested in a Congress of the United States, which shall consist of a Senate and House of Representatives.

SECTION 2. The House of Representatives shall be composed of Members chosen every second Year by the People of the several States, and the Electors in each State shall have the Qualifications requisite for Electors of the most numerous Branch of the State Legislature. No Person shall be a Representative who shall not have attained to the Age of twenty five Years, and been seven Years a Citizen of the United States, and who shall not, when elected, be an Inhabitant of that State in which he shall be chosen.

Representatives and direct Taxes shall be apportioned among the several States which may be included within this Union, according to their respective Numbers, which shall be determined by adding to the whole Number of free Persons, including those bound to Service for a Term of Years, and excluding Indians not taxed, three fifths of all other Persons. The actual Enumeration shall be made within three Years after the first Meeting of the Congress of the United States, and within every subsequent Term of ten Years, in such Manner as they shall by Law direct. The Number of Representatives shall not exceed one for every thirty Thousand, but each State shall have at Least one Representative; and until such enumeration shall be made, the State of New Hampshire shall be entitled to chuse three, Massachusetts eight, Rhode-Island and Providence Plantations one, Connecticut five, New-York six, New Jersey four, Pennsylvania eight, Delaware one, Maryland six, Virginia ten, North Carolina five, South Carolina five, and Georgia three.

When vacancies happen in the Representation from any State, the Executive Authority thereof shall issue Writs of Election to fill such Vacancies.

The House of Representatives shall chuse their Speaker and other Officers; and shall have the sole Power of Impeachment.

SECTION 3. The Senate of the United States shall be composed of two Senators from each State, chosen by the Legislature thereof, for six Years; and each Senator shall have one Vote.

Immediately after they shall be assembled in Consequence of the first Election, they shall be divided as equally as may be into three Classes. The Seats of the Senators of the first Class shall be vacated at the Expiration of the second Year, of the second Class at the Expiration of the fourth Year, and of the third Class at the Expiration of the sixth Year, so that one third may be chosen every second Year; and if Vacancies happen by Resignation, or otherwise, during the Recess of the Legislature of any State, the Executive thereof may make temporary Appointments until the next Meeting of the Legislature, which shall then fill such Vacancies.

No Person shall be a Senator who shall not have attained to the Age of thirty Years, and been nine Years a Citizen of the United States, and who shall not, when elected, be an Inhabitant of that State for which he shall be chosen.

The Vice President of the United States shall be President of the Senate, but shall have no Vote, unless they be equally divided.

The Senate shall chuse their other Officers, and also a President pro tempore, in the Absence of the Vice President, or when he shall exercise the Office of President of the United States. The Senate shall have the sole Power to try all Impeachments. When sitting for that Purpose, they shall be on Oath or Affirmation. When the President of the United States is tried, the Chief Justice shall preside: And no Person shall be convicted without the Concurrence of two thirds of the Members present.

Judgment in Cases of Impeachment shall not extend further than to removal from Office, and disqualification to hold and enjoy any Office of honor, Trust or Profit under the United States: but the Party convicted shall nevertheless be liable and subject to Indictment, Trial, Judgment and Punishment, according to Law.

SECTION 4. The Times, Places and Manner of holding Elections for Senators and Representatives, shall be prescribed in each State by the Legislature thereof; but the Congress may at any time by Law make or alter such Regulations, except as to the Places of chusing Senators. The Congress shall assemble at least once in every Year, and such Meeting shall be on the first Monday in December, unless they shall by Law appoint a different Day.

SECTION 5. Each House shall be the Judge of the Elections, Returns and Qualifications of its own Members, and a Majority of each shall constitute a Quorum to do Business; but a smaller Number may adjourn from day to day, and may be authorized to compel the Attendance of absent Members, in such Manner, and under such Penalties as each House may provide. Each House may determine the Rules of its Proceedings, punish its Members for disorderly Behaviour, and, with the Concurrence of two thirds, expel a Member. Each House shall keep a Journal of its Proceedings, and from time to time publish the same, excepting such Parts as may in their Judgment require Secrecy; and the Yeas and Nays of the Members of either House on any question shall, at the Desire of one fifth of those Present, be entered on the Journal.

Neither House, during the Session of Congress, shall, without the Consent of the other, adjourn for more than three days, nor to any other Place than that in which the two Houses shall be sitting.

SECTION 6. The Senators and Representatives shall receive a Compensation for their Services, to be ascertained by Law, and paid out of the Treasury of the United States. They shall in all Cases, except Treason, Felony and Breach of the Peace, be privileged from Arrest during their Attendance at the Session of their respective Houses, and in going to and returning from the same; and for any Speech or Debate in either House, they shall not be questioned in any other Place.

No Senator or Representative shall, during the Time for which he was elected, be appointed to any civil Office under the Authority of the United States, which shall have been created, or the Emoluments whereof shall have been encreased during such time; and no Person holding any Office under the United States, shall be a Member of either House during his Continuance in Office.

SECTION 7. All Bills for raising Revenue shall originate in the House of Representatives; but the Senate may propose or concur with Amendments as on other Bills.

Every Bill which shall have passed the House of Representatives and the Senate, shall, before it become a Law, be presented to the President of the United States: If he approve he shall sign it, but if not he shall return it, with his Objections to that House in which it shall have originated, who shall enter the Objections at large on their Journal, and proceed to reconsider it. If after such Reconsideration two thirds of that House shall agree to pass the Bill, it shall be sent, together with the Objections, to the other House, by which it shall likewise be reconsidered, and if approved by two thirds of that House, it shall become a Law. But in all such Cases the Votes of both Houses shall be determined by yeas and Nays, and the Names of the Persons voting for and against the Bill shall be entered on the Journal of each House respectively. If any Bill shall not be returned by the President within ten Days (Sundays excepted) after it shall have been presented to him, the Same shall be a Law, in like Manner as if he had signed it, unless the Congress by their Adjournment prevent its Return, in which Case it shall not be a Law.

Every Order, Resolution, or Vote to which the Concurrence of the Senate and House of Representatives may be necessary (except on a question of Adjournment) shall be presented to the President of the United States; and before the Same shall take Effect, shall be approved by him, or being disapproved by him, shall be repassed by two thirds of the Senate and House of Representatives, according to the Rules and Limitations prescribed in the Case of a Bill.

SECTION 8. The Congress shall have Power To lay and collect Taxes, Duties, Imposts and Excises, to pay the Debts and provide for the common Defence and general Welfare of the United

States; but all Duties, Imposts and Excises shall be uniform throughout the United States;

To borrow Money on the credit of the United States;

To regulate Commerce with foreign Nations, and among the several States, and with the Indian Tribes;

To establish an uniform Rule of Naturalization, and uniform Laws on the subject of Bankruptcies throughout the United States;

To coin Money, regulate the Value thereof, and of foreign Coin, and fix the Standard of Weights and Measures;

To provide for the Punishment of counterfeiting the Securities and current Coin of the United States;

To establish Post Offices and post Roads;

To promote the Progress of Science and useful Arts, by securing for limited Times to Authors and Inventors the exclusive Right to their respective Writings and Discoveries;

To constitute Tribunals inferior to the Supreme Court;

To define and punish Piracies and Felonies committed on the high Seas, and Offences against the Law of Nations;

To declare War, grant Letters of Marque and Reprisal, and make Rules concerning Captures on Land and Water;

To raise and support Armies, but no Appropriation of Money to that Use shall be for a longer Term than two Years;

To provide and maintain a Navy;

To make Rules for the Government and Regulation of the land and naval Forces;

To provide for calling forth the Militia to execute the Laws of the Union, suppress Insurrections and repel Invasions;

To provide for organizing, arming, and disciplining, the Militia, and for governing such Part of them as may be employed in the Service of the United States, reserving to the States respectively, the Appointment of the Officers, and the Authority of training the Militia according to the discipline prescribed by Congress;

To exercise exclusive Legislation in all Cases whatsoever, over such District (not exceeding ten Miles square) as may, by Cession of particular States, and the Acceptance of Congress, become the Seat of the Government of the United States, and to exercise like Authority over all Places purchased by the

Consent of the Legislature of the State in which the Same shall be, for the Erection of Forts, Magazines, Arsenals, dock-Yards, and other needful Buildings; –And

To make all Laws which shall be necessary and proper for carrying into Execution the foregoing Powers, and all other Powers vested by this Constitution in the Government of the United States, or in any Department or Officer thereof.

SECTION 9. The Migration or Importation of such Persons as any of the States now existing shall think proper to admit, shall not be prohibited by the Congress prior to the Year one thousand eight hundred and eight, but a Tax or duty may be imposed on such Importation, not exceeding ten dollars for each Person.

The Privilege of the Writ of Habeas Corpus shall not be suspended, unless when in Cases of Rebellion or Invasion the public Safety may require it.

No Bill of Attainder or ex post facto Law shall be passed.

No Capitation, or other direct, Tax shall be laid, unless in Proportion to the Census or Enumeration herein before directed to be taken.

No Tax or Duty shall be laid on Articles exported from any State.

No Preference shall be given by any Regulation of Commerce or Revenue to the Ports of one State over those of another; nor shall Vessels bound to, or from, one State, be obliged to enter, clear, or pay Duties in another.

No Money shall be drawn from the Treasury, but in Consequence of Appropriations made by Law; and a regular Statement and Account of the Receipts and Expenditures of all public Money shall be published from time to time.

No Title of Nobility shall be granted by the United States: And no Person holding any Office of Profit or Trust under them, shall, without the Consent of the Congress, accept of any present, Emolument, Office, or Title, of any kind whatever, from any King, Prince, or foreign State.

SECTION 10. No State shall enter into any Treaty, Alliance, or Confederation; grant Letters of Marque and Reprisal; coin Money; emit Bills of Credit; make any Thing but gold and silver Coin a Tender in Payment of Debts; pass any Bill of

Attainder, ex post facto Law, or Law impairing the Obligation of Contracts, or grant any Title of Nobility.

No State shall, without the Consent of the Congress, lay any Imposts or Duties on Imports or Exports, except what may be absolutely necessary for executing it's [sic] inspection Laws; and the net Produce of all Duties and Imposts, laid by any State on Imports or Exports, shall be for the Use of the Treasury of the United States; and all such Laws shall be subject to the Revision and Controul of the Congress.

No State shall, without the Consent of Congress, lay any Duty of Tonnage, keep Troops, or Ships of War in time of Peace, enter into any Agreement or Compact with another State, or with a foreign Power, or engage in War, unless actually invaded, or in such imminent Danger as will not admit of delay.

Article II.

SECTION 1. The executive Power shall be vested in a President of the United States of America. He shall hold his Office during the Term of four Years, and, together with the Vice President, chosen for the same Term, be elected, as follows:

Each State shall appoint, in such Manner as the Legislature thereof may direct, a Number of Electors, equal to the whole Number of Senators and Representatives to which the State may be entitled in the Congress: but no Senator or Representative, or Person holding an Office of Trust or Profit under the United States, shall be appointed an Elector.

The Electors shall meet in their respective States, and vote by Ballot for two Persons, of whom one at least shall not be an Inhabitant of the same State with themselves. And they shall make a List of all the Persons voted for, and of the Number of Votes for each; which List they shall sign and certify, and transmit sealed to the Seat of the Government of the United States, directed to the President of the Senate. The President of the Senate shall, in the Presence of the Senate and House of Representatives, open all the Certificates, and the Votes shall then be counted. The Person having the greatest Number of Votes shall be the President, if such Number be a Majority of the whole Number of Electors appointed; and if there be more than one who have such Majority, and have an equal Number of Votes, then the House of Representatives shall immediately chuse by

Ballot one of them for President; and if no Person have a Majority, then from the five highest on the List the said House shall in like Manner chuse the President. But in chusing the President, the Votes shall be taken by States, the Representation from each State having one Vote; a quorum for this Purpose shall consist of a Member or Members from two thirds of the States, and a Majority of all the States shall be necessary to a Choice. In every Case, after the Choice of the President, the Person having the greatest Number of Votes of the Electors shall be the Vice President. But if there should remain two or more who have equal Votes, the Senate shall chuse from them by Ballot the Vice President.

The Congress may determine the Time of chusing the Electors, and the Day on which they shall give their Votes; which Day shall be the same throughout the United States.

No Person except a natural born Citizen, or a Citizen of the United States, at the time of the Adoption of this Constitution, shall be eligible to the Office of President; neither shall any Person be eligible to that Office who shall not have attained to the Age of thirty five Years, and been fourteen Years a Resident within the United States.

In Case of the Removal of the President from Office, or of his Death, Resignation, or Inability to discharge the Powers and Duties of the said Office, the Same shall devolve on the Vice President, and the Congress may by Law provide for the Case of Removal, Death, Resignation or Inability, both of the President and Vice President, declaring what Officer shall then act as President, and such Officer shall act accordingly, until the Disability be removed, or a President shall be elected.

The President shall, at stated Times, receive for his Services, a Compensation, which shall neither be increased nor diminished during the Period for which he shall have been elected, and he shall not receive within that Period any other Emolument from the United States, or any of them.

Before he enter on the Execution of his Office, he shall take the following Oath or Affirmation: "I do solemnly swear (or affirm) that I will faithfully execute the Office of President of the United States, and will to the best of my Ability, preserve, protect and defend the Constitution of the United States."

SECTION 2. The President shall be Commander in Chief of the Army and Navy of the United States, and of the Militia of the several States, when called into the actual Service of the United States; he may require the Opinion, in writing, of the principal Officer in each of the executive Departments, upon any Subject relating to the Duties of their respective Offices, and he shall have Power to grant Reprieves and Pardons for Offences against the United States, except in Cases of Impeachment.

He shall have Power, by and with the Advice and Consent of the Senate, to make Treaties, provided two thirds of the Senators present concur; and he shall nominate, and by and with the Advice and Consent of the Senate, shall appoint Ambassadors, other public Ministers and Consuls, Judges of the Supreme Court, and all other Officers of the United States, whose Appointments are not herein otherwise provided for, and which shall be established by Law: but the Congress may by Law vest the Appointment of such inferior Officers, as they think proper, in the President alone, in the Courts of Law, or in the Heads of Departments.

The President shall have Power to fill up all Vacancies that may happen during the Recess of the Senate, by granting Commissions which shall expire at the End of their next Session.

SECTION 3. He shall from time to time give to the Congress Information of the State of the Union, and recommend to their Consideration such Measures as he shall judge necessary and expedient; he may, on extraordinary Occasions, convene both Houses, or either of them, and in Case of Disagreement between them, with Respect to the Time of Adjournment, he may adjourn them to such Time as he shall think proper; he shall receive Ambassadors and other public Ministers; he shall take Care that the Laws be faithfully executed, and shall Commission all the Officers of the United States.

SECTION 4. The President, Vice President and all civil Officers of the United States, shall be removed from Office on Impeachment for, and Conviction of, Treason, Bribery, or other high Crimes and Misdemeanors.

Article III.

SECTION 1. The judicial Power of the United States shall be vested in one Supreme Court, and in such inferior Courts as the Congress may from time to time ordain and establish. The Judges, both of the supreme and inferior Courts, shall hold their Offices during good Behaviour, and shall, at stated Times, receive for their Services a Compensation, which shall not be diminished during their Continuance in Office.

SECTION 2. The judicial Power shall extend to all Cases, in Law and Equity, arising under this Constitution, the Laws of the United States, and Treaties made, or which shall be made, under their Authority; –to all Cases affecting Ambassadors, other public Ministers and Consuls; –to all Cases of admiralty and maritime Jurisdiction; –to Controversies to which the United States shall be a Party; –to Controversies between two or more States; – between a State and Citizens of another State; –between Citizens of different States; –between Citizens of the same State claiming Lands under Grants of different States, and between a State, or the Citizens thereof, and foreign States, Citizens or Subjects.

In all Cases affecting Ambassadors, other public Ministers and Consuls, and those in which a State shall be Party, the Supreme Court shall have original Jurisdiction. In all the other Cases before mentioned, the Supreme Court shall have appellate Jurisdiction, both as to Law and Fact, with such Exceptions, and under such Regulations as the Congress shall make.

The Trial of all Crimes, except in Cases of Impeachment, shall be by Jury; and such Trial shall be held in the State where the said Crimes shall have been committed; but when not committed within any State, the Trial shall be at such Place or Places as the Congress may by Law have directed.

SECTION 3. Treason against the United States shall consist only in levying War against them, or in adhering to their Enemies, giving them Aid and Comfort. No Person shall be convicted of Treason unless on the Testimony of two Witnesses to the same overt Act, or on Confession in open Court.

The Congress shall have Power to declare the Punishment of Treason, but no Attainder of Treason shall work Corruption of Blood, or Forfeiture except during the Life of the Person attainted.

Article IV.

SECTION 1. Full Faith and Credit shall be given in each State to the public Acts, Records, and judicial Proceedings of every other State. And the Congress may by general Laws prescribe the

Manner in which such Acts, Records and Proceedings shall be proved, and the Effect thereof.

SECTION 2. The Citizens of each State shall be entitled to all Privileges and Immunities of Citizens in the several States.

A Person charged in any State with Treason, Felony, or other Crime, who shall flee from Justice, and be found in another State, shall on Demand of the executive Authority of the State from which he fled, be delivered up, to be removed to the State having Jurisdiction of the Crime.

No Person held to Service or Labour in one State, under the Laws thereof, escaping into another, shall, in Consequence of any Law or Regulation therein, be discharged from such Service or Labour, but shall be delivered up on Claim of the Party to whom such Service or Labour may be due.

SECTION 3. New States may be admitted by the Congress into this Union; but no new State shall be formed or erected within the Jurisdiction of any other State; nor any State be formed by the Junction of two or more States, or Parts of States, without the Consent of the Legislatures of the States concerned as well as of the Congress.

The Congress shall have Power to dispose of and make all needful Rules and Regulations respecting the Territory or other Property belonging to the United States; and nothing in this Constitution shall be so construed as to Prejudice any Claims of the United States, or of any particular State.

SECTION 4. The United States shall guarantee to every State in this Union a Republican Form of Government, and shall protect each of them against Invasion; and on Application of the Legislature, or of the Executive (when the Legislature cannot be convened), against domestic Violence.

Article V.

The Congress, whenever two thirds of both Houses shall deem it necessary, shall propose Amendments to this Constitution, or, on the Application of the Legislatures of two thirds of the several States, shall call a Convention for proposing Amendments, which, in either Case, shall be valid to all Intents and Purposes, as Part of this Constitution, when ratified by the Legislatures of three fourths of the several States, or by

Conventions in three fourths thereof, as the one or the other Mode of Ratification may be proposed by the Congress; Provided that no Amendment which may be made prior to the Year One thousand eight hundred and eight shall in any Manner affect the first and fourth Clauses in the Ninth Section of the first Article; and that no State, without its Consent, shall be deprived of its equal Suffrage in the Senate.

Article VI.

All Debts contracted and Engagements entered into, before the Adoption of this Constitution, shall be as valid against the United States under this Constitution, as under the Confederation.

This Constitution, and the Laws of the United States which shall be made in Pursuance thereof; and all Treaties made, or which shall be made, under the Authority of the United States, shall be the supreme Law of the Land; and the Judges in every State shall be bound thereby, any Thing in the Constitution or Laws of any State to the Contrary notwithstanding.

The Senators and Representatives before mentioned, and the Members of the several State Legislatures, and all executive and judicial Officers, both of the United States and of the several States, shall be bound by Oath or Affirmation, to support this Constitution; but no religious Test shall ever be required as a Qualification to any Office or public Trust under the United States.

Article VII.

The Ratification of the Conventions of nine States, shall be sufficient for the Establishment of this Constitution between the States so ratifying the Same.

The Word, "the," being interlined between the seventh and eighth Lines of the first Page, The Word "Thirty" being partly written on an Erazure in the fifteenth Line of the first Page, The Words "is tried" being interlined between the thirty second and thirty third Lines of the first Page and the Word "the" being interlined between the forty third and forty fourth Lines of the second Page.

Attest William Jackson Secretary

done in Convention by the Unanimous Consent of the States present the Seventeenth Day of September in the Year of our Lord one thousand seven hundred and Eighty seven and of the Independence of the United States of America the Twelfth In witness whereof We have hereunto subscribed our Names,

    Go. WASHINGTON, Presidt. and deputy from Virginia

NEW HAMPSHIRE: John Langdon, Nicholas Gilman

MASSACHUSETTS: Nathaniel Gorham, Rufus King

CONNECTICUT: Wm. Saml. Johnson, Roger Sherman

NEW YORK: Alexander Hamilton

NEW JERSEY: Wil. Livingston, David Brearley, Wm. Paterson, Jona. Dayton

PENSYLVANIA [sic]: B. Franklin, Thomas Mifflin, Robt. Morris, Geo. Clymer, Thos. FitzSimons, Jared Ingersoll, James Wilson, Gouv. Morris

DELAWARE: Geo. Read, Gunning Bedford jun., John Dickinson, Richard Bassett, Jaco. Broom

MARYLAND: James McHenry, Dan of St. Thos. Jenifer, Danl. Carroll

VIRGINIA: John Blair, James Madison Jr.

NORTH CAROLINA: Wm. Blount, Richd. Dobbs Spaight, Hu. Williamson

SOUTH CAROLINA: J. Rutledge, Charles Cotesworth Pinckney, Charles Pinckney, Pierce Butler

GEORGIA: William Few, Abr. Baldwin

    Attest: William Jackson, Secretary.

    In Convention Monday, September 17th, 1787. Present The States of New Hampshire, Massachusetts, Connecticut, MR. Hamilton from New York, New Jersey, Pennsylvania, Delaware, Maryland, Virginia, North Carolina, South Carolina and Georgia.

    Resolved,

That the preceeding Constitution be laid before the United States in Congress assembled, and that it is the Opinion of this Convention, that it should afterwards be submitted to a Convention of Delegates, chosen in each State by the People thereof, under the Recommendation of its Legislature, for their Assent and Ratification; and that each Convention assenting to, and ratifying the Same, should give Notice thereof to the United States in Congress assembled.

Resolved, That it is the Opinion of this Convention, that as soon as the Conventions of nine States shall have ratified this Constitution, the United States in Congress assembled should fix a Day on which Electors should be appointed by the States which have ratified the same, and a Day on which the Electors should assemble to vote for the President, and the Time and Place for commencing Proceedings under this Constitution. That after such Publication the Electors should be appointed, and the Senators and Representatives elected: That the Electors should meet on the Day fixed for the Election of the President, and should transmit their Votes certified, signed, sealed and directed, as the Constitution requires, to the Secretary of the United States in Congress assembled, that the Senators and Representatives should convene at the Time and Place assigned; that the Senators should appoint a President of the Senate, for the sole purpose of receiving, opening and counting the Votes for President; and, that after he shall be chosen, the Congress, together with the President, should, without Delay, proceed to execute this Constitution.

By the Unanimous Order of the Convention

Go. WASHINGTON–Presidt. W. JACKSON Secretary.

AMENDMENTS

Articles in Addition to, and Amendment of, the Constitution of the United States of America, Proposed by Congress, and Ratified by the Legislatures of the Several States, Pursuant to the Fifth Article of the Original Constitution.

Article I.

Congress shall make no law respecting an establishment of religion, or prohibiting the free exercise thereof; or abridging the freedom of speech, or of the press, or the right of the people peaceably to assemble, and to petition the Government for a redress of grievances.

Article II.

A well regulated Militia, being necessary to the security of a free State, the right of the people to keep and bear Arms, shall not be infringed.

Article III.

No Soldier shall, in time of peace be quartered in any house, without the consent of the Owner, nor in time of war, but in a manner to be prescribed by law.

Article IV.

The right of the people to be secure in their persons, houses, papers, and effects, against unreasonable searches and seizures, shall not be violated, and no Warrants shall issue, but upon probable cause, supported by Oath or affirmation, and particularly describing the place to be searched, and the persons or things to be seized.

Article V.

No person shall be held to answer for a capital, or otherwise infamous crime, unless on a presentment or indictment of a Grand Jury, except in cases arising in the land or naval forces, or in the Militia, when in actual service in time of War or public danger; nor shall any person be subject for the same offence to be twice put in jeopardy of life or limb, nor shall be compelled in any criminal case to be a witness against himself, nor be deprived of life, liberty, or property, without due process of law; nor shall private property be taken for public use without just compensation.

Article VI.

In all criminal prosecutions, the accused shall enjoy the right to a speedy and public trial, by an impartial jury of the State and district wherein the crime shall have been committed; which district shall have been previously ascertained by law, and to be informed of the nature and cause of the accusation; to be confronted with the witnesses against him; to have compulsory process for obtaining witnesses in his favor, and to have the assistance of counsel for his defence.

Article VII.

In Suits at common law, where the value in controversy shall exceed twenty dollars, the right of trial by jury shall be preserved, and no fact tried by a jury shall be otherwise re-examined in any Court of the United States, than according to the rules of the common law.

Article VIII.

Excessive bail shall not be required, nor excessive fines imposed, nor cruel and unusual punishments inflicted.

Article IX.

The enumeration in the Constitution of certain rights shall not be construed to deny or disparage others retained by the people.

Article X.

The powers not delegated to the United States by the Constitution, nor prohibited by it to the States, are reserved to the States respectively, or to the people.

Article XI.

The Judicial power of the United States shall not be construed to extend to any suit in law or equity, commenced or prosecuted against one of the United States by Citizens of another State, or by Citizens or Subjects of any Foreign State.

Article XII.

The Electors shall meet in their respective states, and vote by ballot for President and Vice President, one of whom, at least, shall not be an inhabitant of the same state with themselves; they shall name in their ballots the person voted for as President, and in distinct ballots the person voted for as Vice-President, and they shall make distinct lists of all persons voted for as President, and of all persons voted for as Vice-President, and of the number of votes for each, which lists they shall sign and certify, and transmit sealed to the seat of the government of the United States, directed to the President of the Senate;

The President of the Senate shall, in the presence of the Senate and House of Representatives, open all the certificates and the votes shall then be counted;

The person having the greatest number of votes for President, shall be the President, if such number be a majority of the whole number of Electors appointed; and if no person have such majority, then from the persons having the highest numbers not exceeding three on the list of those voted for as President, the House of Representatives shall choose immediately, by ballot, the President. But in choosing the President, the votes shall be taken by states, the representation from each state having one vote; a quorum for this purpose shall consist of a member or members from two-thirds of the states, and a majority of all the states shall be necessary to a choice.

And if the House of Representatives shall not choose a President whenever the right of choice shall devolve upon them, before the fourth day of March next following, then the Vice-President shall act as President, as in the case of the death or other constitutional disability of the President. The person having the greatest number of votes as Vice-President, shall be the Vice-President, if such number be a majority of the whole number of Electors appointed, and if no person have a majority, then from the two highest numbers on the list, the Senate shall choose the Vice-President; a quorum for the purpose shall consist of two-thirds of the whole number of Senators, and a majority of the whole number shall be necessary to a choice. But no person constitutionally ineligible to the office of President shall be eligible to that of Vice-President of the United States.

Article XIII.

SECTION 1. Neither slavery nor involuntary servitude, except as a punishment for crime whereof the party shall have been duly convicted, shall exist within the United States, or any place subject to their jurisdiction.

SECTION 2. Congress shall have power to enforce this article by appropriate legislation.

Article XIV.

SECTION 1. All persons born or naturalized in the United States and subject to the jurisdiction thereof, are citizens of the United

States and of the State wherein they reside. No State shall make or enforce any law which shall abridge the privileges or immunities of citizens of the United States; nor shall any State deprive any person of life, liberty, or property, without due process of law; nor deny to any person within its jurisdiction the equal protection of the laws.

SECTION 2. Representatives shall be apportioned among the several States according to their respective numbers, counting the whole number of persons in each State, excluding Indians not taxed. But when the right to vote at any election for the choice of electors for President and Vice President of the United States, Representatives in Congress, the Executive and Judicial officers of a State, or the members of the Legislature thereof, is denied to any of the male inhabitants of such State, being twenty-one years of age, and citizens of the United States, or in any way abridged, except for participation in rebellion, or other crime, the basis of representation therein shall be reduced in the proportion which the number of such male citizens shall bear to the whole number of male citizens twenty-one years of age in such State.

SECTION 3. No person shall be a Senator or Representative in Congress, or elector of President and Vice President, or hold any office, civil or military, under the United States, or under any State, who, having previously taken an oath, as a member of Congress, or as an officer of the United States, or as a member of any State legislature, or as an executive or judicial officer of any State, to support the Constitution of the United States, shall have engaged in insurrection or rebellion against the same, or given aid or comfort to the enemies thereof. But Congress may by a vote of two-thirds of each House, remove such disability.

SECTION 4. The validity of the public debt of the United States, authorized by law, including debts incurred for payment of pensions and bounties for services in suppressing insurrection or rebellion, shall not be questioned. But neither the United States nor any State shall assume or pay any debt or obligation incurred in aid of insurrection or rebellion against the United States, or any claim for the loss or emancipation of any slave; but all such debts, obligations and claims shall be held illegal and void.

SECTION 5. The Congress shall have power to enforce, by appropriate legislation, the provisions of this article.

Article XV.

SECTION 1. The right of citizens of the United States to vote shall not be denied or abridged by the United States or by any State on account of race, color, or previous condition of servitude.

SECTION 2. The Congress shall have power to enforce this article by appropriate legislation.

Article XVI.

The Congress shall have power to lay and collect taxes on incomes, from whatever source derived, without apportionment among the several States, and without regard to any census or enumeration.

Article XVII.

The Senate of the United States shall be composed of two Senators from each State, elected by the people thereof, for six years; and each Senator shall have one vote. The electors in each State shall have the qualifications requisite for electors of the most numerous branch of the State legislatures.

When vacancies happen in the representation of any State in the Senate, the executive authority of such State shall issue writs of election to fill such vacancies: Provided, That the legislature of any State may empower the executive thereof to make temporary appointments until the people fill the vacancies by election as the legislature may direct.

This amendment shall not be so construed as to affect the election or term of any Senator chosen before it becomes valid as part of the Constitution.

Article XVIII.

SECTION 1. After one year from the ratification of this article the manufacture, sale, or transportation of intoxicating liquors within, the importation thereof into, or the exportation thereof from the United States and all territory subject to the jurisdiction thereof for beverage purposes is hereby prohibited.

SECTION 2. The Congress and the several States shall have concurrent power to enforce this article by appropriate legislation.

SECTION 3. This article shall be inoperative unless it shall have been ratified as an amendment to the Constitution by the legislatures of the several States, as provided in the Constitution, within seven years from the date of the submission hereof to the States by the Congress.

Article XIX.

The right of citizens of the United States to vote shall not be denied or abridged by the United States or by any State on account of sex.

Congress shall have power to enforce this article by appropriate legislation.

Article XX.

SECTION 1. The terms of the President and Vice President shall end at noon the 20th day of January, and the terms of Senators and Representatives at noon on the 3d day of January, of the years in which such terms would have ended if this article had not been ratified; and the terms of their successors shall then begin.

SECTION 2. The Congress shall assemble at least once in every year, and such meeting shall begin at noon on the 3d day of January, unless they shall by law appoint a different day.

SECTION 3. If, at the time fixed for the beginning of the term of the President, the President elect shall have died, the Vice President elect shall become President. If a President shall not have been chosen before the time fixed for the beginning of his term, or if the President elect shall have failed to qualify, then the Vice President elect shall act as President until a President shall have qualified; and the Congress may by law provide for the case wherein neither a President elect nor a Vice President elect shall have qualified, declaring who shall then act as President, or the manner in which one who is to act shall be selected, and such person shall act accordingly until a President or Vice President shall have qualified.

SECTION 4. The Congress may by law provide for the case of the death of any of the persons from whom the House of Representatives may choose a President whenever the right of choice shall have devolved upon them, and for the case of the death of any of the persons from whom the Senate may choose a Vice President whenever the right of choice shall have devolved upon them.

SECTION 5. Sections 1 and 2 shall take effect on the 15th day of October following the ratification of this article.

SECTION 6. This article shall be inoperative unless it shall have been ratified as an amendment to the Constitution by the legislatures of three-fourths of the several States within seven years from the date of its submission.

Article XXI.

SECTION 1. The eighteenth article of amendment to the Constitution of the United States is hereby repealed.

SECTION 2. The transportation or importation into any State, Territory, or possession of the United States for delivery or use therein of intoxicating liquors, in violation of the laws thereof, is hereby prohibited.

SECTION 3. This article shall be inoperative unless it shall have been ratified as an amendment to the Constitution by conventions in the several States, as provided in the Constitution, within seven years from the date of the submission hereof to the States by the Congress.

Article XXII.

SECTION 1. No person shall be elected to the office of the President more than twice, and no person who has held the office of President, or acted as President, for more than two years of a term to which some other person was elected President shall be elected to the office of President more than once. But this Article shall not apply to any person holding the office of President when this Article was proposed by the Congress, and shall not prevent any person who may be holding the office of President, or acting as President, during the term within which this Article becomes operative from holding the office of President or acting as President during the remainder of such term.

SECTION 2. This article shall be inoperative unless it shall have been ratified as an amendment to the Constitution by the legislatures of three-fourths of the several States within seven years from the date of its submission to the States by the Congress.

Article XXIII.

SECTION 1. The District constituting the seat of Government of the United States shall appoint in such manner as the Congress may direct:

    A number of electors of President and Vice President equal to the whole number of Senators and Representatives in Congress to which the District would be entitled if it were a State, but in no event more than the least populous State; they shall be in addition to those appointed by the States, but they shall be considered, for the purposes of the election of President and Vice President, to be electors appointed by a State; and they shall meet in the District and perform such duties as provided by the twelfth article of amendment.

SECTION 2. The Congress shall have power to enforce this article by appropriate legislation.

Article XXIV.

SECTION 1. The right of citizens of the United States to vote in any primary or other election for President or Vice President, for electors for President or Vice President, or for Senator or Representative in Congress, shall not be denied or abridged by the United States or any State by reason of failure to pay any poll tax or other tax.

SECTION 2. The Congress shall have power to enforce this article by appropriate legislation.

Article XXV.

SECTION 1. In case of the removal of the President from office or of his death or resignation, the Vice President shall become President.

SECTION 2. Whenever there is a vacancy in the office of the Vice President, the President shall nominate a Vice President who shall take office upon confirmation by a majority vote of both Houses of Congress.

SECTION 3. Whenever the President transmits to the President pro tempore of the Senate and the Speaker of the House of Representatives his written declaration that he is unable to discharge the powers and duties of his office, and until he transmits to them a written declaration to the contrary, such powers and duties shall be discharged by the Vice President as Acting President.

SECTION 4. Whenever the Vice President and a majority of either the principal officers of the executive departments or of such other body as Congress may by law provide, transmit to the President pro tempore of the Senate and the Speaker of the House of Representatives their written declaration that the President is unable to discharge the powers and duties of his office, the Vice President shall immediately assume the powers and duties of the office as Acting President.

Thereafter, when the President transmits to the President pro tempore of the Senate and the Speaker of the House of Representatives his written declaration that no inability exists, he shall resume the powers and duties of his office unless the Vice President and a majority of either the principal officers of the executive department or of such other body as Congress may by law provide, transmit within four days to the President pro tempore of the Senate and the Speaker of the House of Representatives their written declaration that the President is unable to discharge the powers and duties of his office. Thereupon Congress shall decide the issue, assembling within forty-eight hours for that purpose if not in session. If the Congress, within twenty-one days after receipt of the latter written declaration, or, if Congress is not in session, within twenty one days after Congress is required to assemble, determines by two-thirds vote of both Houses that the President is unable to discharge the powers and duties of his office, the Vice President shall continue to discharge the same as Acting President; otherwise, the President shall resume the powers and duties of his office.

Article XXVI.

SECTION 1. The right of citizens of the United States, who are eighteen years of age or older, to vote shall not be denied or abridged by the United States or by any State on account of age.

SECTION 2. The Congress shall have power to enforce this article by appropriate legislation.

Article XXVII.

No law, varying the compensation for the services of the Senators and Representatives, shall take effect, until an election of Representatives shall have intervened.

Where to Learn More

Books

Abraham, Henry J. *Justices, Presidents, and Senators.* Lanham, MD: Rowman & Littlefield Publishers, 1999.

Baum, Lawrence. *The Supreme Court.* Washington, DC: Congressional Quarterly Inc., 1998.

Beard, Charles A. *American Government and Politics.* 10th ed. New York: Macmillan Co., 1949.

Beard, Charles A. *An Economic Interpretation of the Constitution of the United States.* New York: Macmillan, 1935.

Biskupic, Joan, and Elder Witt. *The Supreme Court & the Powers of the American Government.* Washington, DC: Congressional Quarterly Inc., 1997.

Biskupic, Joan, and Elder Witt. *The Supreme Court at Work.* Washington, DC: Congressional Quarterly Inc., 1997.

Brannen, Daniel E., and Richard Clay Hanes. *Supreme Court Drama: Cases That Changed America.* Detroit: UXL, 2001.

Burnham, James. *Congress and the American Tradition.* New Brunswick, NJ: Transaction Publishers, 2003.

Carp, Robert A., and Ronald Stidham. *The Federal Courts.* 2nd ed. Washington, DC: Congressional Quarterly Inc., 1991.

Charleton, James H., Robert G. Ferris, and Mary C. Ryan, eds. *Framers of the Constitution.* Washington, DC: National Archives and Records Administration, 1976.

Choper, Jesse H., ed. *The Supreme Court and Its Justices.* 2nd ed. Chicago: American Bar Association, 2001.

Clark, J. C. D. *The Language of Liberty, 1660–1832.* Cambridge, Eng.: Cambridge University Press, 1994.

Congressional Quarterly Inc. *Guide to the Congress of the United States.* 1st ed. Washington, DC: Congressional Quarterly Service, 1971.

Congressional Quarterly Inc. *Powers of the Presidency.* 2nd ed. Washington, DC: Congressional Quarterly Inc., 1997.

Cronin, Thomas E. *Inventing the American Presidency.* Lawrence: University Press of Kansas, 1989.

Where to Learn More

DiClerico, Robert E. *The American President.* 5th ed. Upper Saddle River, NJ: Prentice Hall, 2000.

Dougherty, J. Hampden. *Power of Federal Judiciary over Legislation.* New York: Putnam's Sons, 1912. Reprint, Clark, NJ: Lawbook Exchange, 2004.

Fisher, Louis. *Constitutional Conflicts between Congress and the President.* 3rd ed. Lawrence: University Press of Kansas, 1991.

Fisher, Louis. *The Politics of Shared Power: Congress and the Executive.* 4th ed. College Station: Texas A&M University Press, 1998.

Goebel, Julius, Jr. *Antecedents and Beginnings to 1801.* Vol. I. New York: Macmillan, 1971.

Green, Mark. *Who Runs Congress?* 3rd ed. New York: The Viking Press, 1979.

Hart, John. *The Presidential Branch.* 2nd ed. Chatham, NJ: Chatham House Publishers, 1995.

Irons, Peter. *A People's History of the Supreme Court.* New York: Penguin Books, 1999.

Janda, Kenneth, Jeffrey M. Berry, and Jerry Goldman. *The Challenge of Democracy.* 5th ed. Boston: Houghton Mifflin Company, 1997.

Kelly, Alfred H., and Winfred A. Harbison. *The American Constitution: Its Origins and Development.* 5th ed. New York: W. W. Norton & Co., 1976.

Kurland, Philip B., and Ralph Lerner. *The Founders' Constitution.* 5 vols. Indianapolis: Liberty Fund, 1987.

Lazarus, Edward P. *Closed Chambers.* New York: Times Books, 1998.

Levy, Leonard W. *Original Intent and the Framers' Constitution.* New York: Macmillan, 1988.

Lintcott, Andrew. *The Constitution of the Roman Republic.* Oxford: Clarendon Press, 1999.

Loomis, Burdett A. *The Contemporary Congress.* 3rd ed. Boston: Bedford/St. Martin's, 2000.

MacNeil, Neil. *Forge of Democracy: The House of Representatives.* New York: David MacKay Co., 1963.

McClenaghan, William A. *Magruder's American Government 2003.* Needham, MA: Prentice Hall School Group, 2002.

McDonald, Forrest. *The American Presidency.* Lawrence: University Press of Kansas, 1994.

Milkis, Sidney M., and Michael Nelson. *The American Presidency: Origins & Development.* 3rd ed. Washington, DC: Congressional Quarterly Inc., 1999.

Millar, Fergus. *The Roman Republic in Political Thought.* Hanover and London: Brandeis University Press and Historical Society of Israel, 2002.

Moran, Thomas Francis. *The Rise and Development of the Bicameral System in America.* Baltimore: The Johns Hopkins Press, 1895.

Nelson, Michael, ed. *The Evolving Presidency.* Washington, DC: Congressional Quarterly Inc., 1999.

Nelson, Michael, ed. *The Presidency and the Political System.* 7th ed. Washington, DC: CQ Press, 2003.

Parenti, Michael. *Democracy for the Few.* 6th ed. New York: St. Martin's Press, 1995.

Pole, J. R. *Political Representation in England and the Origins of the American Republic.* London: Macmillan, 1966.

Ripley, Randall B. *Party Leaders in the House of Representatives.* Washington, DC: Brookings Institution, 1967.

Roelofs, H. Mark. *The Poverty of American Politics.* 2nd ed. Philadelphia: Temple University Press, 1998.

Rozell, Mark J. *Executive Privilege.* Lawrence: University Press of Kansas, 2002.

Rozell, Mark J., William D. Pederson, and Frank J. Williams. *George Washington and the Origins of the American Presidency.* Westport, CT: Praeger, 2000.

Schwartz, Bernard. *A History of the Supreme Court.* New York: Oxford University Press, 1993.

Shelley, Mack C., II. *American Government and Politics Today.* 2004–2005 ed. Belmont, CA: Wadsworth Publishing, 2003.

Surrency, Erwin C. *History of the Federal Courts.* 2nd ed. Dobbs Ferry, NY: Oceana Publications, 2002.

Volkomer, Walter E. *American Government.* 8th ed. Upper Saddle River, NJ: Prentice Hall, 1998.

Wasby, Stephen L. *The Supreme Court in the Federal Judicial System.* 2nd ed. New York: Holt, Rinehart and Winston, 1984.

Wheeler, Russell R., and Cynthia Harrison. *Creating the Federal Judicial System.* Washington, DC: Federal Judicial Center, 1994.

Wilson, Woodrow. *Congressional Government.* Houghton Mifflin Co., 1885. Reprint, New Brunswick, NJ: Transaction Publishers, 2002.

Wolfensberger, Donald R. *Congress and the People.* Washington, DC, and Baltimore: Woodrow Wilson Center Press and Johns Hopkins University Press, 2000.

Woll, Peter. *American Government: Readings and Cases.* 15th ed. New York: Longman, 2003.

Young, Roland. *American Law and Politics: The Creation of Public Order.* New York: Harper & Row, 1967.

Zinn, Howard. *A People's History of the United States.* New York: HarperCollins, 2003.

CD-ROMs

21st Century Complete Guide to U.S. Courts. Progressive Management, 2003.

Web Sites

Federal Judicial Center. http://www.fjc.gov/ (accessed on March 31, 2005).

Federal Judiciary. http://www.uscourts.gov (accessed on February 18, 2005).

Library of Congress. http://www.loc.gov (accessed on March 15, 2005).

O'Hara, James B. "Court History Quizzes." *Supreme Court Historical Society.* http://www.supremecourthistory.org/02_history/subs_history/02_f.html (accessed on March 30, 2005).

Supreme Court of the United States. http://www.supremecourtus.gov (accessed on February 18, 2005).

United States Department of Justice. http://www.usdoj.gov/ (accessed on February 12, 2005).

United States House of Representatives. http://www.house.gov (accessed on March 14, 2005).

United States Senate. http://www.senate.gov (accessed on March 14, 2005).

U.S. Census Bureau. http://www.census.gov (accessed on February 16, 2005).

U.S. Courts: The Federal Judiciary. http://www.uscourts.gov (accessed on March 23, 2005).

U.S. Term Limits. http://www.termlimits.org/ (accessed on March 11, 2005).

The White House. http://www.whitehouse.gov (accessed on February 16, 2005).

Index

Italic type indicates volume number; illustrations are marked by (ill.).

abolitionism, *3:* 430. *See also* slavery
Abraham, Spencer, *1:* 8 (ill.)
Abrams, Elliot, *1:* 153
Ackerman, Gary, *2:* 303
Act for Establishing Religious Freedom, *3:* 389
Act to Establish the Federal Courts of the United States. *See* Judiciary Act of 1789
Adams, Abigail, *1:* 93
Adams, John, *2:* 230 (ill.)
    appointment power of, *1:* 161–63; *3:* 475
    on class, *2:* 210–11, 228–29
    on democracy, *2:* 206
    election of, *1:* 93
    executive orders of, *1:* 76
    Library of Congress and, *2:* 305
    Marbury v. Madison and, *2:* 342; *3:* 424, 497
    Sedition Act of 1798 and, *2:* 244
    on separation of powers, *2:* 220–21
    as vice president, *1:* 93; *2:* 277, 278
    White House and, *2:* 221
Adams, John Quincy, *1:* 69, 69 (ill.), 87; *3:* 442
Adams, Samuel, *2:* 206, 210–11
Administration for Children and Families, *1:* 100
Administration on Aging, *1:* 100
administrative law, *1:* 124–25, 127–28, 169–71; *3:* 481–82. *See also* executive agencies; executive departments; independent regulatory commissions
administrative law judges, *1:* 128
Administrative Office of the United States Courts, *3:* 440, 469

Index

admiralty
- cases concerning, *2:* 346; *3:* 403, 415, 418, 501
- Court of Appeals for, *3:* 391–93
- federal district courts and, *3:* 417

advice and consent
- agency appointments and, *1:* 109, 124, 125
- ambassador appointments and, *1:* 56
- checks and balances and, *1:* 143–46, 173; *2:* 323–27, 349–50, 352–53; *3:* 485–86, 506
- department appointments and, *1:* 95; *3:* 418
- independent regulatory commission appointments and, *1:* 109, 127
- judicial appointments and, *1:* 17, 173; *2:* 195; *3:* 375–76, 433, 437, 439, 485–86
- overview of, *1:* 5, 11, 143–46; *2:* 184, 190, 277, 323–27; *3:* 364, 369
- vice president and, *2:* 352

African Americans, *3:* 500–501. *See also* discrimination; race

Age of Enlightenment, *1:* 26; *2:* 202–3

agencies. *See* executive agencies

Agency for Healthcare Research and Quality, *1:* 100

Agency for International Development, *1:* 105

Agnew, Spiro T., *1:* 96; *3:* 368 (ill.)

Agriculture, Department of, *1:* 95–98

agriculture, secretary of, *1:* 95–97

Air Force, Department of the, *1:* 98

Akerman, Amos Tappan, *3:* 419 (ill.)

Albert, Carl, *3:* 368 (ill.)

Albright, Madeleine, *1:* 85

alcohol, *2:* 258–59

Aldrich, Nelson W., *2:* 255

Allen, Richard, *1:* 105 (ill.)

ambassadors
- appointment of, *2:* 277
- cases concerning, *1:* 14, 15; *2:* 192, 193, 346; *3:* 373, 403–4, 415, 417, 501
- in Constitution, *1:* 55–56
- president and, *1:* 11; *2:* 189; *3:* 369
- work of, *1:* 106

amendments, constitutional. *See also* specific amendments
- checks and balances and, *1:* 17; *2:* 195, 348–49; *3:* 375, 500–501, 504–5
- executive branch and, *1:* 61–62
- judicial interpretation and, *3:* 500–501
- judicial power and, *2:* 348–49; *3:* 504–5
- overview of, *1:* 1, 3; *3:* 504–5
- ratification of, *2:* 236, 255, 257–58, 258–59
- term limits and, *2:* 259–61
- time limit for, *2:* 257–58

American Association for Retired Persons, *2:* 285 (ill.)

American Civil War
- amnesty after, *1:* 52–53
- taxation during, *2:* 254, 350
- war powers and, *3:* 425
- writs of habeas corpus and, *2:* 355; *3:* 510

American Declaration of Independence, *1:* 34 (ill.); *3:* 431 (ill.). *See also* American Revolutionary War
- Constitution and, *3:* 430–31
- Fourteenth Amendment and, *3:* 431
- George III in, *2:* 208
- government under, *1:* 4; *2:* 182; *3:* 362
- grievances in, *1:* 30, 32–34
- inalienable rights in, *3:* 430–31, 500
- military in, *2:* 234
- Parliament in, *2:* 208
- signing of, *1:* 30, 39

American Revolutionary War, *2:* 220, 233, 235. *See also* American Declaration of Independence

amnesty, *1:* 52–53. *See also* pardon power

Annapolis Convention, *1:* 41; *3:* 396

Antiballistic Missile Treaty, *1:* 57

Anti-federalists
- Bill of Rights and, *2:* 241–43; *3:* 418
- Constitution and, *2:* 240–42; *3:* 418
- judicial branch and, *3:* 416–17
- judicial review and, *3:* 418
- Necessary and Proper Clause and, *2:* 246

Index

state power and, *3:* 423–24
Anti-Saloon League, *2:* 258
appeals
   admiralty, *3:* 392
   in American colonies, *3:* 386
   to circuit courts, *3:* 417, 428–29
   to circuit courts of appeals, *3:* 435, 443–45, 446, 447, 458, 460–62
   civil law and, *3:* 418
   criminal law and, *3:* 418
   in Great Britain, *3:* 385
   judicial interpretation and, *3:* 409–11
   overview of, *1:* 13–14; *2:* 191–92; *3:* 371–72, 379–80, 404, 407–9
   purpose of, *3:* 461
   regulatory, *1:* 125
   in Schiavo case, *3:* 381
   in state cases, *3:* 418
   to Supreme Court, *1:* 15; *2:* 193; *3:* 373, 403, 404–5, 415, 417–18, 429, 432–33, 435, 440–43, 462–68
appearance of impropriety, *3:* 476–77
appellate jurisdiction, *3:* 407–8, 415, 417–18, 432–33, 435. *See also* appeals
appointment power. *See also* advice and consent
   agency appointments and, *1:* 109
   ambassador appointments and, *1:* 56
   bureau appointments and, *1:* 109
   checks and balances and, *1:* 11, 17, 143–46, 173; *2:* 190, 195, 323–27, 351–52; *3:* 369, 375–76, 485–86, 506
   department appointments and, *1:* 95, 145–46; *2:* 325; *3:* 418
   independent regulatory commission appointments and, *1:* 109, 127
   judicial appointments and, *1:* 173, 174–75; *3:* 413, 425, 433, 437, 439, 440, 443–44, 445, 447, 458, 485–86
   overview of, *1:* 11, 17, 127; *2:* 195, 349, 351–52; *3:* 369, 375–76, 506
apportionment, *1:* 3; *2:* 181; *3:* 361

appropriations power
   checks and balances and, *1:* 140–43; *2:* 320–23
   debate and, *2:* 293
   federal budget and, *2:* 301
   first bill for, *2:* 288–89
   historic roots of, *1:* 29
   impoundment and, *1:* 141; *2:* 320–22
   line item veto and, *2:* 316
   reprogramming and, *1:* 142–43; *2:* 322–23
   veto power and, *1:* 141; *2:* 321
Arago, 3: 466–67
arbitrators, *3:* 384
Architect of the Capitol, *2:* 305
Aristotle, *2:* 201–2, 202 (ill.)
arms, right to bear, *1:* 6; *2:* 185, 243–45, 268; *3:* 364
Army, Department of the, *1:* 98
Arnold, Benedict, *3:* 407 (ill.)
arraignment, *3:* 457
arrest. *See* search and seizure
Articles of Confederation
   commerce under, *1:* 40–41; *2:* 215, 230–31, 249; *3:* 395
   executive power and, *1:* 31–35, 39
   government under, *1:* 4; *2:* 182, 197, 215; *3:* 362
   judiciary in, *3:* 390–93, 395, 396
   law enforcement under, *1:* 48; *2:* 221
   legislation under, *2:* 215, 221
   military under, *1:* 32–35, 40; *2:* 215
   president under, *1:* 39
   problems under, *1:* 31–35, 37–41, 42–43, 48; *2:* 215, 217, 230–31, 235, 249; *3:* 395–97
   states under, *2:* 217, 235
   taxation under, *1:* 31–32, 39–40; *2:* 215, 217, 235; *3:* 395
Ashcroft, John, *1:* 8 (ill.), 123
assemblies, Roman, *1:* 20–21; *2:* 199, 200
assistant to the president for national security affairs, *1:* 108–9
assistant U.S. attorneys, *1:* 120, 121; *3:* 418, 450
associate attorney general, *1:* 102, 120, 121–22

Index

associate justices, *3:* 439, 440, 441–43, 462, 467. *See also* justices, Supreme court

Attlee, Clement, *1:* 148 (ill.)

attorney general
    appointment of, *3:* 418
    associate attorney general, *1:* 102, 120, 121–22
    creation of, *1:* 50, 73; *3:* 418
    deputy attorney general, *1:* 102, 120, 121–22
    as head of department, *1:* 95, 102, 119–20
    work of, *1:* 121–22

attorneys, *1:* 66; *3:* 450–51. *See also* specific posts

b

bail, *3:* 423

Bailey, Joseph W., *2:* 255

balanced budget amendment, *2:* 261–62, 272

Bank of the United States, *2:* 247–49

bankruptcy, *3:* 432, 460

bench trials, *3:* 379, 409, 446–47, 459, 460

bicameralism
    checks and balances and, *2:* 209–10
    class and, *2:* 212–15, 312
    in colonies, American, *2:* 212–15
    Constitution and, *2:* 197, 223–24
    Federal Convention and, *2:* 198–99, 223–24
    Madison, James, on, *2:* 312
    states and, *2:* 212–15

Bill of Rights, *2:* 242 (ill.). *See also* specific amendments
    Anti-federalists and, *2:* 241–43; *3:* 418
    civil liberties in, *1:* 16; *2:* 194, 243–46; *3:* 374–75, 430
    Federal Convention and, *2:* 239–40
    Federalist Party and, *2:* 241–43; *3:* 418
    judicial power and, *3:* 418–23
    legislative power and, *1:* 6; *2:* 185, 239–46; *3:* 364
    Madison, James, and, *1:* 63; *2:* 242–43; *3:* 418, 430
    Magna Carta and, *1:* 24
    ratification of, *1:* 6; *2:* 185, 242–43, 257; *3:* 364, 418–19
    ratification of Constitution and, *1:* 62–63; *2:* 240–43; *3:* 418
    states and, *3:* 430

bills. *See* legislation

bills of attainder
    legislative power and, *1:* 6; *2:* 184, 355; *3:* 364, 510
    liberty and, *2:* 205

Black Codes, *3:* 427, 428 (ill.), 500–501

Black, Hugo L., *1:* 166; *3:* 439 (ill.)

Black, Jeremiah, *2:* 187 (ill.)

Black, Shirley Temple, *1:* 56 (ill.)

Blackmun, Harry A., *3:* 372 (ill.), 463 (ill.)

Blackstone, Sir William, *1:* 25; *2:* 210

Blount, William, *1:* 155, 155 (ill.); *2:* 333

Blumenthal, Richard, *3:* 451 (ill.)

Board of Trade, *3:* 387

Board of Veterans Appeals, *3:* 458

Body of Civil Law, *3:* 383

Boies, David, *3:* 451 (ill.)

Boland Amendment, *1:* 153

bootlegging, *2:* 258

Bork, Robert H., *1:* 17; *2:* 195, 326 (ill.), 352; *3:* 376

Boston Gazette, *2:* 302

Boston Tea Party, *1:* 39

breach of the peace, *1:* 131–32; *2:* 309–10, 337; *3:* 493

Brennan, William J., Jr., *3:* 372 (ill.), 439 (ill.), 463 (ill.)

bribery
    as impeachable offense, *1:* 5, 91, 153–54; *2:* 182–84, 333, 353–54; *3:* 437, 508
    impeachments for, *3:* 363

briefs, *3:* 441, 444, 448, 461, 465

British Empire. *See* Great Britain

Broom, Jacob, *1:* 46
Brown, Henry B., *3:* 466–67, 467 (ill.)
Brown v. Board of Education of Topeka, 2: 345; *3:* 499–500
Brutus, *2:* 236, 237
Buchanan, James, *2:* 187 (ill.)
budget. *See* federal budget
Budget and Accounting Act of 1921, *1:* 72–73; *2:* 299
Budget and Impoundment Control Act of 1974, *1:* 141; *2:* 299–301, 321–22
Bureau of Competition, *1:* 127
Bureau of Consumer Protection, *1:* 127
Bureau of Indian Affairs, *1:* 102
Bureau of Labor Statistics, *1:* 103
Bureau of Land Management, *1:* 102
Bureau of Reclamation, *1:* 102
Bureau of the Budget, *1:* 72; *2:* 299. *See also* Office of Management and Budget
bureaus, *1:* 109. *See also* specific bureaus
Burger, Warren, *3:* 372 (ill.), 463 (ill.), 486 (ill.), 488–89
Burr, Aaron, *1:* 48, 66–67, 68–69
Bursey, Brett A., *1:* 122–23
Bush, Barbara, *1:* 119 (ill.)
Bush, George (forty-first president), *1:* 10 (ill.), 119 (ill.)
  appointment power of, *2:* 352
  debate by, *1:* 86
  Iran-Contra scandal and, *1:* 153
  Noriega, Manuel, and, *1:* 82
  pardons by, *1:* 52, 153, 176; *3:* 490
  as vice president, *1:* 104–5, 118
  War Powers Resolution and, *1:* 82
Bush, George W. (forty-third president), *1:* 8 (ill.), 145 (ill.); *2:* 189 (ill.), 260 (ill.), 318 (ill.); *3:* 370 (ill.)
  appointment power of, *1:* 144, 145; *2:* 324–25
  cabinet of, *1:* 8 (ill.), 107
  congressional messages of, *1:* 10; *2:* 188; *3:* 368
  election of, *1:* 13–14, 66, 84, 87; *2:* 191–92; *3:* 371–72, 464–65
  Iraq and, *1:* 122–23

Office of Faith-Based and Community Initiatives and, *1:* 75–76
Office of Homeland Security and, *1:* 100
reprogramming by, *1:* 142; *2:* 322
Schiavo case and, *3:* 381
State of the Union address of, *1:* 51–52
treaties made by, *1:* 11, 57; *2:* 190; *3:* 369
vetoes by, *1:* 136; *2:* 315
Bush, Laura, *1:* 103; *3:* 370 (ill.)
Bush v. Gore, 3: 464–65
business. *See* commerce
Butler, Pierce, *1:* 174
Butterfield, Alexander, *3:* 488
Byrd, Robert, *2:* 189 (ill.), 280
Byrne, James F., *3:* 442
Byrns, Joseph, *2:* 188 (ill.)

cabinet
  appointment power and, *1:* 145–46; *2:* 325
  of Buchanan, James, *2:* 187 (ill.)
  of Bush, George W., *1:* 8 (ill.)
  chief of staff in, *1:* 8; *2:* 186; *3:* 366
  composition of, *1:* 7–8, 95, 107; *2:* 186; *3:* 366
  executive heads in, *1:* 7–8; *2:* 186; *3:* 366
  of Lincoln, Abraham, *3:* 366 (ill.)
  of Monroe, James, *1:* 98 (ill.)
  vice president in, *1:* 8, 94, 115; *2:* 186; *3:* 366
  of Washington, George, *1:* 74 (ill.), 77
calendars, *2:* 293
campaign finance reform, *1:* 85; *2:* 288
campaigning, *2:* 268, 303–5. *See also* elections
Cannon, Joseph G., *2:* 268 (ill.), 270, 270 (ill.), 271
capital crime, *1:* 65, 165; *3:* 422, 479–80
capital punishment, *2:* 245–46
capitalism, *1:* 152
Card, Andrew, *1:* 8 (ill.)

Index

Carrington, Edward, *1:* 44
Carswell, G. Harrold, *1:* 17; *2:* 195; *3:* 376, 508 (ill.)
Carter, Jimmy, *1:* 52, 53, 96
"case of the mutinous mariner," *3:* 391
cases and controversies. *See also* jurisdiction
    checks and balances and, *2:* 346–47; *3:* 501–3
    friendly suits and, *2:* 346–47; *3:* 503
    historic roots of, *3:* 390–93
    judicial power and, *2:* 339; *3:* 495
    mootness and, *2:* 347; *3:* 503–4
    overview of, *1:* 14–15; *2:* 192–93; *3:* 373, 402–5
    ripeness and, *2:* 347; *3:* 503–4
    test cases and, *2:* 346–47; *3:* 503
casework, *2:* 267, 275, 276, 301–3
Cass, Lewis, *2:* 187 (ill.)
Catron, John, *3:* 426
ceilings, personnel, *1:* 143; *2:* 323
Center on Budget and Policy Priorities, *2:* 262
Centers for Disease Control and Protection, *1:* 100
Centers for Medicare and Medicaid Services, *1:* 100
Centinel, *1:* 41; *2:* 237
Central Intelligence Agency, *1:* 109, 124, 152–53
centuriate assembly, *1:* 21; *2:* 199
Chamber of Commerce, *1:* 116
Chamorro, Edgar, *1:* 152
chancellors, *3:* 385
chancery courts, *3:* 386
Chao, Elaine, *1:* 8 (ill.)
Chase, Salmon P., *3:* 440, 442, 484 (ill.)
Chase, Samuel, *2:* 354 (ill.); *3:* 438 (ill.), 511 (ill.)
    impeachment of, *1:* 18; *2:* 196, 354; *3:* 376, 438, 510, 511
checks and balances
    advice and consent and, *1:* 143–46, 173; *2:* 323–27, 349–50, 352–53; *3:* 485–86, 506
    amendment power and, *1:* 17; *2:* 195, 348–49; *3:* 375, 500–501, 504–5
    appointment power and, *1:* 11, 17, 143–46, 173; *2:* 190, 195, 323–27, 351–52; *3:* 369, 375–76, 485–86, 506
    appropriations power and, *1:* 140–43; *2:* 320–23
    bicameralism and, *2:* 209–10
    bills of attainder and, *2:* 355; *3:* 510
    in British Empire, *1:* 31
    cases and controversies and, *2:* 346–47; *3:* 501–3
    class and, *2:* 201–2, 312–13
    commander in chief and, *1:* 6; *2:* 185; *3:* 364
    in Constitution, *1:* 1; *2:* 179, 222–23, 339; *3:* 359, 495
    Democratic Party and, *2:* 313
    executive branch and, *1:* 133; *2:* 222, 310–14
    executive power and, *1:* 45–46
    executive privilege and, *1:* 173–76; *3:* 486–87
    Federal Convention and, *1:* 45–46, 133, 160–61; *2:* 217–18, 222–23, 310–14, 339; *3:* 474–75, 495
    Federalist on, *2:* 222
    Fifth Amendment and, *1:* 165–68; *3:* 479–81
    Founding Fathers and, *2:* 312
    Fourth Amendment and, *1:* 163–65; *3:* 478–79
    historic roots of, *1:* 21–22
    House of Representatives and, *2:* 312–13
    impeachment and, *1:* 11–12, 17–18, 151–55, 172–73; *2:* 190, 195–96, 332–33, 353–54; *3:* 369, 376, 483–85, 508–10
    income tax and, *2:* 350–51
    Iran-Contra scandal and, *1:* 152–53
    judicial branch and, *2:* 222, 339; *3:* 495
    judicial interpretation and, *1:* 169–71; *2:* 344–45; *3:* 481–82, 498–501
    judicial power and, *2:* 348–54, 354–55; *3:* 369–70, 504–10, 510–12
    judicial review and, *1:* 6–7, 15–16, 161–69; *2:* 185, 193–94, 339–44; *3:* 364–65, 374–75, 412, 475–78, 495–98
    law enforcement and, *1:* 6, 12; *2:* 185, 190; *3:* 364, 369
    legislation and, *1:* 16–17, 51–54; *2:* 194–95, 349; *3:* 375, 506
    legislative branch and, *1:* 6–7, 133; *2:* 185, 209–10, 222–23, 310–14, 339; *3:* 364–65, 495

Index

legislative oversight and, *1:* 150–51; *2:* 331
legislative power and, *1:* 6–7; *2:* 185, 354–55; *3:* 364, 510–12
Madison, James, on, *2:* 222
Marbury v. Madison and, *1:* 6–7; *2:* 185, 341–44; *3:* 365, 497–98
overview of, *1:* 133, 160–61; *2:* 310–14, 339; *3:* 474–75, 495
pardon power and, *1:* 176; *3:* 487–90
Parliament and, *2:* 209–10
political parties and, *2:* 313
political question doctrine and, *2:* 347–48; *3:* 504
prosecution and, *1:* 165–68; *3:* 479–81
Republican Party and, *2:* 313
in Roman Republic, *1:* 21–22
search and seizure and, *1:* 163–65; *3:* 478–79
Senate and, *2:* 312–13
Sixth Amendment and, *1:* 168–69; *3:* 481
special interest groups and, *2:* 313
treaties and, *1:* 11, 146–47; *2:* 190, 327–28; *3:* 369
veto power and, *1:* 11, 133–39; *2:* 189–90, 222, 314–19; *3:* 369
war powers and, *1:* 147–49; *2:* 329–31
writs of habeas corpus and, *1:* 171; *2:* 354–55; *3:* 482–86, 510
writs of mandamus and, *1:* 171–72; *3:* 483
writs of prohibition and, *1:* 171–72; *3:* 483
Cheney, Dick, *1:* 8 (ill.); *2:* 279 (ill.); *3:* 476–77
chief judges, *3:* 443
chief justice
    administrative duties of, *3:* 440, 469–70
    appointment of, *3:* 440
    compensation for, *3:* 440
    impeachment trials and, *1:* 151–52, 152–53, 172–73; *2:* 332–33; *3:* 413, 440, 483–85
    Marshall, John, appointed to, *2:* 342; *3:* 497
    removal of, *3:* 440
    role of, *3:* 417, 439–40, 443, 462, 466–67
chief of staff
    in cabinet, *1:* 8, 107; *2:* 186; *3:* 366
    work of, *1:* 75, 107–8
chief of state, *1:* 90, 113
Chipman, Nathaniel, *3:* 397–400
Chipman, Norton P., *2:* 286
Chisholm v. Georgia, *3:* 423
Choate, Joseph, *2:* 254
Christianity, *3:* 388–89
Church of England, *3:* 388
Cicero, Marcus Tillius, *3:* 382, 382 (ill.)
circuit courts, *3:* 416–17, 425, 428–29. *See also* circuit courts of appeals
circuit courts of appeals. *See also* circuit courts
    appeals to, *3:* 444–45, 446, 447, 458, 460–62
    clerk of the court of, *3:* 449–50
    creation of, *3:* 429
    decision-making by, *3:* 461–62
    judges of, *3:* 443–44, 448
    Judicial Conference of the United States and, *3:* 469
    judicial interpretation in, *3:* 462
    judicial review in, *3:* 462
    law clerks at, *3:* 448–49
    opinions of, *3:* 461–62
    oral argument in, *3:* 461
    organization of, *3:* 435, 443, 444, 460–61
    overview of, *1:* 13; *2:* 191; *3:* 371, 379–80, 432, 435
    Schiavo case and, *3:* 381
    summary judgment and, *3:* 446
Circuit Courts of Appeals Act of 1891, *3:* 429
citizens
    African Americans as, *3:* 500–501
    cases concerning, *1:* 14; *2:* 192; *3:* 373, 403, 415, 417, 418, 432
Citizens for Term Limits, *2:* 261
civil cases
    in American colonies, *3:* 386–87
    appeals concerning, *3:* 418
    in circuit courts, *3:* 417

Index

in Constitution, *3:* 406–7
in federal district courts, *1:* 13; *2:* 191; *3:* 371, 379, 417, 432, 435, 445–47, 459–60
in Great Britain, *3:* 384–85
Justice, Department of, and, *1:* 64–65, 122
magistrate judges and, *3:* 448
civil liberties. *See also* inalienable rights; liberty
in Bill of Rights, *2:* 243–46
Fourteenth Amendment and, *2:* 252–53; *3:* 430–31
Interstate Commerce Clause and, *2:* 251–53
judicial branch and, *1:* 16; *2:* 194; *3:* 374–75
judicial review and, *3:* 427–28
Magna Carta and, *1:* 23–24
Civil Rights Act of 1875, *2:* 251
Civil Rights Act of 1964, *2:* 251–53
Civil War. *See* American Civil War
civilians, *1:* 8–9, 78–79; *2:* 186, 234–35; *3:* 366–67
Claiborne, Harry, *2:* 354; *3:* 510
Clark, Tom C., *3:* 421
Clarridge, Duane R., *1:* 153
class. *See also* property
Adams, John, on, *2:* 228–29
Aristotle on, *2:* 201–2
bicameralism and, *2:* 212–15, 312
checks and balances and, *2:* 201–2, 312–13
Constitution and, *2:* 226–29
democracy and, *1:* 133; *2:* 311
elections and, *2:* 226–29, 255–57
Federal Convention and, *1:* 133; *2:* 198–99, 217–19, 226–29, 311
House of Lords and, *2:* 210
House of Representatives and, *2:* 226–28, 312–13
income tax and, *2:* 254–55
legislation and, *2:* 202
legislative branch and, *2:* 198–99, 201–2, 206, 214, 226–29, 312–13
liberty and, *2:* 210–11
monarchy and, *2:* 202

Parliament and, *2:* 208–9
representatives, *2:* 202
Senate and, *2:* 202, 210–11, 228–29, 312–13
senators and, *2:* 202
separation of powers and, *2:* 201–2; *3:* 400–402
unicameralism, *2:* 312
voting rights and, *2:* 226–29, 255–57
war and, *2:* 245
Clay, Henry, *1:* 69
Clean Air Act, *1:* 169; *2:* 251; *3:* 482
Clean Water Act, *1:* 125, 169; *3:* 482
clerk of the court, *3:* 449–50
Cleveland, Grover, *1:* 78–79
Clifford, Nathan, *3:* 442
Clinton, Bill, *1:* 59 (ill.), 76 (ill.); *2:* 296 (ill.), 313 (ill.), 317 (ill.)
Clinton, Hillary, and, *1:* 103
Contract with America and, *2:* 272
election of, *1:* 86; *2:* 272
executive privilege of, *1:* 79
impeachment of, *1:* 5, 59, 91, 154, 173; *2:* 184, 333; *3:* 363, 440, 485
line item veto and, *2:* 316
State of the Union address of, *2:* 316
vetoes by, *1:* 11; *2:* 190, 272, 296 (ill.), 297; *3:* 369
Clinton, Hillary, *1:* 85, 103, 103 (ill.); *2:* 304 (ill.)
Clinton v. City of New York, *2:* 316
closing argument, *3:* 457, 459, 460
cloture rule, *2:* 294
Coard, Bernard, *1:* 149; *2:* 331
Coast Guard, U.S., *1:* 98
Coats, Dan, *2:* 316
Cobb, Howell, *2:* 187 (ill.)
Cold War, *1:* 99
Coleman, William T., Jr., *1:* 116
Colfax, Schuyler, *3:* 431
colonies, American, *1:* 28–29; *2:* 211–15; *3:* 386–87, 388–89. *See also* states
commander in chief

checks and balances and, *1:* 6, 147–49; *2:* 185, 329–31; *3:* 364
role of, *1:* 6, 8–9, 54–55, 80–82, 113; *2:* 185, 186; *3:* 364, 366–67
steel seizure case and, *1:* 166

Commentaries on the Constitution, 3: 398–99

Commentaries on the Laws of England, 1: 25; *2:* 210

commerce. *See also* economy
under Articles of Confederation, *1:* 40–41; *2:* 215, 230–31, 249; *3:* 395
Constitution and, *2:* 230–32, 239, 241
executive power and, *1:* 38–39
Federal Convention and, *2:* 218–19, 230–32, 239
Federalist on, *2:* 232
Federalist Party and, *2:* 241
Great Britain and, *1:* 38–39; *2:* 231, 249
Hamilton, Alexander, on, *2:* 229–30, 231, 247
Interstate Commerce Clause and, *2:* 249–53
legislative branch and, *1:* 2; *2:* 180, 205, 215, 239; *3:* 360
legislative power and, *2:* 230–32
lobbying and, *2:* 284–85
Madison, James, on, *2:* 230–31, 232
military and, *2:* 232
with Native Americans, *2:* 232
Sherman Antitrust Act and, *2:* 344–45; *3:* 499
taxation and, *2:* 231–32, 249
Washington, George, on, *2:* 231

Commerce, Chamber of, *1:* 116

Commerce, Department of, *1:* 97

commerce, secretary of, *1:* 97

commissioners, *1:* 109, 127, 144; *2:* 324

Committee of Detail, *3:* 398

Committee of the States, *1:* 39

committees, congressional. *See also* political action committees; specific committees
composition of, *2:* 291
conference, *2:* 276, 295–96
federal budget and, *2:* 299–301

iron triangles and, *2:* 292
issue networks and, *2:* 292
joint, *2:* 270, 276, 299
legislation and, *2:* 266–67, 270, 271, 276, 290–93, 295–96, 299
legislative oversight by, *2:* 297
lobbying and, *2:* 286
majority party and, *2:* 291
minority party and, *2:* 291
select, *2:* 298–99
Senate, *2:* 276, 281
Speaker of the House and, *2:* 270, 295
staff for, *2:* 275, 281
standing, *2:* 266–67, 290, 291, 297, 299–301
Washington, D.C., and, *2:* 286
work of, *2:* 266–67

common law
American colonies and, *3:* 386
in Great Britain, *3:* 384–85
infamous crimes under, *1:* 166–68; *3:* 480
judicial interpretation and, *3:* 410
reception provisions and, *3:* 387–90
Seventh Amendment and, *3:* 422–23

Common Sense, 1: 31

communism, *1:* 52

compensation
in American Revolutionary War, *2:* 220, 233
in Congress, *2:* 257–58
of judges, *2:* 338; *3:* 413, 437, 440, 443, 445, 447, 458, 494
of president, *1:* 132; *2:* 310

competition, *1:* 127

"Completing the Constitution," *3:* 431

Concord Coalition, *2:* 262

concurring opinions, *3:* 442, 448, 462, 467

conference committees, *2:* 276, 295–96. *See also* joint committees

confirmation power. *See* advice and consent

Confrontation Clause, *1:* 168–69; *3:* 481

Index

Congress, *2:* 313 (ill.), 321 (ill.); *3:* 367 (ill.). *See also* Congress (under Articles of Confederation); Continental Congress; House of Representatives; legislative branch; Senate
   bicameralism and, *2:* 223–24
   checks and balances on, *1:* 6–7, 133; *2:* 185; *3:* 495
   checks and balances within, *2:* 209–10, 312–13
   class and, *2:* 198–99, 201–2, 226–29, 312–13
   commerce and, *1:* 2; *2:* 180, 205, 215, 239; *3:* 360
   composition of, *2:* 197, 223–24, 265, 283, 312–13
   in Constitution, *1:* 1, 3–5; *2:* 179, 181–85, 283; *3:* 359–65
   economy and, *1:* 82
   election to, *1:* 131; *2:* 223–24, 226–29, 309, 312, 337; *3:* 493
   federal budget and, *1:* 72–73, 108; *2:* 316
   Federal Convention and, *2:* 197–99, 312
   Founding Fathers and, *2:* 312
   historic roots of, *1:* 24–25; *2:* 197–215
   introduction of a bill in, *2:* 289
   Iran-Contra scandal and, *1:* 152–53
   iron triangles and, *2:* 292
   issue networks and, *2:* 292
   judicial branch and, *3:* 429
   judicial interpretation and, *2:* 344–45; *3:* 498–500
   judicial review and, *2:* 339–44; *3:* 424–25, 495–98
   judicial system created by, *1:* 12–13; *2:* 190–91; *3:* 370–71
   legislative courts of, *3:* 458
   liberty and, *2:* 203–6
   military and, *1:* 2, 54–55; *2:* 180, 215, 239; *3:* 360
   money and, *1:* 2; *2:* 180; *3:* 360
   naturalization and, *1:* 2; *2:* 180; *3:* 360
   oversight by, *1:* 150–51; *2:* 331
   overview of, *1:* 1–7; *2:* 179–85; *3:* 359–65
   Parliament and, *2:* 208–11
   political philosophers and, *2:* 201–8
   property and, *2:* 203–6, 239
   qualifications to serve in, *1:* 131; *2:* 309
   Reconstruction and, *3:* 425–26
   representation and, *2:* 210–11, 223–26
   republicanism and, *2:* 206–8
   Roman Republic and, *2:* 199–200
   Schiavo case and, *3:* 381
   Senate minority leader and, *2:* 280–81
   separation of powers and, *1:* 131–32; *2:* 203, 209, 219–22, 309–10, 337–38; *3:* 397–400, 400–402, 493–94
   slavery and, *2:* 225–26
   special interest groups and, *2:* 313
   State of the Union address and, *1:* 9–10; *2:* 187–88; *3:* 367–68
   Supreme Court and, *3:* 425–26
   taxation and, *1:* 2; *2:* 180, 215; *3:* 360
   terms in, *2:* 272
   veto power and, *1:* 136–38; *2:* 316–19
   voting in, *1:* 133–34; *2:* 314
   war powers and, *1:* 22, 54–55, 80–82, 147–49; *2:* 329–31
   in Washington, D.C., *2:* 221
Congress (under the Articles of Confederation). *See also* Continental Congress
   executive power of, *1:* 31–33, 39–40; *2:* 221
   invasion of, *2:* 220
   judicial power of, *3:* 395, 396
   legislative power of, *2:* 215, 221
   problems with, *2:* 217
Congressional Budget Office, *2:* 300
congressional districts
   constituents in, *2:* 267, 301, 305
   gerrymandering and, *2:* 302
   organization of, *2:* 265, 267, 283
congressional staff, *2:* 275–76, 281, 301–3
Conklin, Scott, *2:* 267
Connecticut Compromise, *2:* 224

constituents, *2:* 267, 301–3

Constitution, *1:* 4 (ill.), xxxvii–l; *2:* 183 (ill.), 242 (ill.), xxxvii–l; *3:* xxxvii–l. *See also* amendments, constitutional; Federal Convention; specific amendments and clauses

   ambassadors in, *1:* 55–56

   American Declaration of Independence and, *3:* 430–31

   Anti-federalists and, *2:* 240–42; *3:* 418

   avoiding questions concerning, *2:* 347; *3:* 504

   bicameralism and, *2:* 223–24

   Bill of Rights and, *1:* 62–63, 240–43; *3:* 418

   cases concerning, *1:* 14–15; *2:* 192–93, 346; *3:* 373, 402, 415, 417–18, 424, 501

   checks and balances in, *1:* 1; *2:* 179, 222–23, 339; *3:* 359, 495

   class and, *2:* 226–29

   commerce and, *2:* 230–32, 239, 241

   Congress in, *1:* 1, 3–5; *2:* 179, 181–85, 283; *3:* 359–65

   on criminal trials, *3:* 406

   duration of, *3:* 420

   elections under, *2:* 226–29

   executive departments in, *1:* 7, 50; *2:* 186; *3:* 365–66

   executive power in, *1:* 48–49

   executive privilege in, *3:* 488

   Federalist Party and, *2:* 240–42; *3:* 418

   House of Representatives in, *1:* 1, 3–5; *2:* 179, 181–85, 223–24, 265; *3:* 359, 361–64

   inalienable rights in, *3:* 430–31

   interpretation of, *3:* 410, 420, 462

   Interstate Commerce Clause in, *1:* 2; *2:* 180; *3:* 360

   Jefferson, Thomas, on, *3:* 420

   judicial branch in, *3:* 395

   judicial power in, *2:* 339; *3:* 495

   judicial review and, *1:* 6; *2:* 185, 340, 342–44; *3:* 365, 411–12, 424, 495–96, 498

   law enforcement and, *1:* 49–50

   legislative power in, *1:* 2–3; *2:* 180–81; *3:* 360–61

   Madison, James, and, *2:* 241–43

   military in, *1:* 2, 54–55; *2:* 180, 232–35, 239; *3:* 360

   money in, *1:* 2; *2:* 180; *3:* 360

   naturalization in, *1:* 2; *2:* 180; *3:* 360

   original intent of, *3:* 410

   overview of, *1:* 1; *2:* 179; *3:* 359

   preamble of, *3:* 398–99, 430

   property and, *2:* 239

   ratification of, *1:* 1, 4, 62–63; *2:* 179, 182, 220, 234, 236, 237, 239, 240–43; *3:* 359, 362, 417, 418, 430

   representation and, *2:* 223–26

   Senate in, *1:* 1, 3–5; *2:* 179, 181–85, 223–24, 276; *3:* 359, 361–64

   separation of powers in, *1:* 1, 131–32; *2:* 179, 219–22, 309–10, 337–38; *3:* 359, 415, 493–94

   slavery and, *2:* 225–26, 232; *3:* 430

   Speaker of the House in, *2:* 269

   states and, *2:* 240–42

   Supreme Court in, *1:* 12; *2:* 190–91; *3:* 370, 402, 415, 417–18, 462

   taxation and, *1:* 2; *2:* 180, 231–32, 235–36, 253–55; *3:* 360

   voting rights and, *2:* 226–29

Constitution of England, 1: 27–28

constitutional amendments. *See* amendments, constitutional

Constitutional Convention of 1787. *See* Federal Convention

constitutional courts, *3:* 458

consuls

   cases concerning, *3:* 403–4, 415, 417

   in Roman Republic, *1:* 20–21; *2:* 199

consumers, *1:* 127

Continental Congress. *See also* Congress (under Articles of Confederation)

   executive power of, *1:* 31, 37–39

   government under, *1:* 4; *2:* 182; *3:* 362

   judicial power of, *3:* 390

Index

Continentalist, 2: 231
Contract with America, 2: 261, 272–73, 273 (ill.)
Contras, 1: 152–53
Coolidge, Calvin, 1: 9, 135 (ill.); 2: 187; 3: 367
Corpus Juris Civilus, 3: 383
Council of Economic Advisors, 1: 75
counsel, right to, 3: 422
Court of Appeals (prize cases), 3: 392–93
Court of Appeals for the Armed Services, 3: 458
Court of Appeals for the Federal Circuit, 3: 443, 444, 458, 460, 468
Court of Appeals for Veterans Claims, 3: 458
Court of Common Pleas, 3: 384–85
Court of Exchequer, 3: 384–85
Court of Federal Claims, 3: 443, 468
Court of International Trade, 3: 432, 443, 460, 468, 469
Court of King's Bench, 3: 384–85
Court of Queen's Bench, 3: 384–85
court stenographers, 3: 450
court-martial, 3: 458
court-packing plans, 1: 174–75; 3: 425
courts. *See* judicial branch; specific courts
Cox, Archibald, 3: 488
Crawford, William H., 1: 69
criminal cases. *See also* prosecution
   in American colonies, 3: 386
   appeals concerning, 3: 418
   arraignment, 3: 457
   in circuit courts, 3: 417
   in Constitution, 3: 406
   Eighth Amendment and, 3: 423
   in federal district courts, 1: 13; 2: 191; 3: 371, 379, 417, 432, 435, 445–47, 456–59
   Fifth Amendment and, 1: 64–65; 3: 422
   in Great Britain, 3: 384–85
   Interstate Commerce Clause and, 2: 251
   Justice, Department of, and, 1: 122
   magistrate judges and, 3: 447
   sentencing, 3: 459
   Sixth Amendment and, 1: 65–66; 3: 422
Cromwell, Oliver, 2: 235
cross-examination, 1: 65; 3: 422
Cushing, William, 3: 425, 425 (ill.)

d

Daniels, Mitch, 1: 8 (ill.)
Daschle, Tom, 2: 294 (ill.)
death penalty, 2: 245–46
debate
   appropriations power and, 2: 293
   filibuster and, 2: 293–94
   in House of Representatives, 2: 271, 293–95
   in Senate, 2: 278, 279, 280, 281, 293–95
   Speech and Debate Clause, 1: 131–32; 2: 309–10, 337; 3: 493
Debs, Eugene, 2: 245, 245 (ill.)
Declaration of Independence. *See* American Declaration of Independence
declarations of war. *See also* military; war powers
   by Congress, 1: 54–55, 149; 2: 329–31
   separation of powers and, 1: 22, 147, 149; 2: 234–35, 329
   War Powers Resolution and, 1: 80–82
Defence of the Constitutions of Government of the United States, 2: 220–21, 228–29, 230
defense. *See* military
Defense, Department of, 1: 50, 97–99, 142; 2: 323. *See also* War, Department of
defense, secretary of, 1: 97–99, 108–9
DeLay, Tom, 2: 274 (ill.), 288
Delolme, Jean Louis, 1: 25, 27–28
democracy
   class and, 1: 133; 2: 206, 311
   elections and, 1: 46; 2: 255–57
   Federal Convention and, 1: 133; 2: 255–56, 311
   French Revolution and, 2: 256

Index

Montesquieu, Charles, on, *2:* 206–8
   representation and, *2:* 206, 255–57
   voting rights and, *2:* 226, 255–57
   war and, *2:* 245
Democratic Caucus, *2:* 269, 271, 273, 274–75
Democratic Conference, *2:* 281
Democratic Federalist, *2:* 234
Democratic National Committee, *3:* 488
Democratic Party
   checks and balances and, *2:* 313
   elections and, *2:* 267
   income tax and, *2:* 254
   presidency and, *1:* 84, 85–86
   prohibition and, *2:* 258
Democratic-Republican Party
   election of 1800 and, *1:* 48, 66–67
   gerrymandering and, *2:* 302
   Marbury v. Madison and, *2:* 341–44; *3:* 497–98
   Sedition Act of 1798 and, *2:* 244
Department of Agriculture, *1:* 95–98
Department of Commerce, *1:* 97
Department of Defense, *1:* 50, 97–99, 142; *2:* 323. *See also* Department of War
Department of Education, *1:* 99
Department of Energy, *1:* 99
Department of Health & Human Services, *1:* 99–100
Department of Homeland Security, *1:* 100–101
Department of Housing & Urban Development, *1:* 101–2
Department of Justice. *See* Justice, Department of
Department of Labor, *1:* 102–3, 119
Department of State, *1:* 31, 50, 56, 73, 104–6
Department of the Interior, *1:* 102
Department of the Navy, *1:* 31, 98
Department of the Treasury. *See* Treasury, Department of the
Department of Transportation, *1:* 98, 106
Department of Veterans Affairs, *1:* 107
Department of War, *1:* 31, 97. *See also* Department of Defense

deputy attorney general, *1:* 102, 120, 121–22
Dickinson, John, *1:* 46
Discourses on the First Ten Books of Titus Livius, *2:* 200
discovery, *3:* 445–46, 447, 459
discretionary acts, *1:* 172; *2:* 347–48; *3:* 483, 504
discrimination. *See also* African Americans; race
   by Black Codes, *3:* 427
   in education, *1:* 99
   Fifteenth Amendment and, *2:* 256
   Fourteenth Amendment and, *2:* 345; *3:* 499–500, 500–501
   gerrymandering and, *2:* 302
   in housing, *1:* 101
   Interstate Commerce Clause and, *2:* 251–53
   in jury selection, *3:* 446
   in voting, *1:* 70–71; *3:* 427
dissenting opinions, *3:* 442, 448, 462, 467
Dissertation on the First Principles of Government, *2:* 226
District of Columbia. *See* Washington, D.C.
Double Jeopardy Clause, *1:* 65, 168; *3:* 422, 480
Douglas, William O., *1:* 166; *2:* 252; *3:* 439 (ill.), 511
Drug Enforcement Agency, *1:* 123–24
drugs, *1:* 75, 100, 107, 123–24
dual service, *3:* 442
Due Process Clause
   in Fifth Amendment, *1:* 65, 168; *3:* 422, 430, 480–81
   in Fourteenth Amendment, *3:* 427, 430–31

East India Company, *1:* 39
Eckhardt, Christopher, *3:* 408–9
economy, *1:* 75, 82–83, 91; *2:* 299. *See also* commerce
Edmunds, George, *2:* 254
education, *2:* 201

Index

Education, Department of, *1:* 99

education, secretary of, *1:* 99

Eighteenth Amendment, *1:* lv–lvi; *2:* 258–59, lv–lvi; *3:* lv–lvi

Eighth Amendment, *1:* lii; *2:* lii; *3:* lii
   civil liberties and, *1:* 16; *2:* 194; *3:* 375
   criminal law and, *3:* 423
   judicial power and, *3:* 423
   legislative power and, *1:* 6; *2:* 185, 245–46; *3:* 364

elections. *See also* electoral system; voting rights
   campaign finance reform and, *1:* 85; *2:* 288
   campaigning for, *2:* 268, 303–5
   casework and, *2:* 303
   class and, *2:* 226–29, 255–57
   congressional, *1:* 131; *2:* 223–24, 226–29, 255–57, 265–66, 267–68, 276–77, 303–5, 309, 312–13, 337; *3:* 493
   under Constitution, *2:* 226–29
   democracy and, *1:* 46; *2:* 255–57
   Democratic Party and, *2:* 267
   Federal Convention and, *1:* 46; *2:* 226–29
   First Amendment and, *1:* 85
   gender and, *1:* 84–85
   House of Representatives and, *2:* 202, 208
   incumbency and, *2:* 268
   instant runoff, *1:* 87
   judicial, *3:* 433
   legislative branch and, *2:* 226–29
   lobbying and, *2:* 268
   monarchy and, *1:* 46–47
   money and, *1:* 85
   political parties and, *1:* 85–86, 87; *2:* 267
   popular, *1:* 87
   presidential, *1:* 13–14, 46–48, 66–69, 91; *2:* 191–92, 257, 286; *3:* 371–72
   property and, *2:* 256
   proportional representation and, *2:* 267
   representation and, *2:* 226–29
   Republican Party and, *2:* 267
   Senate and, *2:* 202
   Seventeenth Amendment and, *2:* 255–57
   of 2000, *1:* 13–14; *2:* 191–92; *3:* 371–72, 464–65
   vice presidential, *1:* 47–48, 58, 66–69, 93–94

electoral system, *1:* 47–48, 66–69, 87; *3:* 464–65. *See also* elections

Eleventh Amendment, *1:* lii; *2:* 348, lii; *3:* 403, 423–24, 505, lii

Elk Grove Unified School District v. Newdow, *1:* 15–16; *2:* 193–94; *3:* 374

Ellsworth, Oliver, *2:* 236

Emerson, John, *3:* 500

Employee Standards Administration, *1:* 103

en banc review, *3:* 445, 461

Energy, Department of, *1:* 99

energy policy, *3:* 476–77

energy, secretary of, *1:* 99

English Bill of Rights, *1:* 24–25

Environmental Hearings Board, *1:* 125

environmental law, *2:* 251

Environmental Protection Agency, *1:* 107, 124–25, 169–70; *3:* 482

Equal Protection Clause, *2:* 345; *3:* 427, 430–31, 464–65, 499–500

equity, *3:* 385, 386, 402

espionage, *1:* 124

Espionage Act of 1917, *2:* 244–45

Establishment Clause, *1:* 15–16, 76; *2:* 193–94; *3:* 374

Evans, Donald, *1:* 8 (ill.)

evidence, *3:* 446, 457, 460

ex post facto laws, *1:* 6; *2:* 184–85, 205; *3:* 364

Excellencie of a Free-State, *2:* 199

exclusionary rule
   Fourteenth Amendment and, *3:* 457
   search and seizure and, *1:* 165; *3:* 421–22, 457, 479
   self-incrimination and, *1:* 168; *3:* 480

Index

executive agencies. *See also* administrative law; executive departments; specific agencies
    appointment to, *1:* 109, 124, 125, 144; *2:* 323–24
    growth of, *1:* 73–74
    heads of, *1:* 144; *2:* 324
    judicial interpretation and, *1:* 169–71; *3:* 481–82
    law enforcement by, *1:* 7–8, 169–71; *2:* 186; *3:* 365–66, 482
    legislative veto and, *1:* 139; *2:* 319
    oversight of, *2:* 297
    overview of, *1:* 109, 124
    regulatory power of, *1:* 7; *2:* 186; *3:* 365–66
executive agreements, *1:* 147; *2:* 328
executive branch. *See also* executive agencies; executive departments; executive power; president; specific departments and agencies; vice president
    checks and balances and, *2:* 222
    in Constitution, *1:* 1; *2:* 179; *3:* 359
    constitutional amendments and, *1:* 61–62
    future of, *1:* 83–87
    historic roots of, *1:* 19–35, 39
    iron triangles and, *2:* 292
    issue networks and, *2:* 292
    law enforcement by, *3:* 419–22
    oversight of, *1:* 150–51; *2:* 331
    overview of, *1:* 7–12, 19, 37, 61–62; *2:* 185–90; *3:* 365–70
    separation of powers and, *1:* 131–32, 159–60; *2:* 199–200, 203, 209, 309–10, *3.* 473–74, 488–89
executive bureaus, *1:* 109
executive departments. *See also* administrative law; executive agencies; specific departments
    appointment to, *1:* 95, 144; *2:* 323–24
    in Constitution, *1:* 7, 50; *2:* 186; *3:* 365–66
    growth of, *1:* 73–74
    heads of, *1:* 7–8, 95, 144; *2:* 186, 324; *3:* 366
    historic roots of, *1:* 31
    law enforcement by, *1:* 7–8, 119; *2:* 186; *3:* 365–66
    oversight of, *2:* 297
    overview of, *1:* 7, 37, 95; *2:* 186; *3:* 365–66
    regulatory power of, *1:* 7; *2:* 186; *3:* 365–66
    removal from, *1:* 146; *2:* 325–26
Executive Office of the President, *1:* 72, 74–75, 107–9
executive orders, *1:* 75–77, 114
executive power. *See also* executive branch; specific powers
    in American colonies, *1:* 28–29
    Articles of Confederation and, *1:* 31–35, 39
    checks and balances and, *1:* 45–46
    commerce and, *1:* 38–39
    in Constitution, *1:* 48–49
    Continental Congress and, *1:* 37–39
    Delolme, Jean Louis, on, *1:* 27–28
    Federal Convention and, *1:* 41–45
    foreign relations and, *1:* 11, 55–57; *2:* 190; *3:* 369
    in Great Britain, *1:* 22–25, 45–46
    Hamilton, Alexander, on, *1:* 49
    historic roots of, *1:* 21–22; *2:* 199
    judicial interpretation and, *1:* 169–71; *3:* 481–82
    judicial review and, *1:* 161–69; *3:* 475–78
    limits on, *1:* 11–12; *2:* 189–90; *3:* 369–70
    Locke, John, on, *1:* 49
    military and, *1:* 54–55
    overview of, *1:* 7–12, 89–91; *2:* 185–90; *3:* 365–70
    political philosophers on, *1:* 25–28
    in Roman Republic, *1:* 21–22
    search and seizure and, *3:* 419–22
    separation of powers and, *3:* 397–400
executive privilege, *2:* 321 (ill.)
    checks and balances and, *1:* 173–76; *3:* 486–87
    Cheney, Dick, and, *3:* 476–77
    in Constitution, *3:* 488
    judicial branch and, *1:* 173–76; *3:* 486–87
    judicial review and, *3:* 488–89
    legislative oversight and, *1:* 151; *2:* 331

military and, *3:* 488–89

national security and, *3:* 488–89

Nixon, Richard M., and, *1:* 78–79; *3:* 488–89

overview of, *1:* 77–79

separation of powers and, *3:* 476–77, 488–89

Fauntroy, Walter E., *2:* 286

Federal Aviation Administration, *1:* 73, 106

federal budget

    appropriations power and, *2:* 301

    balanced budget amendment, *2:* 261–62, 272

    committees and, *2:* 299–301

    impoundment and, *1:* 141; *2:* 320–22

    legislative branch and, *1:* 72–73, 108; *2:* 316

    legislative power and, *2:* 299–301

    line item veto and, *2:* 316

    Office of Management and Budget and, *1:* 72–73, 75, 108; *2:* 300

    president and, *1:* 11, 72–73, 114; *2:* 188–89, 299–301, 316; *3:* 368

    reprogramming and, *1:* 142–43; *2:* 322–23

Federal Bureau of Investigation, *1:* 50, 64, 120

Federal Convention, *1:* 43 (ill.); *3:* 362 (ill.). *See also* Constitution; Founding Fathers

    bicameralism and, *2:* 198–99, 223–24

    Bill of Rights and, *2:* 239–40

    checks and balances and, *1:* 45–46, 133, 160–61; *2:* 217–18, 222–23, 310–14, 339; *3:* 474–75, 495

    class and, *1:* 133; *2:* 198–99, 217–19, 226–29, 311

    commerce and, *2:* 218–19, 230–32, 239

    Committee of, *3:* 398

    Congress and, *2:* 197–99, 312

    Connecticut Compromise, *2:* 224

    democracy and, *1:* 133; *2:* 206, 255–56, 311

    elections and, *1:* 46; *2:* 226–29

    executive branch and, *1:* 41–45

    judicial review and, *1:* 6; *2:* 185, 340; *3:* 365, 411–12, 496

    legality of, *1:* 42–43

    military and, *2:* 232–35, 239

    monarchy and, *1:* 19–20

    original intent of, *3:* 410

    overview of, *1:* 4; *2:* 182; *3:* 362

    pardon power and, *1:* 51

    political philosophers and, *1:* 25–28; *2:* 201–8

    preamble and, *3:* 398–99

    property and, *2:* 239

    purpose of, *2:* 197–98, 217–19; *3:* 396–97

    representation and, *2:* 223–26

    resolution for, *1:* 35, 41; *3:* 396

    seat of government and, *2:* 220

    separation of powers and, *1:* 41–45; *2:* 219–22; *3:* 397–402

    Shays's Rebellion and, *1:* 41

    slavery and, *2:* 218–19, 225–26

    states at, *1:* 4; *2:* 182, 197–98, 223–24; *3:* 361, 362

    taxation and, *2:* 231–32, 235–36

    vice president and, *2:* 277

    Virginia Plan, *1:* 47; *2:* 223–24

    voting rights and, *2:* 226–29

    war powers and, *1:* 148–49; *2:* 329

federal district courts

    admiralty and, *3:* 417

    bankruptcy and, *3:* 432, 460

    civil cases in, *3:* 417, 432, 435, 459–60

    clerk of the court of, *3:* 449–50

    creation of, *3:* 416–17

    criminal cases in, *3:* 417, 432, 435, 456–59

    error in, *3:* 461

    growth of, *3:* 425, 428–29

    historic roots of, *3:* 387

    judges of, *3:* 445–47, 448

    Judicial Conference of the United States and, *3:* 469

law clerks at, *3:* 448–49
magistrate judges of, *3:* 447–48
motions in, *3:* 449
organization of, *3:* 432, 435, 445, 455–56
overview of, *1:* 13; *2:* 191; *3:* 371, 379, 435, 455–56
Schiavo case and, *3:* 381
trials in, *3:* 416–17, 428–29, 432, 435, 445–47, 455–60
work of, *3:* 429–32
Federal Highway Administration, *1:* 106
Federal Housing Administration, *1:* 101
Federal Judicial Center, *3:* 440, 469–70
Federal Magistrates Act, *3:* 447
Federal Motor Carrier Safety Administration, *1:* 106
federal public defenders, *3:* 450
federal question jurisdiction, *2:* 355; *3:* 512
Federal Railroad Administration, *1:* 106
Federal Reporter, 3: 451
Federal Supplement, 3: 451–52
Federal Trade Commission, *1:* 127–28
Federal Transit Administration, *1:* 106
Federalist, 3: 401 (ill.)
  on checks and balances, *2:* 222
  on commerce, *2:* 232
  on elections, *2:* 228
  on federal government, *2:* 229–30
  on foreign relations, *2:* 229–30
  on high crimes and misdemeanors, *1:* 154; *2:* 333
  on judicial branch, *3:* 400–402
  on judicial review, *2:* 340; *3:* 412, 496
  on military, *2:* 234
  on Necessary and Proper Clause, *2:* 237
  purpose of, *2:* 219
  on representation, *2:* 228
  on separation of powers, *1:* 43–44; *2:* 219–20; *3:* 400–402
Federalist Party
  Bill of Rights and, *2:* 241–43; *3:* 418

commerce and, *2:* 241
Constitution and, *2:* 240–42; *3:* 418
election of 1800 and, *1:* 48, 66–67, 68–69
gerrymandering and, *2:* 302
judicial branch and, *3:* 416–17
Marbury v. Madison and, *2:* 341–44; *3:* 497–98
Sedition Act of 1798 and, *2:* 244
state power and, *3:* 423–24
Supreme Court and, *3:* 425
felonies
  congresspersons and, *1:* 131–32; *2:* 309–10
  as infamous crime, *1:* 166–67; *3:* 480
  Speech and Debate Clause and, *2:* 337; *3:* 493
Ferraro, Geraldine, *1:* 84
Field, Stephen J., *2:* 254–55; *3:* 425, 426 (ill.)
Fiers, Alan, *1:* 153
Fifteenth Amendment, *1:* 70, lv; *2:* 256, lv; *3:* 426–28, lv
Fifth Amendment, *1:* 64–65, 165–68, li; *2:* li; *3:* 422, 479–81, li
filibuster, *1:* 145; *2:* 293–94, 325
fines, *3:* 423
First Amendment, *1:* l–li; *2:* l–li; *3:* l–li
  campaign finance and, *2:* 288
  civil liberties and, *1:* 16; *2:* 194; *3:* 374
  elections and, *1:* 85
  Espionage Act of 1917 and, *2:* 244–45
  freedom of religion under, *3:* 388
  freedom of speech under, *1:* 122–23
  judicial review and, *1:* 15–16; *2:* 193–94; *3:* 374
  legislative power and, *1:* 6; *2:* 185, 243; *3:* 364
  Office of Faith-Based and Community Initiatives and, *1:* 76
  prosecution and, *1:* 165–68; *3:* 479–81
  protest and, *3:* 408–9
  Sedition Act of 1798 and, *2:* 244
first lady, *1:* 103
Fish and Wildlife Service, *1:* 102
floor procedure, *2:* 293–95

Index

floors, personnel, *1:* 143; *2:* 323
Floyd, John B., *2:* 187 (ill.)
Food and Drug Administration, *1:* 73, 74, 100
Ford, Betty, *1:* 116
Ford, Gerald, *1:* 53 (ill.), 56 (ill.), 96 (ill.), 117 (ill.)
    pardons by, *1:* 52, 53, 96
    as president, *1:* 96, 116–17
    Rockefeller, Nelson, and, *1:* 95
    as vice president, *1:* 96
foreign relations. *See also* treaties
    executive privilege and, *1:* 77
    Federalist on, *2:* 229–30
    Hamilton, Alexander, on, *2:* 229–30
    president in, *1:* 11, 55–57, 113; *2:* 189; *3:* 369
    Senate and, *2:* 280
    State, Department of, and, *1:* 56, 104–6
    vice president and, *1:* 94, 118
formulary system, *3:* 384
Fortas, Abe, *3:* 408–9, 439 (ill.), 511
Founding Fathers, *3:* 362 (ill.), 431 (ill.). *See also* Federal Convention
    checks and balances and, *2:* 312
    Congress and, *2:* 312
    democracy and, *2:* 206, 255–56
    education of, *2:* 201
    original intent of, *3:* 410
    separation of powers and, *3:* 397–402
    vice president and, *2:* 277
Fourteenth Amendment, *1:* liii–liv; *2:* liii–liv; *3:* liii–liv
    American Declaration of Independence and, *3:* 431
    civil liberties and, *2:* 252–53; *3:* 430–31
    Civil Rights Act of 1875 and, *2:* 251
    Civil Rights Act of 1964 and, *2:* 252–53
    discrimination and, *2:* 345; *3:* 499–500, 500–501
    exclusionary rule and, *3:* 457
    freedom of religion under, *3:* 388
    inalienable rights in, *3:* 430–31
    judicial interpretation and, *2:* 345; *3:* 499–500
    judicial power and, *3:* 426–28
    ratification of, *2:* 348; *3:* 427, 505
Fourth Amendment, *1:* li; *2:* li; *3:* li
    checks and balances and, *1:* 163–65; *3:* 478–79
    civil liberties and, *1:* 16; *2:* 194; *3:* 374–75
    judicial power and, *3:* 419–22
    judicial review and, *1:* 163–65; *3:* 478–79
    law enforcement and, *1:* 64, 163–65; *3:* 478–79
    search and seizure and, *1:* 63–64; *3:* 419–22
Frank, Barney, *1:* 123
Franklin, Benjamin, *1:* 29; *2:* 214, 214 (ill.); *3:* 388, 389 (ill.)
free speech. *See* freedom of speech
freedom of assembly
    civil liberties and, *1:* 16; *2:* 194; *3:* 374
    legislative power and, *1:* 6; *2:* 185; *3:* 364
Freedom of Information Act, *1:* 173–74; *3:* 486–87
freedom of religion
    civil liberties and, *1:* 16; *2:* 194; *3:* 374
    history of, *3:* 388–89
    judicial review and, *1:* 15–16; *2:* 193–94; *3:* 374
    legislative power and, *1:* 6; *2:* 185, 243; *3:* 364
freedom of speech
    campaign finance and, *2:* 288
    civil liberties and, *1:* 16; *2:* 194; *3:* 374
    Espionage Act of 1917 and, *2:* 244–45
    legislative power and, *1:* 6; *2:* 185, 243; *3:* 364
    protest and, *1:* 122–23; *3:* 408–9
    regulation of, *2:* 243
    Sedition Act of 1798 and, *2:* 244
French Revolution, *2:* 244, 256
friendly suits, *2:* 346–47; *3:* 503
Frist, Bill, *2:* 294 (ill.)

Index

Gandhi, Indira, *1:* 84
Garfield, James A., *1:* 136; *2:* 315–16
Garner, John Nance, *1:* 93; *2:* 188 (ill.)
gender, *1:* 84–85. *See also* women
George, Clair, *1:* 153
George III, *1:* 30 (ill.)
    American Declaration of Independence and, *1:* 22, 30, 32–34; *2:* 208
    executive power and, *1:* 38
    military of, *2:* 234
    presidency and, *1:* 47
Gerry, Elbridge, *1:* 55 (ill.); *3:* 411 (ill.)
    Bill of Rights and, *2:* 239–40
    in Continental Congress, *2:* 217
    gerrymandering by, *2:* 302
    on judicial review, *3:* 411–12
    military power and, *1:* 54
gerrymandering, *2:* 302, 302 (ill.)
Gibbons v. Ogden, 2: 250
Gingrich, Newt, *2:* 272–73, 273 (ill.)
Ginsburg, Douglas H., *2:* 352, 353 (ill.)
Ginsburg, Ruth Bader, *1:* 84
Glorious Revolution, *1:* 24, 26
Goldberg, Arthur J., *2:* 252–53
Gonzalez, Henry, *1:* 153
Gore, Al, *2:* 279 (ill.)
    election of 2000 and, *1:* 13–14, 66; *2:* 191–92; *3:* 371–72, 464–65
    as vice president, *1:* 103
Gore, Tipper, *2:* 279 (ill.)
Government Printing Office, *2:* 305
grand juries, *1:* 65, 165–68; *3:* 422, 457, 479–80. *See also* juries
Grant, Ulysses S., *3:* 426
Great Britain
    American colonies and, *3:* 386–87
    checks and balances in, *1:* 31
    commerce and, *1:* 38–39; *2:* 231, 249
    executive power in, *1:* 22–25, 45–46
    freedom of religion in, *3:* 389
    judiciary in, *3:* 384–85
    legislative power in, *2:* 208–11
    military of, *2:* 234
    monarchy in, *1:* 22–25, 45–46
    separation of powers in, *1:* 22–23
    tyrants in, *1:* 22–25
Great Depression, *1:* 82, 174; *2:* 258
Grenada, *1:* 149; *2:* 331
Guam, *2:* 236
Guarantee Clause, *1:* 22

Haig, Alexander, *1:* 104–5, 105 (ill.), 119 (ill.)
Haig, Patricia, *1:* 119 (ill.)
Halonen, Tarja, *1:* 84
Hamilton, Alexander, *1:* 74 (ill.); *2:* 229 (ill.)
    Bank of the United States and, *2:* 247
    on commerce, *2:* 229–30, 231, 247
    Constitution and, *2:* 241
    Delolme, Jean Louis, and, *1:* 27
    on elections, *1:* 46
    on executive power, *1:* 49
    on federal government, *2:* 229–30
    Federalist and, *2:* 219; *3:* 400
    on foreign relations, *2:* 229–30
    on high crimes and misdemeanors, *1:* 154; *2:* 333
    on judicial branch, *3:* 400–402
    on judicial review, *2:* 340; *3:* 412, 496
    on military, *2:* 229, 234
    on Necessary and Proper Clause, *2:* 237, 246–47
    on pardon power, *1:* 51
    on representation, *2:* 224

as secretary of the treasury, *2:* 247
on separation of powers, *3:* 400–402
on taxation, *2:* 231–32
Hancock, John, *1:* 39
happiness, *3:* 430
Harding, Warren G., *2:* 245
Harlan, John Marshall, *3:* 439 (ill.), 467, 467 (ill.)
Harrison, Benjamin, *1:* 87
Harrison, William Henry, *1:* 75, 92
Hartzok, Alanna, *2:* 267
Hastert, Dennis, *2:* 189 (ill.), 274 (ill.)
Hastings, Alcee L., *2:* 354; *3:* 509 (ill.), 510
Hawaii, *2:* 355; *3:* 510
Hayes, George, *3:* 502 (ill.)
Hayes, Rutherford B., *1:* 87
Haynsworth, Clement, Jr., *1:* 17; *2:* 195, 349 (ill.); *3:* 376
Health & Human Services, Department of, *1:* 99–100
health & human services, secretary of, *1:* 99–100
Health Resources and Services Administration, *1:* 100
Heart of Atlanta Motel v. United States, 2: 251–53, 252 (ill.)
Henry, Patrick, *2:* 232; *3:* 389
Heston, Charlton, *2:* 269 (ill.)
high crimes and misdemeanors
Federalist on, *1:* 154; *2:* 333
as impeachable offense, *1:* 5, 91, 154; *2:* 182–84, 333, 353–54; *3:* 363, 437, 508–9
Hill, Anita F., *2:* 352–53
Hinckley, John, *1:* 104
Holt, Joseph, *2:* 187 (ill.)
Homeland Security, Department of, *1:* 100–101, 144; *2:* 324–25
homeland security, secretary of, *1:* 100
Hoover, Herbert, *2:* 258
Hoover, J. Edgar, *1:* 121 (ill.)
House Appropriations Committee, *2:* 286, 293, 301
House Committee on Homeland Security, *2:* 298–99
House Government Reform Committee, *2:* 286

House of Commons, *1:* 22; *2:* 208–9, 284
House of Lords, *1:* 22; *2:* 208–9, 210
House of Representatives, *2:* 268 (ill.). *See also* Congress; legislative branch; legislative power; representatives
 apportionment of, *1:* 3; *2:* 181; *3:* 361
 calendars of, *2:* 293
 campaigning and, *2:* 268
 casework in, *2:* 267, 275, 301–3
 checks and balances and, *2:* 312–13
 class and, *2:* 226–28, 312–13
 committees of, *2:* 266–67, 270, 271, 275, 286, 290–93, 297–99, 299–301
 composition of, *1:* 3; *2:* 181, 265–76; *3:* 361
 in Constitution, *1:* 1, 3–5; *2:* 179, 181–85, 223–24, 265; *3:* 359, 361–64
 debate in, *2:* 271, 293–95, 337; *3:* 493
 Democratic Caucus in, *2:* 269, 271, 273, 274–75
 districts covered by, *2:* 265, 267, 283, 301, 302, 305
 election to, *1:* 131; *2:* 202, 208, 223–24, 226–28, 256, 265–66, 267–68, 303–5, 309, 312, 337; *3:* 493
 electoral system and, *1:* 48, 67, 68–69
 executive privilege and, *1:* 77
 floor procedure in, *2:* 293, 295
 impeachment by, *1:* 5, 58–59, 91, 151–55, 172; *2:* 182–84, 332–33, 354; *3:* 363, 412, 437, 484, 509–10, 511
 legislation and, *2:* 266, 289
 lobbying and, *2:* 268, 275, 283–88
 majority leader of, *2:* 270–71, 274, 293
 majority party in, *2:* 269–70, 271, 272–73, 291
 minority leader of, *2:* 271–72, 274
 minority party in, *2:* 291
 powers exclusive to, *1:* 5; *2:* 182–84; *3:* 363
 powers shared with Senate, *1:* 4–5; *2:* 181–82; *3:* 361–63
 proportional representation in, *2:* 267
 qualifications to serve in, *2:* 228, 265–66, 337; *3:* 493

redistricting for, *1:* 3; *2:* 181; *3:* 361

removal from, *1:* 154–55; *2:* 333

Republican Conference in, *2:* 269, 271, 273, 274–75

rules of, *1:* 131, 155; *2:* 309, 333, 337; *3:* 493

slavery and, *2:* 226

Speaker of the House in, *2:* 269–70, 270–71, 293

staff for, *2:* 275–76, 301–3

terms in, *2:* 228, 259–61, 272, 303

treaties and, *1:* 147; *2:* 327

voting in, *1:* 133–34; *2:* 265, 271, 314

whips in, *2:* 273–74

work of, *2:* 265–76

House Rules Committee, *2:* 270, 293

House Ways and Means Committee, *2:* 301

Housing & Urban Development, Department of, *1:* 101–2

housing & urban development, secretary of, *1:* 101

Houston, E. & W. Tex. Ry. v. United States, 2: 251

Houston, Thomas, *3:* 391

Hughes, Charles Evans, *3:* 462, 462 (ill.)

Hume, David, *2:* 206, 207 (ill.)

Humphreys, West H., *1:* 5; *2:* 183–84; *3:* 363

hung jury, *3:* 459

Hussein, Saddam, *1:* 122

Ickes, Harold, *1:* 175, 175 (ill.)

immigration. *See* naturalization

impeachment

checks and balances and, *1:* 11–12, 17–18, 151–55, 172–73; *2:* 190, 195–96, 332–33, 353–54; *3:* 369, 376, 483–85, 508–10

chief justice role in, *1:* 151–52, 152–53, 172–73; *2:* 332–33; *3:* 413, 440, 483–85

of congresspersons, *1:* 154–55; *2:* 333

federal courts and, *1:* 159–60; *3:* 473

House of Representatives and, *1:* 91

of judges, *1:* 17–18, 146, 159, 173; *2:* 195–96, 327, 338, 353–54; *3:* 376, 413, 433, 437–38, 444, 445, 473, 485, 494, 508–10, 511

judicial power and, *3:* 412–13

offenses covered by, *1:* 5, 51, 91, 153–54, 159; *2:* 182–84, 333, 353–54; *3:* 363, 437, 473, 508–9

overview of, *1:* 5, 58–59, 172; *2:* 182–84; *3:* 363, 483–85

pardon power and, *1:* 51

of president, *1:* 5, 11–12, 58–59, 91, 138, 159–60, 172–73; *2:* 184, 190, 318; *3:* 363, 369, 412–13, 440, 473–74, 484–85

Senate and, *1:* 91

vice president role in, *1:* 152–53, 172; *2:* 332; *3:* 413, 484–85

Watergate scandal and, *1:* 52

imports, *2:* 253–54, 255. *See also* commerce

impoundment, *1:* 141; *2:* 320–22, 321 (ill.)

inalienable rights, *3:* 430–31, 500. *See also* civil liberties

income tax, *2:* 253–55, 346–47, 350–51, 351 (ill.); *3:* 503. *See also* taxation

incumbency, *2:* 268

independent regulatory commissions. *See also* regulatory power; specific commissions

appointment to, *1:* 127, 144; *2:* 324

removal from, *1:* 146; *2:* 326–27

work of, *1:* 73–74, 109, 127

Independents, *2:* 275

Indian Health Service, *1:* 100

indictments, *3:* 457

Industrial Revolution, *2:* 250, 254

infamous crimes, *1:* 65, 165–68; *3:* 422, 479–80

INS v. Chadha, 1: 139, 141, 142; *2:* 319, 322, 323

instant runoff voting, *1:* 87

Interior, Department of the, *1:* 102

interior, secretary of the, *1:* 102

Internal Revenue Code, *3:* 458

Internal Revenue Service, *1:* 107, 119

International Space Station, *1:* 126

Index

Interstate Commerce Clause, *1:* 2; *2:* 180, 249–53; *3:* 360
involuntary servitude, *3:* 466–67. *See also* slavery
Iran-Contra scandal, *1:* 52, 152–53, 176; *2:* 298; *3:* 490
Iraq, *1:* 122–23
iron triangles, *2:* 292
issue networks, *2:* 292
Istook, Ernest, *2:* 262

Jackson, Andrew, *1:* 69, 137; *2:* 311 (ill.)
Jacobson, Henning, *3:* 399
Jacobson v. Massachusetts, 3: 399
James II, *1:* 23, 24–25
Jaworski, Leon, *3:* 488
Jay, John, *2:* 219, 231; *3:* 400
Jefferson, Thomas, *1:* 44 (ill.), 74 (ill.); *2:* 248 (ill.); *3:* 389 (ill.), 421 (ill.)
   American Declaration of Independence and, *1:* 30, 32; *3:* 430
   appointment power of, *3:* 425
   Bank of the United States and, *2:* 247
   Bill of Rights and, *2:* 242
   Chase, Samuel, and, *1:* 18; *2:* 196; *3:* 376, 511
   on Constitution, *3:* 420
   election of, *1:* 48, 66–67, 68–69, 93
   executive orders of, *1:* 76
   on freedom of religion, *3:* 388, 389
   Library of Congress and, *2:* 305
   Marbury v. Madison and, *1:* 162; *2:* 341–42; *3:* 476–77, 497
   Necessary and Proper Clause and, *2:* 247
   Sedition Act of 1798 and, *2:* 244
   on separation of powers, *1:* 44–45
   slavery and, *2:* 232
   State of the Union address of, *1:* 9; *2:* 187; *3:* 367
Jet Propulsion Laboratory, *1:* 126

John, king of England, *1:* 23 (ill.), 23–24
Johnson, Andrew
   appointment power of, *3:* 425–26
   impeachment of, *1:* 5, 59, 91, 138, 173; *2:* 184, 318; *3:* 363, 440, 485
   pardons by, *1:* 52–53
   Reconstruction and, *3:* 425–26
   as senator, *3:* 442
   veto power and, *1:* 72, 138; *2:* 318
Johnson, Lyndon B., *1:* 149, 150 (ill.); *2:* 329
Johnson Space Center, *1:* 126
Joint Chiefs of Staff, Office of, *1:* 98, 109
Joint Committee on Taxation, *2:* 299
joint committees, *2:* 270, 299. *See also* conference committees
Joint Economic Committee, *2:* 299
judex, *3:* 384
judges. *See also* justices, Supreme Court
   appearance of impropriety of, *3:* 476–77
   appointment of, *2:* 277, 349–50; *3:* 413, 425, 433, 439, 443, 445, 458, 506
   of circuit courts of appeals, *3:* 443, 448
   compensation of, *2:* 338; *3:* 413, 437, 440, 443, 445, 447, 458, 494
   decision-making by, *3:* 444–45, 461–62
   election of, *3:* 433
   fairness of, *3:* 382
   of federal district courts, *3:* 445–47, 448
   good behavior of, *2:* 338; *3:* 413, 437, 443, 445, 494
   historic roots of, *3:* 383–84
   impeachment of, *1:* 173; *2:* 353–54; *3:* 413, 433, 437–38, 444, 445, 485, 508–10, 511
   law clerks for, *3:* 448–49
   of legislative courts, *3:* 458
   magistrate, *3:* 447–48
   recusal of, *3:* 476–77
   removal of, *3:* 413, 433, 444, 445, 458, 462
   term limits for, *3:* 433
   work of, *3:* 444–45, 445–47, 455–62

judgment, *3:* 445–46, 447. *See also* verdicts
judicial branch. *See also* specific courts
    administration of, *3:* 440, 468–70
    in American colonies, *3:* 386–87
    Anti-federalists and, *3:* 416–17
    appeals in, *1:* 13; *2:* 191–92; *3:* 371–72
    appointment to, *1:* 173, 174–75; *2:* 277; *3:* 485–86
    Articles of Confederation and, *3:* 390–93, 395, 396
    cases and controversies heard by, *1:* 14–15; *2:* 192–93; *3:* 373, 402–3
    checks and balances and, *2:* 222, 339; *3:* 412, 495
    Circuit Courts of Appeals Act of 1891 and, *3:* 429
    composition of, *1:* 12–14; *2:* 190–92; *3:* 370–73, 379–81, 429–33, 435
    in Constitution, *1:* 1; *2:* 179; *3:* 359, 395
    Continental Congress and, *3:* 390
    executive privilege and, *1:* 173–76; *3:* 486–87
    Federalist on, *3:* 400–402
    Federalist Party and, *3:* 416–17
    Great Britain and, *3:* 384–85
    Hamilton, Alexander, on, *3:* 400–402
    historic roots of, *3:* 379–93, 395–97
    judicial interpretation and, *1:* 15; *2:* 193; *3:* 373–74
    judicial review and, *1:* 15; *2:* 193–94; *3:* 374–75
    Judiciary Act of 1789 and, *3:* 416–18
    Judiciary Act of 1869 and, *3:* 428–29
    Judiciary Act of 1875 and, *3:* 429
    legislative branch and, *3:* 424–25, 429
    legislative power over, *3:* 402, 404–5, 415–18
    limits on, *1:* 16–18; *2:* 194–96; *3:* 375–76
    overview of, *1:* 12–18; *2:* 190–96; *3:* 370–76, 379–81, 455
    pardon power and, *1:* 176; *3:* 487–90
    powers of, *1:* 14–16; *2:* 192–94; *3:* 370–76
    Roman Republic and, *3:* 382–84
    separation of powers and, *1:* 159–60; *2:* 337–38; *3:* 397–402, 413, 473–74, 488–89, 493–94
    in states, *3:* 387–90, 418, 424
    trials in, *1:* 13; *2:* 191; *3:* 371
Judicial Conference of the United States, *3:* 440, 469
judicial interpretation. *See also* judicial review
    administrative law and, *1:* 169–71; *3:* 481–82
    checks and balances and, *1:* 169–71; *2:* 344–45; *3:* 481–82, 498–500
    in circuit courts of appeals, *3:* 462
    constitutional amendment and, *3:* 500–501
    executive agencies and, *1:* 169–71; *3:* 481–82
    executive power and, *1:* 169–71; *3:* 481–82
    Fourteenth Amendment and, *2:* 345; *3:* 499–500
    legislative branch and, *2:* 344–45; *3:* 498–500
    limits on, *2:* 345–48; *3:* 500–504
    original intent and, *3:* 410
    overview of, *1:* 15; *2:* 193; *3:* 373–74, 409–11
judicial power. *See also* cases and controversies; judicial interpretation; judicial review
    appeals, *3:* 407–9
    Bill of Rights and, *3:* 418–23
    checks and balances and, *2:* 348–54, 354–55; *3:* 369–70, 504–10, 510–12
    in Constitution, *2:* 339; *3:* 495
    constitutional amendments and, *2:* 348–49; *3:* 504–5
    Eighth Amendment and, *3:* 423
    Eleventh Amendment and, *3:* 423–24
    Fifteenth Amendment and, *3:* 426–28
    Fifth Amendment and, *3:* 422
    Fourteenth Amendment and, *3:* 426–28
    Fourth Amendment and, *3:* 419–22
    impeachment and, *3:* 412–13
    Judiciary Act of 1789 and, *3:* 416–19
    Judiciary Act of 1869 and, *3:* 428–29
    Judiciary Act of 1875 and, *3:* 429
    legislation and, *2:* 349; *3:* 506

limits on, *1:* 16–18; *2:* 194–96, 345–48; *3:* 375–76, 500–504

overview of, *1:* 14–16; *2:* 192–94; *3:* 370–76, 405–13

Seventh Amendment and, *3:* 422–23

Sixth Amendment and, *3:* 422

Thirteenth Amendment and, *3:* 426–28

trials, *3:* 406–7

writs of habeas corpus and, *3:* 409

judicial review. *See also* judicial interpretation

Anti-federalists and, *3:* 418

checks and balances and, *1:* 6–7, 15–16, 161–69; *2:* 185, 193–94, 339–44; *3:* 364–65, 374–75, 475–78, 495–98

in circuit courts of appeals, *3:* 462

civil liberties and, *3:* 427–28

Constitution and, *1:* 6; *2:* 185, 340, 342–44; *3:* 365, 411–12, 424, 495–96, 498

creation of, *1:* 161–63; *3:* 475–78

executive power and, *1:* 161–69; *3:* 475–78

executive privilege and, *3:* 488–89

Federal Convention and, *1:* 6; *2:* 185, 340; *3:* 365, 411–12, 496

Fourth Amendment and, *1:* 163–65; *3:* 478–79

Hamilton, Alexander, on, *2:* 340; *3:* 496

historic roots of, *3:* 386–87, 387–90

Judiciary Act of 1789 and, *3:* 424

legislative branch and, *2:* 339–44; *3:* 495–98

limits on, *2:* 345–48; *3:* 500–504

Marbury v. Madison and, *2:* 341–44; *3:* 424–25, 462, 497–98

overview of, *1:* 15; *2:* 193–94; *3:* 374–75, 411–12, 424–25

states and, *3:* 418, 424

Supremacy Clause and, *3:* 411, 412, 424

Judicial Watch, *3:* 476–77

Judiciary Act of 1789

judicial power and, *3:* 416–18

judicial review and, *3:* 424

Marbury v. Madison and, *1:* 162–63; *2:* 342–44; *3:* 424–25, 477–78, 497–98

overview of, *3:* 416–18

Supreme Court justices in, *2:* 351; *3:* 425, 437, 506

Judiciary Act of 1869, *3:* 428–29

Judiciary Act of 1875, *3:* 429

juries. *See also* grand juries

fairness of, *1:* 65, 168–69; *2:* 355; *3:* 382, 446, 481, 512

historic roots of, *3:* 384

selection of, *3:* 446, 457, 460

Sixth Amendment and, *1:* 16; *2:* 194; *3:* 375

trial by, *2:* 205, 355; *3:* 379, 406, 409, 422, 446–47, 457–59, 460, 510–12

jurisdiction. *See also* cases and controversies

appellate, *1:* 15; *2:* 193; *3:* 403, 404–5, 407–8, 415, 417–18, 432–33, 435

federal question, *2:* 355; *3:* 512

Marbury v. Madison and, *2:* 342–44; *3:* 497–98

original, *1:* 15; *2:* 193; *3:* 373, 403–4, 417, 424–25

overview of, *3:* 373

Justice, Department of

creation of, *1:* 50; *3:* 418

Federal Trade Commission and, *1:* 128

head of, *1:* 95, 119–20; *3:* 418

investigation by, *1:* 120

law enforcement by, *1:* 50, 64–65, 102, 119–24

U.S. attorneys in, *3:* 450

justices, Supreme Court, *3:* 372 (ill.), 439 (ill.), 463 (ill.). *See also* chief justice; judges; Supreme Court

appearance of impropriety of, *3:* 476–77

appointment of, *1:* 144–45; *2:* 324, 325, 349, 352–53; *3:* 413, 425, 433, 437, 439, 506

associate justices, *3:* 439, 440, 441–43, 462, 467

circuit court duties of, *3:* 417, 425, 429

compensation of, *3:* 413, 437, 440, 494

decision-making by, *2:* 352; *3:* 440–43, 448, 465–68, 507

election of, *3:* 433
good behavior of, *2:* 338; *3:* 413, 437, 494
impeachment of, *1:* 146, 173; *2:* 327, 338, 353–54; *3:* 413, 433, 437–38, 485, 494, 508–10, 511
law clerks for, *3:* 448
number of, *1:* 16, 174–75; *2:* 194, 351–52; *3:* 375, 417, 425–26, 436–37, 462, 506–7
opinions of, *3:* 441–43, 448, 451–52, 466–68
overview of, *3:* 436–43
recusal of, *3:* 476–77
removal of, *1:* 146; *2:* 327, 338; *3:* 413, 433, 437, 494
term limits for, *3:* 433
work of, *3:* 439–43
Justinian I, *3:* 383

Katzenbach v. McClung, *2:* 251–53
Kennedy, Edward M., *2:* 281
Kennedy Space Center, *1:* 125, 126 (ill.)
Kensinger, John, II, *2:* 267
Kerik, Bernard, *1:* 144, 145 (ill.); *2:* 324–25
King, Rufus, *2:* 217; *3:* 411–12, 412 (ill.)
Kissinger, Henry A., *1:* 116
Klein, Joel, *3:* 451 (ill.)
Knox, Henry, *1:* 34, 42–43, 74 (ill.)
Korean War, *1:* 55

labor, *1:* 78–79, 166–67; *2:* 345; *3:* 466–67, 499
Labor, Department of, *1:* 102–3, 119
labor, secretary of, *1:* 102
Lamar, Lucius Q., *3:* 442
law clerks, *3:* 448–49

law enforcement
    under Articles of Confederation, *1:* 48; *2:* 221
    checks and balances and, *1:* 6, 12; *2:* 185, 190; *3:* 364, 369
    by Congress (under the Articles of Confederation), *2:* 221
    Constitution and, *1:* 49–50
    Drug Enforcement Agency and, *1:* 123–24
    by executive agencies, *1:* 7–8, 169–71; *2:* 186; *3:* 365–66, 482
    by executive branch generally, *1:* 6, 7, 49–50; *2:* 185–86; *3:* 364, 365–66
    by executive departments, *1:* 7–8; *2:* 186; *3:* 365–66
    Fourth Amendment and, *1:* 64, 163–65; *3:* 419–22, 478–79
    Justice, Department of, and, *1:* 50, 64–65, 102, 119–24
    Magna Carta and, *1:* 24
    ripeness and, *2:* 347; *3:* 503
Law of the Twelve Tables, *3:* 382–83
lawmaking. *See* legislation
lawsuits. *See* cases and controversies; trials
lawyers. *See* attorneys
Lazio, Rick, *1:* 103
League of Nations, *1:* 147; *2:* 290 (ill.), 327
legislation
    under Articles of Confederation, *2:* 221
    bills of attainder, *1:* 6; *2:* 184; *3:* 364
    calendars for, *2:* 293
    cases concerning, *2:* 346; *3:* 402, 415, 417–18, 501
    checks and balances and, *1:* 16–17, 51–54; *2:* 194–95, 349; *3:* 375, 506
    class and, *2:* 202
    committees and, *2:* 266–67, 270, 271, 276, 290–93, 295–96, 299
    Congress (under the Articles of Confederation) and, *2:* 221
    congressional staff and, *2:* 275
    debate on, *2:* 293–95

Index

ex post facto laws, *1:* 6; *2:* 184–85; *3:* 364
filibuster and, *2:* 293–94
in Great Britain, *3:* 385
historic roots of, *3:* 382–83
House of Representatives and, *2:* 266, 289
introduction of, *2:* 289
judicial interpretation of, *3:* 409–11, 462
judicial power and, *2:* 349; *3:* 506
legislative oversight and, *2:* 297
lobbying and, *2:* 283–88
majority leader and, *2:* 271
minority leader and, *2:* 271
Montesquieu, Charles, on, *2:* 203–6
overview of, *1:* 4–5; *2:* 182, 265, 288–97; *3:* 363
reception provisions and, *3:* 387–90
recommendation power and, *1:* 11, 114; *2:* 189; *3:* 368–69
representatives and, *2:* 266
Senate and, *2:* 276, 289
Senate majority leader and, *2:* 280
senators and, *2:* 276
separation of powers and, *1:* 26, 28; *2:* 209; *3:* 400–402
Speaker of the House and, *2:* 270, 296
State of the Union address and, *1:* 51–52; *2:* 289
veto power and, *1:* 5, 52–54, 72, 114, 133–39; *2:* 182, 314–19; *3:* 363
vice president and, *1:* 115, 133–34; *2:* 277–78, 295, 296, 314
voting on, *2:* 295
whips and, *2:* 273–74, 281
legislative branch. *See also* Congress; legislative power
in American colonies, *2:* 211–15
checks and balances and, *2:* 209–10
class and, *2:* 201–2, 206, 214
democracy and, *2:* 206
separation of powers and, *2:* 199–200, 202–3
legislative courts, *3:* 458
legislative oversight, *1:* 150–51; *2:* 297, 331

legislative power. *See also* legislative branch; specific powers
Bill of Rights and, *1:* 6; *2:* 185, 239–46; *3:* 364
checks and balances and, *1:* 6–7; *2:* 185, 354–55; *3:* 364, 510–12
commerce and, *2:* 230–32
compensation and, *2:* 257–58
in Constitution, *1:* 2–3; *2:* 180–81; *3:* 360–61
constitutional amendments, *2:* 258–59
Eighteenth Amendment and, *2:* 258–59
Eighth Amendment and, *2:* 245–46
federal budget and, *2:* 261–62, 299–301
First Amendment and, *2:* 243
historic roots of, *1:* 21–22
Interstate Commerce Clause and, *2:* 249–53
judicial branch and, *3:* 402, 404–5, 415–18
legislative veto, *1:* 138–39, 141, 142–43; *2:* 318–19, 322, 323
liberty and, *2:* 205–6
life and, *2:* 205
limits on, *1:* 6–7; *2:* 185; *3:* 364–65
military and, *1:* 2; *2:* 180, 232–35; *3:* 360
money and, *1:* 2; *2:* 180, 232; *3:* 360
naturalization and, *1:* 2; *2:* 180; *3:* 360
Necessary and Proper Clause and, *1:* 2–3; *2:* 180–81, 236–37, 246–49; *3:* 360–61
overview of, *2:* 219, 229–37
of president, *1:* 51–54, 90, 114, 137; *2:* 276, 289
prohibition and, *2:* 258–59
property and, *2:* 205
resolutions, *1:* 138; *2:* 319
Second Amendment and, *2:* 243–45
Sixteenth Amendment and, *2:* 253–55
slavery and, *2:* 232
taxation and, *1:* 2; *2:* 180, 231–32, 235–36; *3:* 360
Tenth Amendment and, *2:* 246
treaty power, *1:* 5, 11; *2:* 184, 190; *3:* 363–64, 369
Twenty-seventh Amendment and, *2:* 257–58

veto override, *1:* 5, 11; *2:* 182, 189–90, 265; *3:* 363, 369

writs of habeas corpus and, *1:* 171; *3:* 483

legislative veto

impoundment and, *1:* 141; *2:* 322

overview of, *1:* 138–39; *2:* 318–19

reprogramming and, *1:* 142–43; *2:* 323

letters of marque, *3:* 391–93

Lever Act, *2:* 258

Lewinsky, Monica, *1:* 79, 154; *2:* 333

liberty. *See also* civil liberties

in American Declaration of Independence, *3:* 430

bills of attainder and, *2:* 205

class and, *2:* 210–11

in Constitution, *3:* 430

in Due Process Clause, *3:* 422, 427, 430

ex post facto laws and, *2:* 205

legislative branch and, *2:* 203–6

property as, *2:* 230

representation and, *2:* 225–26

slavery and, *2:* 205–6

writs of habeas corpus and, *2:* 205

Library of Congress, *2:* 305

Lieberman, Joseph, *2:* 286

life, *2:* 205; *3:* 422, 427, 430

Lincoln, Abraham, *3:* 366 (ill.)

Agriculture, Department of, and, *1:* 95

cabinet of, *3:* 366 (ill.)

executive orders of, *1:* 76

pardons by, *1:* 52–53

vetoes by, *1:* 71

war powers of, *3:* 425

Lincoln Memorial, *2:* 287 (ill.)

line item veto, *1:* 141; *2:* 272, 316–17, 321

lobbying, *2:* 268, 275, 276, 283–88, 292

local courts, *3:* 384

Locke, John, *1:* 26 (ill.)

on executive power, *1:* 49

on property, *2:* 205

on separation of powers, *1:* 25–26; *2:* 202–3, 209

Lomen, Lucille, *3:* 449 (ill.)

Long, Russell B., *2:* 281

Love Fellowship Tabernacle, *2:* 304 (ill.)

Lyons, Lisa, *1:* 116

m

Machiavelli, Niccolò, *2:* 200, 201 (ill.)

Maddox, Lester, *2:* 253 (ill.)

Madison, James, *1:* 46 (ill.), 162 (ill.), 164 (ill.); *2:* 222 (ill.); *3:* 421 (ill.), 424 (ill.)

on bicameralism, *2:* 312

Bill of Rights and, *1:* 63; *2:* 242–43; *3:* 418, 430

on checks and balances, *2:* 222

on commerce, *2:* 230–31, 232

Constitution and, *2:* 241–43

executive power and, *1:* 19

Federalist and, *2:* 219–20; *3:* 400

on humanity, *2:* 219

on judicial interpretation, *3:* 410

Marbury v. Madison and, *1:* 162–63; *2:* 341–44; *3:* 424–25, 476–77, 497–98

military power and, *1:* 54

on representation, *2:* 224, 228

on seat of government, *2:* 220

on separation of powers, *1:* 43–44

on taxation, *2:* 235

Twenty-seventh Amendment and, *2:* 257

Virginia Plan and, *1:* 47

on war powers, *1:* 148–49; *2:* 329

magistrate judges, *3:* 447–48

Magna Carta, *1:* 23 (ill.), 23–24

majority leader, *2:* 270–71, 279–80, 293, 295

majority party

committees and, *2:* 291

in House of Representatives, *2:* 269–70, 271, 272–73

Index

in Senate, *2:* 280
whips and, *2:* 274
manorial courts, *3:* 384
Mansfield, Mike, *2:* 281
Mapp, Dollree, *3:* 420–22
Mapp v. Ohio, 3: 420–22
Marbury v. Madison, 1: 162 (ill.)
    checks and balances and, *1:* 6–7; *2:* 185, 341–44; *3:* 365, 497–98
    judicial review and, *1:* 161–63; *2:* 341–44; *3:* 424–25, 462, 475–78, 497–98
Marbury, William, *2:* 342–44, 343 (ill.); *3:* 424–25, 497–98
Marine Corps, U.S., *1:* 98
maritime. *See* admiralty
Marshall, John, *2:* 250 (ill.), 341 (ill.)
    as chief justice, *2:* 342; *3:* 497–98
    federal service of, *3:* 442
    Gibbons v. Ogden and, *2:* 250
    Interstate Commerce Clause and, *2:* 250
    Marbury v. Madison and, *1:* 161–63; *2:* 341–44; *3:* 424–25, 475–78, 497–98
    McCulloch v. Maryland and, *2:* 249
Marshall, Thurgood, *2:* 352; *3:* 372 (ill.), 439 (ill.), 463 (ill.), 502 (ill.)
Martinez, Mel, *1:* 8 (ill.)
Marxism, *1:* 152
Mary II, *1:* 24
Maryland, *2:* 248–49
Mason, George, *2:* 220, 239–40
Massachusetts
    legislature in, *2:* 211–12
    ratification and, *2:* 241, 242
    religion in, *2:* 243; *3:* 388–89
    voting rights in, *2:* 228
McAleese, Mary, *1:* 84
McClurg, James, *1:* 46
McCord, James W., Jr., *3:* 488
McCulloch, James W., *2:* 249
McCulloch v. Maryland, 2: 247–49

McFarlane, Robert, *1:* 153
McGovern, George, *3:* 488
McReynolds, James C., *1:* 174
Meese, Edwin, III, *1:* 104
Meir, Golda, *1:* 84
Mercer, John Francis, *1:* 46
Mexican-American War, *1:* 54, 80, 149; *2:* 329
Middle Ages, *3:* 384
military. *See also* declarations of war; war powers
    in American Declaration of Independence, *2:* 234
    under Articles of Confederation, *1:* 32–35, 40; *2:* 215
    civilians and, *1:* 8–9, 78–79; *2:* 186, 234–35; *3:* 366–67
    commerce and, *2:* 232
    Congress and, *2:* 215
    in Constitution, *1:* 2, 54–55; *2:* 180, 232–35, 239; *3:* 360
    Court of Appeals for the Armed Services, *3:* 458
    executive power and, *1:* 54–55
    Federal Convention and, *2:* 232–35, 239
    Federalist on, *2:* 234
    of Great Britain, *2:* 234
    Hamilton, Alexander, on, *2:* 229, 234
    labor strikes and, *1:* 78–79
    legislative branch and, *1:* 2, 54–55; *2:* 180, 239; *3:* 360
    legislative power and, *2:* 232–35
    overview of, *1:* 8–9; *2:* 186; *3:* 366–67
    president and, *1:* 54–55
    quartering soldiers, *1:* 62–63
    separation of powers and, *2:* 234–35
    Shays's Rebellion and, *2:* 232–34
Militia Clause, *1:* 78
Minerals Management Service, *1:* 102
Mineta, Norman, *1:* 8 (ill.)
ministerial acts, *1:* 171–72; *3:* 483
minor parties, *2:* 267, 275
minority leader, *2:* 271–72, 274, 280–81, 293
minority party, *2:* 280–81, 291

Minton, Sherman, *3:* 442
Mitchell, John N., *3:* 488
monarchy
    class and, *2:* 202
    elections and, *1:* 46–47
    Federal Convention and, *1:* 19–20
    French Revolution and, *2:* 256
    in Great Britain, *1:* 22–25, 45–46
    president and, *1:* 19–20
Mondale, Walter, *1:* 84, 95
money
    in Constitution, *1:* 2; *2:* 180; *3:* 360
    legislative power and, *1:* 2; *2:* 180, 232; *3:* 360
    paper, *2:* 233
    presidency and, *1:* 84, 85
Monroe, James, *1:* 98 (ill.); *3:* 397 (ill.), 398
Montesquieu, Charles, *1:* 27 (ill.)
    on democracy, *2:* 206–8
    influence of, *1:* 25
    on legislation, *2:* 203–6
    on republicanism, *2:* 206–8
    on separation of powers, *1:* 27
mootness, *2:* 347; *3:* 503–4
Morris, Gouverneur, *1:* 46
Moscow Treaty on Strategic Offensive Reductions, *1:* 11, 57; *2:* 190; *3:* 369
motions, *3:* 446–47, 449, 459

N

Nabrit, James M., *3:* 502 (ill.)
Nader, Ralph, *1:* 86 (ill.)
National Aeronautics and Space Administration, *1:* 125–27
National Economic Council, *1:* 75, 108
National Energy Policy Development Group, *3:* 476–77
National Guard, U.S., *1:* 98
National Highway System, *1:* 106
National Highway Traffic Safety Administration, *1:* 106
National Institutes of Health, *1:* 100
National Military Establishment, *1:* 50
National Parks Service, *1:* 102
National Prohibition Act of 1919, *2:* 258
National Reserve, U.S., *1:* 98
National Rifle Association, *2:* 268, 269 (ill.)
national security
    executive privilege and, *1:* 77; *3:* 488–89
    legislative oversight and, *1:* 151; *2:* 331
    National Security Council and, *1:* 75, 94, 108–9, 115, 116, 124
    vice president and, *1:* 94
national security advisor, *1:* 108–9
National Security Council
    Central Intelligence Agency in, *1:* 124
    in Executive Office of the President, *1:* 75
    Ford, Gerald, and, *1:* 116
    vice president in, *1:* 94, 115
    work of, *1:* 108–9
National Union of Christian Schools, *1:* 116
Native Americans, *1:* 100, 102; *2:* 232
natural law, *3:* 382, 399
naturalization, *1:* 2; *2:* 180; *3:* 360, 427
navigable waters. *See* admiralty
Navigation Acts, *3:* 386–87
Navy, Department of the, *1:* 31, 98
Nebraska, *2:* 197
Necessary and Proper Clause
    in Constitution, *1:* 2–3; *2:* 180–81; *3:* 360–61
    Hamilton, Alexander, on, *2:* 237, 246–47
    legislative power and, *2:* 246–49
    overview of, *2:* 236–37
New Deal, *1:* 174
New Hampshire, *2:* 241
New Haven, *3:* 388
New Jersey, *2:* 212–15
New York, *2:* 241

Index

Newdow, Michael, *1:* 15–16; *2:* 193–94; *3:* 374

Nicaragua, *1:* 152–53

Nineteenth Amendment, *1:* 70, 71 (ill.), lvi; *2:* 257, 349, lvi; *3:* 505, lvi

Ninth Amendment, *1:* lii; *2:* lii; *3:* 430, lii

Nixon, Richard M., *1:* 170 (ill.); *2:* 278 (ill.), 321 (ill.), 330 (ill.); *3:* 368 (ill.), 489 (ill.)
  appointment power of, *1:* 17; *2:* 195; *3:* 376
  executive privilege of, *1:* 78–79, 176; *3:* 487, 488–89
  Ford, Gerald, and, *1:* 96
  impeachment discussions surrounding, *1:* 52, 91, 96
  impoundment by, *1:* 141; *2:* 320–21
  Office of Management and Budget and, *1:* 72
  pardon of, *1:* 52, 96
  vetoes by, *1:* 80
  as vice president, *2:* 277
  Vietnam War and, *1:* 149; *2:* 329
  War Powers Resolution and, *1:* 80
  Watergate scandal and, *1:* 52, 78–79, 96, 176; *3:* 487

Nixon, Walter L., Jr., *2:* 354; *3:* 510

No Taxation Without Representation Act, *2:* 286

nobility, *2:* 210–11

nominations. *See* appointment power

Noriega, Manuel, *1:* 81 (ill.)

Norman dynasty, *3:* 384

North Carolina, *2:* 241; *3:* 417

North Korea, *1:* 166

North, Oliver, *2:* 298 (ill.)

Norton, Eleanor Holmes, *2:* 286

Norton, Gale, *1:* 8 (ill.)

Notes on the State of Virginia, 3: 388

notice, *3:* 422

Observations on the Government of Pennsylvania, 2: 226–27

Observations upon the Proposed Plan of Federal Government, 3: 398

Occupational Safety and Health Administration, *1:* 73–74, 103

O'Connor, John J., *3:* 486 (ill.)

O'Connor, Sandra Day, *1:* 84; *3:* 372 (ill.), 463 (ill.), 486 (ill.)

Office of Administration, *1:* 75

Office of Chief of Staff. *See* chief of staff

Office of Faith-Based and Community Initiatives, *1:* 75–76

Office of Homeland Security, *1:* 100

Office of Management and Budget, *1:* 72–73, 75. *See also* Bureau of the Budget
  in cabinet, *1:* 107
  creation of, *2:* 299
  director of, *1:* 107, 108
  federal budget and, *1:* 108, 114; *2:* 300
  overview of, *1:* 108
  personnel ceilings and, *1:* 143; *2:* 323

Office of National Drug Control Policy, *1:* 75, 107

Office of Surface Mining Reclamation and Enforcement, *1:* 102

Office of the Attorney General, *1:* 50, 73. *See also* attorney general

Office of the Solicitor General, *1:* 102. *See also* solicitor general

Old Whig, *2:* 237

Olmstead, Gideon, *3:* 391

O'Neill, Paul, *1:* 8 (ill.)

O'Neill, Tip, *1:* 10 (ill.), 140 (ill.); *2:* 288

opening statement, *3:* 457, 459, 460

opinions, *3:* 441–43, 448, 461–62, 466–68

oral argument, *3:* 441, 444, 448, 461, 465

original intent, *3:* 410
original jurisdiction, *3:* 403–4, 417, 424–25
oversight, legislative, *1:* 150–51; *2:* 297, 331

P

Paige, Roderick, *1:* 8 (ill.)
Paine, Thomas, *1:* 31; *2:* 226
Panama, *1:* 82
pardon power
    checks and balances and, *1:* 176; *3:* 487–90
    examples of, *1:* 52–53, 96, 153
    judicial branch and, *1:* 176; *3:* 487–90
    overview of, *1:* 50–51
Parliament
    American colonies and, *3:* 386–87
    American Declaration of Independence and, *1:* 32–34; *2:* 208
    checks and balances and, *2:* 209–10
    class and, *2:* 208–9
    composition of, *1:* 22; *2:* 208–11
    English Bill of Rights and, *1:* 24–25
    lobbying in, *2:* 284
    representation and, *2:* 210–11
    separation of powers and, *1:* 22
    whips in, *2:* 273
patents, *2:* 232; *3:* 460
Pearl Harbor, *1:* 108
Pelosi, Nancy, *2:* 274 (ill.)
Pennsylvania, *2:* 214; *3:* 388
perjury, *1:* 167, 168; *3:* 479, 480
Permanent Representative to the United Nations, *1:* 105
Perot, H. Ross, *1:* 86
Persian Gulf Wars, *1:* 55
personnel ceilings, *1:* 143; *2:* 323
personnel floors, *1:* 143; *2:* 323
Peterson, David A., *1:* 116
Philippines, *2:* 355; *3:* 510

Pickering, John, *1:* 17–18; *2:* 195–96; *3:* 376
Pierce, Franklin, *1:* 83, 137
Pitts, Lewis, *1:* 123
pleadings, *3:* 384, 445, 459
Plessy v. Ferguson, *2:* 345; *3:* 499–500
pocket vetoes, *1:* 54, 134–35, 136, 138; *2:* 315, 318
political action committees, *2:* 288, 304
political parties. *See also* specific parties
    checks and balances and, *2:* 313
    elections and, *1:* 85–86; *2:* 267
    independents, *2:* 275
    presidency and, *1:* 84, 87
    third parties, *2:* 267, 275
    veto power and, *1:* 138; *2:* 318
    vice president and, *1:* 93–94
political philosophers, *1:* 25–28; *2:* 201–8; *3:* 382. *See also* specific philosophers
political question doctrine, *2:* 347–48; *3:* 504
poll taxes, *2:* 228, 256, 257
Pollock, Charles, *2:* 350
Pollock v. Farmers' Loan and Trust Co., *2:* 346–47, 350–51; *3:* 503
post-trial motions, *3:* 446–47
Potsdam Conference, *1:* 148 (ill.)
Powell, Colin, *1:* 8 (ill.)
Powell, Lewis F., Jr., *2:* 352; *3:* 372 (ill.), 463 (ill.)
praetors, *3:* 383
preamble, *3:* 398–99, 430
president. *See also* executive branch; specific powers
    appropriations power and, *1:* 140–43; *2:* 320–23
    under Articles of Confederation, *1:* 39
    checks and balances and, *1:* 133; *2:* 310–14
    as chief of state, *1:* 90, 113
    compensation of, *1:* 132; *2:* 310
    day in the life of, *1:* 113–14, 116–17
    economy and, *1:* 75, 82–83, 91
    election of, *1:* 13–14, 46–48, 66–69, 83–87, 91; *2:* 191–92, 257, 286; *3:* 371–72
    executive powers of, *1:* 7–11, 48–51, 61, 89–91, 113–14; *2:* 185–89; *3:* 365–69

Index

federal budget and, *1:* 11, 72–73, 114; *2:* 188–89, 299–301, 316; *3:* 368
foreign relations and, *1:* 11, 55–57, 113; *2:* 189; *3:* 369
future of, *1:* 83–87
historic roots of, *1:* 21, 24–25, 28–29, 30–31; *2:* 199
impeachment of, *1:* 5, 11–12, 58–59, 91, 138, 159–60, 172–73; *2:* 184, 190, 318; *3:* 363, 369, 412–13, 473–74, 484–85
impoundment by, *1:* 141; *2:* 320–22
law enforcement by, *1:* 6, 7, 49–50; *2:* 185–86; *3:* 364, 365–66
legislative power of, *1:* 51–54, 90, 114, 137; *2:* 276, 289, 296–97
limits on, *1:* 11–12; *2:* 189–90; *3:* 369–70
monarchy and, *1:* 19–20
money and, *1:* 84, 85
pardon power and, *1:* 50–51
qualifications to be, *1:* 47, 89
recommendation power of, *1:* 9, 11; *2:* 187–89, 289, 319–20; *3:* 367, 368–69
replacement of, *1:* 58, 61, 92–93, 104–5, 115; *2:* 278; *3:* 413
reprogramming by, *1:* 142–43; *2:* 322–23
State of the Union address of, *1:* 9, 51–52, 139–40; *2:* 187–88, 289, 316, 319–20; *3:* 367–68
terms of, *1:* 19, 37, 58, 66, 67–68, 91; *2:* 260
title of, *1:* 47
treaty power of, *1:* 56–57; *2:* 277
veto power of, *1:* 5, 11, 71–72, 133–36; *2:* 182, 189, 296–97, 314–19; *3:* 363, 368–69
vice president and, *1:* 93–95, 104–5
president *pro tempore,* *1:* 115; *2:* 278–79, 280
Principi, Anthony, *1:* 8 (ill.)
Private Securities Litigation Reform Act, *1:* 11; *2:* 190; *3:* 369
Privileges and Immunities Clause, *3:* 427, 430–31
Privy Council, *3:* 386
prize cases, *3:* 391–93, 396
probable cause, *1:* 64, 120, 164; *3:* 419–22, 478–79

Progressive Party, *2:* 275
Prohibition, *2:* 258–59, 259 (ill.)
Prohibition Party, *2:* 275
Project Exile, *2:* 269 (ill.)
property. *See also* class
    Constitution and, *2:* 239
    in Due Process Clause, *3:* 422, 427, 430
    elections and, *2:* 256
    Federal Convention and, *2:* 239
    legislative branch and, *2:* 203–6, 239
    legislative power and, *2:* 205
    as liberty, *2:* 230
    Locke, John, on, *2:* 205
    republicanism and, *2:* 230
    taking of, *3:* 422
    voting rights and, *2:* 202, 228, 229, 233, 256
proportional representation, *2:* 267
prosecution, *1:* 64–65, 121–22, 165–69; *3:* 479–81. *See also* criminal cases; trials
Protection Clause, *1:* 78
protest, *1:* 122–23; *3:* 408–9
Protestants, *3:* 388–89
public ministers, *3:* 403–4, 415, 417
Puerto Rico, *1:* 3–4; *2:* 181–82, 236; *3:* 361
Pullman Palace Car Company, *1:* 78
Pullman Strike of 1894, *1:* 78–79, 79 (ill.)
punishment, capital, *2:* 245–46
punishment, cruel and unusual
    civil liberties and, *1:* 16; *2:* 194; *3:* 375
    legislative power and, *1:* 6; *2:* 185, 245–46; *3:* 364
    Supreme Court on, *3:* 423
Puritans, *3:* 388
Putin, Lyumilla, *3:* 370 (ill.)
Putin, Vladimir, *1:* 11, 57; *2:* 190; *3:* 369, 370 (ill.)

quaestors, *3:* 383
Quakers, *3:* 388
quartering soldiers, *1:* 62–63
Queries and Remarks Respecting Alterations in the Constitution of Pennsylvania, 2: 214
quorum, *1:* 138; *2:* 318

race, *1:* 70; *2:* 267, 302. *See also* African Americans; discrimination
Randolph, Edmund, *1:* 22, 47, 74 (ill.); *2:* 223
Reagan, Nancy, *1:* 119 (ill.)
Reagan, Ronald, *1:* 140 (ill.); *2:* 300 (ill.), 317 (ill.), 353 (ill.)
    appointment power of, *1:* 17; *2:* 195, 352; *3:* 376
    assassination attempt on, *1:* 104–5
    election of, *1:* 84
    impeachment of threatened, *1:* 153
    Iran-Contra scandal and, *1:* 52, 152–53; *2:* 298
    line item veto and, *2:* 316
    recommendation power of, *1:* 139–40; *2:* 320
    State of the Union address of, *1:* 10 (ill.); *2:* 316
    on Twenty-second Amendment, *1:* 68
reception provisions, *3:* 387–90
recommendation power
    legislation and, *2:* 289
    legislative power and, *1:* 51–52; *2:* 319–20
    overview of, *1:* 9–11, 139–40; *2:* 187–89; *3:* 367–69
Reconstruction
    Supreme Court and, *3:* 404–5, 425–26
    veto override and, *1:* 138; *2:* 318
    writs of habeas corpus and, *2:* 355; *3:* 510
Records of the Federal Convention, 1: 22, 29
recusal, *3:* 476–77

redistricting, *1:* 3; *2:* 181, 302; *3:* 361
regulatory commissions. *See* independent regulatory commissions
regulatory power, *1:* 7, 125; *2:* 186; *3:* 365–66. *See also* independent regulatory commissions
Rehnquist, William, *1:* 154 (ill.); *3:* 372 (ill.), 440, 441 (ill.), 463 (ill.)
Reid, Harry, *2:* 294 (ill.)
religion, *1:* 75–76, 84. *See also* freedom of religion
Religious Tolerance, 3: 389
removal power. *See also* impeachment
    from executive branch, *1:* 146; *2:* 325–27
    from judicial branch, *3:* 413, 437, 440, 444, 445, 447, 458, 462
    from legislative branch, *1:* 154–55; *2:* 333
Reno, Janet, *3:* 451 (ill.)
reporter of decisions, *3:* 451–52
representation. *See also* republicanism
    Constitution and, *2:* 223–26
    democracy and, *2:* 255–57
    elections and, *2:* 226–29
    Federal Convention and, *2:* 223–26
    Federalist on, *2:* 228
    Hamilton, Alexander, on, *2:* 224
    legislative branch and, *2:* 223–26
    liberty and, *2:* 225–26
    Madison, James, on, *2:* 224, 228
    Montesquieu, Charles, on, *2:* 206–8
    in Parliament, *2:* 210–11
    proportional, *2:* 267
    Sherman, Roger, on, *2:* 224
    slavery and, *2:* 225–26
    voting rights and, *2:* 226–29
    Washington, D.C., and, *2:* 286–87
representatives
    campaigning by, *2:* 268, 303–5
    casework of, *2:* 267, 275, 301–3
    class and, *2:* 202
    committee work of, *2:* 266–67, 270, 275
    compensation of, *2:* 257–58

Index

criminal liability of, *1:* 131–32; *2:* 309–10, 337; *3:* 493
election of, *2:* 226–28, 267–68, 303–5, 312, 337; *3:* 493
impeachment of, *1:* 154–55; *2:* 333
legislation and, *2:* 266
lobbying and, *2:* 268, 275
qualifications to be, *2:* 228, 265–66
staff for, *2:* 275–76
terms of, *2:* 228, 259–61, 303
votes of, *2:* 265, 271
whips for, *2:* 273–74
work of, *2:* 265–76
reprieves. *See* pardon power
reprogramming, *1:* 142–43; *2:* 322–23
Republican Conference (House), *2:* 269, 271, 273, 274–75
Republican Conference (Senate), *2:* 281
Republican Party
    checks and balances and, *2:* 313
    Contract with America and, *2:* 261
    elections and, *2:* 267
    presidency and, *1:* 84, 85–86
    Republican Revolution of 1994 and, *2:* 272
    Twenty-second Amendment and, *1:* 67–68
    Watergate scandal and, *1:* 78–79, 91, 96
Republican Revolution of 1994, *2:* 272–73
republicanism
    Guarantee Clause and, *1:* 22
    property and, *2:* 230
    representation and, *2:* 206–8
    in Roman Republic, *1:* 20; *2:* 199; *3:* 382
requisitions, *2:* 235. *See also* taxation
resolutions, *1:* 138; *2:* 319
restraint of trade, *2:* 344–45; *3:* 499
return vetoes
    number of, *1:* 136, 138; *2:* 318
    override of, *1:* 138; *2:* 296–97, 318
    overview of, *1:* 53–54, 134; *2:* 314–15

Revolutionary War. *See* American Revolutionary War
Rhode Island, *2:* 197, 241; *3:* 417
Rice, Condoleezza, *1:* 85
Ridge, Tom, *1:* 101 (ill.)
right to bear arms, *1:* 6; *2:* 185, 243–45, 268; *3:* 364
ripeness, *2:* 347; *3:* 503–4
Robertson v. Baldwin, 3: 466–67
Robinson, Mary, *1:* 84
Rockefeller, Nelson, *1:* 95, 116
Roe v. Wade, 1: 16–17; *2:* 195; *3:* 375
Rolleston, Morton, *2:* 252 (ill.)
Roman codes, *3:* 382–83
Roman Empire, *3:* 382, 383. *See also* Roman Republic
Roman Forum, *3:* 382–83
Roman Republic. *See also* Roman Empire
    assemblies in, *1:* 20–21; *2:* 199, 200
    checks and balances in, *1:* 21–22
    codes of law in, *3:* 382–83
    consuls in, *1:* 20–21; *2:* 199
    democracy in, *2:* 206
    executive power in, *1:* 21–22
    formulary system in, *3:* 384
    judiciary in, *3:* 382–84
    legislature in, *2:* 199–200
    republicanism and, *2:* 199
    Senate in, *2:* 199–200
    separation of powers in, *2:* 199–200
Roosevelt, Franklin D., *1:* 70 (ill.), 83 (ill.), 94 (ill.), 175 (ill.); *2:* 188 (ill.)
    Bureau of the Budget and, *1:* 72
    court-packing plan of, *1:* 174–75
    death of, *1:* 115–18
    executive agreements and, *1:* 147; *2:* 328
    Executive Office of the President and, *1:* 74, 107
    New Deal of, *1:* 82, 174
    prohibition and, *2:* 258
    terms of, *1:* 58, 67, 91
    vetoes by, *1:* 72, 136, 137; *2:* 315
    vice president of, *1:* 93

Roosevelt, Theodore, *1:* 76
Ross, George, *3:* 391
Rother, John, *2:* 285 (ill.)
royal courts, *3:* 384
Ruckelshaus, William D., *1:* 170 (ill.)
Rumsfeld, Donald, *1:* 8 (ill.)
Rush, Benjamin, *2:* 226–27, 227 (ill.)

St. Clair, Arthur, *1:* 77
salaries. *See* compensation
Sanders, Bernard, *2:* 275
Sandinista National Liberation Front, *1:* 152
Sanford, John F. A., *3:* 500
Sawyer, Charles, *1:* 166
Scalia, Antonin, *3:* 476–77, 477 (ill.)
Schiavo, Michael, *3:* 381
Schiavo, Terri, *3:* 381
Schindler, Mary, *3:* 381
Schindler, Robert, *3:* 381
Schlesinger, James R., *1:* 116
Scott, Dred, *3:* 500, 501 (ill.)
Scott v. Sandford, 3: 500
Scowcroft, Brent, *1:* 116
search and seizure
    checks and balances and, *1:* 163–65; *3:* 478–79
    civil liberties and, *1:* 16; *2:* 194; *3:* 374–75
    exclusionary rule and, *3:* 457
    executive power and, *3:* 419–22
    by Federal Bureau of Investigation, *1:* 120
    Fourth Amendment and, *1:* 63–64; *3:* 419–22
    law enforcement and, *3:* 419–22
    probable cause and, *3:* 419–22
search warrants, *1:* 64, 120, 163–64; *3:* 419–22, 478–79. *See also* search and seizure
Second Amendment, *1:* 6, li; *2:* 185, 243–45, li; *3:* 364, li
Secret Service, *1:* 122–23

Sedition Act of 1798, *2:* 244
seizure. *See* search and seizure
select committees, *2:* 298–99
self-incrimination, privilege against, *1:* 65, 168; *3:* 422, 480
Senate. *See also* Congress; legislative branch; legislative power; senators
    calendars of, *2:* 293
    campaigning for, *2:* 276
    casework in, *2:* 276, 301–3
    checks and balances and, *2:* 312–13
    class and, *2:* 202, 210–11, 228–29, 312–13
    cloture rule in, *2:* 294
    committees of, *2:* 270, 276, 277, 281, 286, 290–93, 297–99, 299–301
    composition of, *1:* 3; *2:* 181, 276–81; *3:* 361
    in Constitution, *1:* 1, 3–5; *2:* 179, 181–85, 223–24, 276; *3:* 359, 361–64
    debate in, *2:* 276, 278, 279, 280, 281, 293–95, 337; *3:* 493
    Democratic Conference in, *2:* 281
    election to, *1:* 131; *2:* 202, 223–24, 228–29, 255–57, 276–77, 303–5, 309, 312–13, 337; *3:* 493
    electoral system and, *1:* 48, 68–69
    executive privilege and, *1:* 78–79
    filibuster in, *1:* 145; *2:* 293–94, 325
    floor procedure in, *2:* 293–95
    foreign relations and, *2:* 280
    historic roots of, *1:* 21–22; *2:* 210–11
    impeachment trials by, *1:* 5, 58–59, 91, 151–55, 172–73; *2:* 184, 332–33, 354; *3:* 363, 437–38, 484–85, 509–10, 511
    legislation and, *2:* 276, 289
    lobbying and, *2:* 276, 283–88
    majority leader of, *2:* 279–80, 293, 295
    majority party in, *2:* 280, 291
    minority leader of, *2:* 280–81, 293
    minority party in, *2:* 280–81, 291
    powers exclusive to, *1:* 5, 11; *2:* 184, 190, 277; *3:* 363–64, 369

Index

powers shared with House of Representatives, *1:* 4–5; *2:* 181–82; *3:* 361–63
president of, *1:* 58, 61, 92, 115, 133–34, 152–53, 172; *2:* 277–78, 280, 295, 314, 332, 352; *3:* 413, 484–85
president *pro tempore* of, *1:* 115; *2:* 278–79
qualifications to serve in, *2:* 229, 276, 337; *3:* 493
removal from, *1:* 154–55; *2:* 333
Republican Conference in, *2:* 281
rules of, *1:* 131, 155; *2:* 309, 333, 337; *3:* 493
staff for, *2:* 281, 301–3
terms in, *2:* 259–61, 303
treaty power of, *1:* 5, 11, 57; *2:* 184, 190, 277; *3:* 363–64, 369
unanimous consent in, *2:* 280, 293
vice president in, *1:* 58, 61, 92, 115, 133–34, 152–53, 172; *2:* 277–78, 280, 295, 314, 332, 352; *3:* 413, 484–85
voting in, *1:* 133–34; *2:* 265, 314
whips in, *2:* 281
work of, *2:* 276–81
Senate Appropriations Committee, *2:* 286, 301
Senate Finance Committee, *2:* 301
Senate Foreign Relations Committee, *1:* 146; *2:* 277, 327
Senate Governmental Affairs Committee, *2:* 286
Senate Judiciary Committee, *1:* 144–45; *2:* 277, 325, 352; *3:* 437
Senate, Roman, *1:* 21; *2:* 199–200
senatorial courtesy, *1:* 146; *2:* 325
senators
   campaigning by, *2:* 276–77, 303–5
   casework of, *2:* 276, 301–3
   class and, *2:* 202
   committee work of, *2:* 277
   compensation of, *2:* 257–58
   criminal liability of, *1:* 131–32; *2:* 309–10, 337; *3:* 493
   debate by, *2:* 276
   election of, *2:* 228–29, 276, 303–5, 312–13, 337; *3:* 493
   impeachment of, *1:* 154–55; *2:* 333
   legislation and, *2:* 276
   lobbying and, *2:* 276
   qualifications to be, *2:* 229, 276
   terms of, *2:* 229, 259–61, 303
   votes of, *2:* 265
   work of, *2:* 276–81
sentencing, *3:* 447, 458, 459
separation of powers
   Adams, John, on, *2:* 220–21
   Cheney, Dick, and, *3:* 476–77
   class and, *2:* 201–2; *3:* 400–402
   in Constitution, *1:* 1, 131–32; *2:* 179, 219–22, 309–10, 337–38; *3:* 359, 415, 493–94
   declarations of war and, *2:* 234–35
   dual service and, *3:* 442
   executive branch and, *1:* 131–32, 159–60; *2:* 199–200, 203, 209, 309–10; *3:* 397–400, 473–74, 488–89
   executive privilege and, *3:* 476–77, 488–89
   Federal Convention and, *1:* 41–45; *2:* 219–22; *3:* 397–402
   Founding Fathers and, *3:* 397–402
   in Great Britain, *1:* 22–23
   Hamilton, Alexander, on, *3:* 400–402
   Jefferson, Thomas, on, *1:* 44–45
   judicial branch and, *1:* 159–60; *2:* 337–38; *3:* 397–402, 413, 473–74, 488–89, 493–94
   legislation and, *1:* 26, 28; *2:* 209; *3:* 400–402
   legislative branch and, *1:* 131–32; *2:* 199–200, 202–3, 209, 219–22, 309–10, 337–38; *3:* 397–400, 400–402, 493–94
   Locke, John, on, *1:* 26; *2:* 202–3, 209
   Madison, James, on, *1:* 43–44; *2:* 219–20
   military and, *2:* 234–35
   Montesquieu, Charles, on, *1:* 27
   Parliament and, *2:* 209
   political question doctrine and, *2:* 347–48; *3:* 504
   in Roman Republic, *2:* 199–200
   Scalia, Antonin, and, *3:* 476–77

tyranny and, *2:* 337; *3:* 493
veto power and, *2:* 209
war powers and, *1:* 22, 54–55, 80–82
Washington, George, on, *2:* 221–22
September 11, 2001, terrorist attacks
    Department of Homeland Security and, *1:* 144; *2:* 324–25
    Office of Homeland Security and, *1:* 100
    presidential message after, *1:* 10; *2:* 188, 189 (ill.); *3:* 368
    select committees after, *2:* 298–99
Seventeenth Amendment, *1:* lv; *2:* 255–57, 312–13, lv; *3:* lv
Seventh Amendment, *1:* lii; *2:* lii; *3:* 422–23, lii
Seward, William H., *1:* 19
Shays, Daniel, *1:* 33–34, 40; *2:* 232–34, 233 (ill.)
Shays's Rebellion, *1:* 33–35, 40, 41; *2:* 232–34, 233 (ill.)
Sherman Antitrust Act, *2:* 344–45; *3:* 499
Sherman, Roger, *2:* 224, 225 (ill.)
shoestring district, *2:* 302
Shuster, William, *2:* 267
Siegal, Dorothy, *3:* 452 (ill.)
Sierra Club, *3:* 476–77
Sirica, John, *3:* 488
Sixteenth Amendment, *1:* lv; *2:* lv; *3:* lv
    overview of, *2:* 253–55
    ratification of, *2:* 347, 348–49, 350–51; *3:* 503, 504–5
Sixth Amendment, *1:* li–lii; *2:* li–lii; *3:* li–lii
    checks and balances and, *1:* 168–69; *3:* 481
    civil liberties and, *1:* 16; *2:* 194; *3:* 375
    criminal cases and, *1:* 64–66, 168–69; *3:* 422, 481
    judicial power and, *3:* 422
    jury trials and, *2:* 355; *3:* 512
Sketches of the Principles of Government, *3:* 397–400
slavery
    in Constitution, *2:* 205–6, 225–26, 232; *3:* 430
    Federal Convention and, *2:* 218–19, 225–26

    House of Representatives and, *2:* 226
    legislative power and, *2:* 232
    representation and, *2:* 225–26
    taxation and, *2:* 226
    Thirteenth Amendment ends, *2:* 345; *3:* 426–27, 430, 499, 500
Sloop Active, *3:* 391
Smith, Adam, *2:* 234–35
Socialist Party, *2:* 275
soldiers, quartering, *1:* 62–63
solicitor general, *1:* 102, 120; *3:* 450
South Carolina, *2:* 228
South Korea, *1:* 166
space exploration, *1:* 125–27
Spanish-American War
    declaration of war for, *1:* 54, 80, 149; *2:* 329
    writs of habeas corpus and, *2:* 355; *3:* 510
Speaker of the House
    committees and, *2:* 295
    debate and, *2:* 293
    Gingrich, Newt, as, *2:* 272
    House majority leader and, *2:* 270–71
    legislation and, *2:* 296
    overview of, *2:* 269–70
    Senate majority leader compared with, *2:* 280
special interest groups, *2:* 283–85, 288, 292, 313
speech. *See* freedom of speech
Speech and Debate Clause, *1:* 131–32; *2:* 309–10, 337; *3:* 493
spending power. *See* appropriations power
Spirit of Laws, *1:* 27; *2:* 203–5
spying, *1:* 124
Stalin, Joseph, *1:* 148 (ill.)
standing committees, *2:* 266–67, 290, 291, 297, 299–301
state conventions, *2:* 236, 241–42, 258, 348; *3:* 504
State, Department of
    creation of, *1:* 50, 73, 104

foreign relations and, *1:* 56
historic roots of, *1:* 31
overview of, *1:* 104–6
State of the Union address, *2:* 188 (ill.), 313 (ill.); *3:* 368 (ill.)
   legislation and, *2:* 289
   line item veto and, *2:* 316
   overview of, *1:* 9–10, 51–52, 139–40; *2:* 187–88, 319–20; *3:* 367–68
state, secretary of, *1:* 104–6, 108–9
states. *See also* colonies, American
   admission of, *1:* 3–4; *2:* 181–82, 236; *3:* 361
   under Articles of Confederation, *2:* 217, 235
   Bank of the United States and, *2:* 247–49
   bicameralism and, *2:* 212–15
   Bill of Rights and, *3:* 430
   cases concerning, *1:* 14, 15; *2:* 192, 193, 346; *3:* 373, 403–4, 415, 417, 423–24, 501
   Constitution and, *2:* 240–42
   electoral system and, *1:* 47–48, 66
   Eleventh Amendment and, *3:* 423–24
   at Federal Convention, *1:* 3, 4; *2:* 181, 182, 197–98, 223–24; *3:* 361, 362
   freedom of religion in, *3:* 389
   governments of, *1:* 30–31
   judicial review and, *3:* 418, 424
   judicial systems of, *1:* 13–14; *2:* 191–92; *3:* 371–72, 387–90, 417, 424
   line item veto in, *2:* 316
   term limits and, *2:* 261
   voting rights in, *1:* 70–71; *2:* 256–57
statutory law. *See* legislation
steel seizure case, *1:* 166–67
stenographers, *3:* 450
stenotype, *3:* 450
Stevens, John Paul, *3:* 372 (ill.), 463 (ill.)
Stewart, Potter, *3:* 439 (ill.)
Stimson, Henry L., *1:* 118, 118 (ill.)
Stockman, David, *2:* 300 (ill.)
Story, Joseph, *3:* 398–99, 399 (ill.)

subpoena power, *1:* 65–66, 168–69; *3:* 422, 481, 488–89
Substance Abuse and Mental Health Services Administration, *1:* 100
suffrage, *1:* 70, 71 (ill.); *2:* 256. *See also* voting rights
summary judgment, *3:* 446
Sumners, Hatton W., *1:* 137, 137 (ill.)
superior common law courts, *3:* 384–85
Supremacy Clause, *2:* 340; *3:* 411, 412, 424, 495–96
Supreme Court, *1:* 12 (ill.); *3:* 439 (ill.), 463 (ill.), 465 (ill.). *See also* justices, Supreme Court
   appeals to, *3:* 380–81, 407–8, 415, 417–18, 429, 432–33, 435, 440–43, 462–68
   appointment to, *1:* 144; *2:* 324, 325, 349, 352–53; *3:* 413, 425, 433, 437, 439, 506
   chief justice in, *3:* 417, 462
   civil liberties and, *2:* 251–53
   clerk of the court of, *3:* 449–50
   Congress and, *3:* 425–26
   in Constitution, *1:* 12; *2:* 190–91; *3:* 370, 402, 415, 417–18, 462
   decision-making by, *1:* 16; *2:* 194, 352; *3:* 375, 439–43, 448, 465–68, 507
   election of 2000 and, *3:* 464–65
   on equal protection, *2:* 345; *3:* 499–500
   Federalist Party and, *3:* 425
   First Amendment and, *2:* 243, 244
   on gerrymandering, *2:* 302
   historic roots of, *3:* 386, 387, 392–93
   income tax and, *2:* 254–55, 346–47; *3:* 503
   Interstate Commerce Clause and, *2:* 250–51, 251–53
   on judicial review, *2:* 342–44; *3:* 498
   jurisdiction of, *1:* 15; *2:* 193, 342–44; *3:* 373, 403–5, 424–25, 497–98
   law clerks at, *3:* 448
   line item veto and, *2:* 316
   Necessary and Proper Clause and, *2:* 249
   opinions of, *3:* 448, 451–52, 466–68
   oral argument in, *3:* 465

overview of, *3:* 380–81
preamble to Constitution and, *3:* 399
on protest, *3:* 408–9
Reconstruction and, *3:* 425–26
on removal power, *1:* 146; *2:* 325–26
reporter of decisions in, *3:* 451–52
Roosevelt, Franklin D., and, *1:* 174–75
Schiavo case and, *3:* 381
on search and seizure, *3:* 420–22
size of, *1:* 16, 174–75; *2:* 194, 351–52; *3:* 375, 417, 425–26, 436–37, 462, 506–7
solicitor general and, *1:* 102
state cases reviewed by, *3:* 418
on state power, *3:* 423
term limits and, *2:* 261
treaties and, *1:* 147; *2:* 327
trials in, *1:* 15; *2:* 193; *3:* 373, 415, 417, 424–25
veto power and, *1:* 135; *2:* 315
work of, *3:* 462–68
writs of certiorari in, *1:* 14; *2:* 192; *3:* 372–73
surveillance, *1:* 120
Sutherland, George, *1:* 174
symbolic speech, *3:* 408–9

Taft, William Howard, *2:* 255; *3:* 442, 442 (ill.)
Taft-Hartley Act, *1:* 166
Takings Clause, *3:* 422
Taney, Roger B., *3:* 500
Tax Court, U.S., *3:* 432, 458
taxation
under Articles of Confederation, *1:* 31–32, 39–40; *2:* 215, 217, 235; *3:* 395
commerce and, *2:* 231–32, 249
Congress and, *2:* 215
in Constitution, *1:* 2; *2:* 180, 231–32, 235–36, 253–55; *3:* 360
Federal Convention and, *2:* 231–32, 235–36

Hamilton, Alexander, on, *2:* 231–32
on imports, *2:* 253–54
income tax, *2:* 253–55, 346–47, 350–51; *3:* 503
Internal Revenue Service and, *1:* 107, 119
Joint Committee on Taxation and, *2:* 299
legislative power and, *2:* 231–32, 235–36
Madison, James, on, *2:* 235
Sixteenth Amendment and, *2:* 253–55, 347; *3:* 503
slavery and, *2:* 226
Tax Court and, *3:* 458
Washington, D.C., and, *2:* 286
Tenth Amendment, *1:* lii; *2:* 246, lii; *3:* lii
term limits, *2:* 259–61, 272; *3:* 433
territories, *1:* 4; *2:* 182, 236; *3:* 361–63
test cases, *2:* 346–47; *3:* 503
That Politics May Be Reduced to a Science, *2:* 206
Thatcher, Margaret, *1:* 84
Third Amendment, *1:* 62–63, li; *2:* li; *3:* li
third parties, *2:* 267, 275
Thirteenth Amendment, *1:* liii; *2:* liii; *3:* liii
enforcement of, *3:* 427–28
as labor amendment, *3:* 466–67
ratification of, *3:* 426–27, 430
slavery ended by, *2:* 345; *3:* 499, 500
Thomas, Clarence, *2:* 352–53
Thompson, Jacob, *2:* 187 (ill.)
Thompson, Tommy, *1:* 8 (ill.)
three-fifths compromise, *2:* 226
Thurmond, J. Strom, *1:* 154 (ill.); *2:* 260, 260 (ill.), 294
Tinker, John P., *3:* 408–9
Tinker, Mary Beth, *3:* 408–9
Tinker v. Des Moines Independent Community School District, *3:* 408–9
Tisdale, Elkanah, *2:* 302
torts, *3:* 468
Toucey, Isaac, *2:* 187 (ill.)
trade. *See* commerce

Index

Train, Russell, *1:* 170 (ill.)
Transportation, Department of, *1:* 98, 106
transportation, secretary of, *1:* 106
treason
    bills of attainder and, *2:* 205
    definition of, *3:* 406
    as impeachable offense, *1:* 5, 91, 153; *2:* 182–84, 333, 353–54; *3:* 363, 437, 508
    as infamous crime, *1:* 65, 166–67; *3:* 480
    Speech and Debate Clause and, *1:* 131–32; *2:* 309–10, 337; *3:* 493
Treasury, Department of the
    Bureau of the Budget and, *1:* 72
    creation of, *1:* 50, 73, 104
    head of, *1:* 106–7; *2:* 229, 247
    historic roots of, *1:* 31
    work of, *1:* 119; *2:* 229, 247
treasury, secretary of the, *1:* 106–7, 108–9; *2:* 247
treaties. *See also* foreign relations
    Antiballistic Missile Treaty, *1:* 57
    cancellation of, *1:* 57, 147; *2:* 327
    cases concerning, *2:* 346; *3:* 402, 415, 418, 501
    checks and balances and, *1:* 11, 146–47; *2:* 190, 327–28; *3:* 369
    executive agreements, *1:* 147; *2:* 328
    House of Representatives and, *1:* 147; *2:* 327
    Moscow Treaty on Strategic Offensive Reductions, *1:* 11, 57; *2:* 190; *3:* 369
    president and, *1:* 56–57; *2:* 277
    Senate approval of, *1:* 5, 11, 57; *2:* 184, 190, 277; *3:* 363–64, 369
    Supreme Court and, *1:* 147; *2:* 327
Treaty of Versailles, *1:* 147; *2:* 327, 328 (ill.)
trials
    in American colonies, *3:* 386
    bench, *3:* 379, 409, 446–47, 459, 460
    in circuit courts, *3:* 417, 428–29
    civil cases, *3:* 445–47, 459–60
    closing argument, *3:* 457, 459, 460
    Constitution on, *3:* 406–7
    criminal cases, *3:* 445–47, 456–59
    discovery for, *3:* 445–46, 447, 459
    evidence at, *3:* 446, 457, 460
    in federal district courts, *3:* 379, 416–17, 428–29, 432, 435, 445–47, 455–60
    Fifth Amendment and, *1:* 64–65
    First Amendment and, *3:* 422
    friendly suits, *2:* 346–47; *3:* 503
    judgment in, *3:* 445–46, 447
    judicial interpretation in, *1:* 15; *2:* 193; *3:* 373–74, 409–11
    jury, *2:* 205, 355; *3:* 379, 406, 409, 422, 446–47, 457–59, 460, 510–12
    jury selection for, *3:* 457, 460
    location of, *3:* 406, 422
    magistrate judges and, *3:* 447–48
    motions in, *3:* 449, 459
    opening statement, *3:* 457, 459, 460
    original jurisdiction and, *3:* 403–4
    overview of, *1:* 13; *2:* 191; *3:* 371, 406–7, 445–47
    phases of, *3:* 445–47
    pleadings for, *3:* 384, 445, 459
    post-trial motions, *3:* 447
    pretrial motions, *3:* 447
    public, *1:* 65, 168–69; *2:* 355; *3:* 422, 481, 512
    sentencing, *3:* 459
    Seventh Amendment and, *3:* 422–23
    Sixth Amendment and, *1:* 16, 64–66, 168–69; *2:* 194; *3:* 375, 422, 481
    speedy, *1:* 65, 168–69; *2:* 355; *3:* 422, 481, 512
    summary judgment before, *3:* 446
    in Supreme Court, *1:* 15; *2:* 193; *3:* 373, 415, 417, 424–25
    test cases, *2:* 346–47; *3:* 503
    verdicts in, *3:* 447, 458–59
tribal assembly, *1:* 21; *2:* 199, 200
Truman, Harry S., *1:* 118 (ill.), 148 (ill.); *3:* 367 (ill.)
    Defense, Department of, and, *1:* 50
    executive agreements of, *1:* 147; *2:* 328
    State of the Union address of, *1:* 9; *2:* 187; *3:* 367

steel seizure case and, *1:* 166–67

as vice president, *1:* 115–18

Trumbull, John, *3:* 431 (ill.)

Twelfth Amendment, *1:* 48, 66–67, 69, 92, lii–liii; *2:* lii–liii; *3:* lii–liii

Twentieth Amendment, *1:* lvi–lvii; *2:* lvi–lvii; *3:* lvi–lvii

Twenty-fifth Amendment, *1:* 93, 96, lviii–lix; *2:* lviii–lix; *3:* lviii–lix

Twenty-first Amendment, *1:* lvii; *2:* 258, lvii; *3:* lvii

Twenty-fourth Amendment, *1:* 70–71, lviii; *2:* 257, lviii; *3:* lviii

Twenty-second Amendment, *1:* 19, 58, 67–68, 91, lvii–lviii; *2:* lvii–lviii; *3:* lvii–lviii

Twenty-seventh Amendment, *1:* lx; *2:* 257–58, lx; *3:* lx

Twenty-sixth Amendment, *1:* 71, lix–lx; *2:* 257, 349, lix–lx; *3:* 505, lix–lx

Twenty-third Amendment, *1:* 68–69, lviii; *2:* 286, lviii; *3:* lviii

Two Treatises of Government, 1: 26, 49; *2:* 203, 204 (ill.), 205

Tyler, John, *1:* 92, 92 (ill.), 137; *3:* 442, 507 (ill.)

tyranny, *1:* 22–25, 159–60; *2:* 337; *3:* 473, 493

unanimous consent, *2:* 280, 293

unicameralism, *2:* 197, 211–15, 223, 312

Unified Commands, *1:* 98–99

Uniform Code of Military Justice, *3:* 458

United Nations, *1:* 105–6, 147; *2:* 327

United States of America (as litigant), *1:* 14; *2:* 192; *3:* 373, 403, 415, 418

United States Reports, 3: 451

United States v. Nixon, 1: 151; *2:* 331; *3:* 488–89

United Steel Workers of America, *1:* 166–67

Uribe, Alvaro, *2:* 294 (ill.)

U.S. attorneys, *1:* 50, 120, 121–22; *3:* 450, 455, 456–57. *See also* attorney general

U.S. Botanic Garden, *2:* 305

U.S. Capitol, *2:* 287 (ill.), 305, 313 (ill.)

U.S. Chamber of Commerce, *1:* 116; *2:* 268

U.S. Department of Agriculture, *1:* 95–98

U.S. Department of Commerce, *1:* 97

U.S. Department of Education, *1:* 99

U.S. Department of Energy, *1:* 99

U.S. Department of Health & Human Services, *1:* 99–100

U.S. Department of Homeland Security, *1:* 100–101

U.S. Department of Housing & Urban Development, *1:* 101–2

U.S. Department of Interior, *1:* 102

U.S. Department of Justice. *See* Justice, Department of

U.S. Department of Labor, *1:* 102–3, 119

U.S. Department of State. *See* State, Department of

U.S. Department of the Treasury. *See* Treasury, Department of the

U.S. Department of Transportation, *1:* 98, 106

U.S. Department of Veterans Affairs, *1:* 107

U.S. Fish and Wildlife Service, *1:* 102

U.S. Geological Survey, *1:* 102

U.S. Term Limits, *2:* 261

U.S. Term Limits v. Thornton, 2: 261

U.S. trade representative, *1:* 107

Van Devanter, Willis, *1:* 174, 175

Veneman, Ann, *1:* 8 (ill.)

verdicts, *3:* 447, 458–59. *See also* judgment

veterans, *3:* 458

Veterans Affairs, Department of, *1:* 107; *3:* 458

veterans affairs, secretary of, *1:* 107

veto power, *2:* 321 (ill.)

appropriations power and, *1:* 141; *2:* 321

checks and balances and, *1:* 11, 133–39; *2:* 189–90, 222, 314–19; *3:* 369

historic roots of, *1:* 29

Index

legislation and, *1:* 52–54, 72, 114, 133–39; *2:* 314–19

legislative veto, *1:* 138–39, 141, 142–43; *2:* 318–19, 322, 323

line item veto, *1:* 141; *2:* 272, 316–17, 321

override of, *1:* 5, 11, 54, 72, 80, 136–38; *2:* 182, 189–90, 209, 222, 265, 296–97, 316–18; *3:* 363, 369

overview of, *1:* 52–54, 133–36; *2:* 265, 296–97, 314–19

pocket vetoes, *1:* 54, 134–35, 136, 138; *2:* 315, 318

as policy tool, *1:* 71–72, 137

political parties and, *1:* 138; *2:* 318

recommendation power and, *1:* 11; *2:* 189; *3:* 368–69

return vetoes, *1:* 53–54, 134, 136, 138; *2:* 296–97, 314–15, 318

separation of powers and, *2:* 209

Supreme Court and, *1:* 135; *2:* 315

vice president

advice and consent and, *2:* 352

in cabinet, *1:* 8, 94, 107, 115; *2:* 186; *3:* 366

ceremonial duties of, *1:* 118

day in the life of, *1:* 115–18

debate by, *2:* 278

election of, *1:* 58, 66–69, 93–94

Federal Convention and, *2:* 277

in foreign relations, *1:* 94, 118

Founding Fathers and, *2:* 277

history of, *1:* 21, 93–95; *2:* 277–78

impeachment trials and, *1:* 152–53, 172; *2:* 332; *3:* 413, 484–85

legislation and, *1:* 115, 133–34; *2:* 277–78, 295, 296, 314

in National Security Council, *1:* 108, 115

office of, *2:* 277

political parties and, *1:* 93–94

powers of, *1:* 57–58, 61, 92–95, 115–18

president and, *1:* 93–95, 104–5

as president temporarily, *1:* 104–5, 115

qualifications to be, *1:* 92

replacement of, *1:* 96

in Senate, *1:* 58, 61, 92, 115, 133–34, 152–53, 172; *2:* 277–78, 280, 295, 314, 332, 352; *3:* 413, 484–85

term of, *1:* 37, 58, 66, 92

Vices of the Political System of the United States, 2: 230–31

Vietnam War, *1:* 150 (ill.); *2:* 330 (ill.)

amnesty after, *1:* 53

end of, *1:* 116–17

protest of, *3:* 408–9

as undeclared, *1:* 55

War Powers Resolution and, *1:* 149; *2:* 329

Vinson, Frederick M., *1:* 166–67

Virginia, *2:* 241, 243, 244; *3:* 388, 389

Virginia Declaration of Rights, *3:* 389

Virginia Plan, *1:* 47; *2:* 223–24

Volstead Act, *2:* 258

Volstead, Andrew J., *2:* 258

voting rights

class and, *2:* 226–29, 255–57

Congress and, *2:* 226–29

in Constitution, *2:* 226–29

democracy and, *2:* 226, 255–57

Federal Convention and, *2:* 226–29

Fifteenth Amendment and, *2:* 256; *3:* 427

Fifth Amendment and, *1:* 70

House of Representatives and, *2:* 208

Nineteenth Amendment and, *1:* 70; *2:* 257

property and, *2:* 202, 228, 229, 233, 256

representation and, *2:* 226–29

Senate and, *2:* 255–57

states and, *1:* 70–71; *2:* 256–57

Twenty-fourth Amendment and, *1:* 70–71; *2:* 257

Twenty-sixth Amendment and, *1:* 70–71; *2:* 257

in Washington, D.C., *2:* 286

W

Walker, Clement, *2:* 209
Walker, Hezekiah, *2:* 304 (ill.)
Wallace, Henry A., *1:* 93, 94 (ill.)
War, Department of, *1:* 31, 50, 73, 97, 104. *See also* Defense, Department of
War of 1812, *1:* 54, 80, 149; *2:* 305, 329
war powers. *See also* commander in chief; military
    appointment power and, *3:* 425
    checks and balances and, *1:* 147–49; *2:* 329–31
    Federal Convention and, *1:* 54–55, 148–49; *2:* 329
    historic roots of, *1:* 21, 22
    separation of powers and, *1:* 22, 54–55, 80–82
    War Powers Resolution and, *1:* 80–82, 149; *2:* 329–31
War Powers Resolution, *1:* 80–82, 149; *2:* 329–31
warrants, search, *1:* 64, 120, 163–64; *3:* 419–22, 478–79. *See also* search and seizure
Warren, Earl, *3:* 439 (ill.)
Warren, James, *2:* 231
Washington, D.C., *2:* 221 (ill.)
    creation of, *2:* 220–21
    government of, *2:* 286–87, 287 (ill.)
    statehood for, *1:* 3–4; *2:* 181–82; *3:* 361
    Twenty-third Amendment and, *1:* 68–69; *2:* 286
Washington, George, *1:* 43 (ill.); *3:* 362 (ill.), 392 (ill.)
    admiralty courts and, *3:* 392
    appropriations power and, *2:* 288–89
    Bank of the United States and, *2:* 247
    cabinet of, *1:* 74 (ill.), 77
    on commerce, *2:* 231
    election of, *1:* 67
    executive departments under, *1:* 31, 104
    executive orders of, *1:* 76
    executive privilege of, *1:* 77
    Federal Convention and, *1:* 42–43
    Necessary and Proper Clause and, *2:* 247
    pardons by, *1:* 52
    on power, *2:* 231
    on separation of powers, *2:* 221–22
    Shays's Rebellion and, *1:* 34–35
    State of the Union address of, *1:* 9; *2:* 187; *3:* 367
    terms of, *1:* 67, 91
    treaties and, *1:* 146; *2:* 327
    vetoes by, *1:* 71
Washington Monument, *2:* 287 (ill.)
Watergate scandal
    executive privilege and, *1:* 78–79, 176; *3:* 487, 488–89
    impeachment threat during, *1:* 91
    pardon power and, *1:* 52, 96
Wayne, James M., *3:* 426
Wealth of Nations, 2: 234–35
Weinberger, Caspar W., *1:* 119 (ill.), 176 (ill.)
    pardon of, *1:* 153, 176; *3:* 490
    as secretary of health, education, and welfare, *1:* 116
whips, *2:* 273–74, 281
Whiskey Rebellion, *1:* 52
White, Byron R., *3:* 372 (ill.), 439 (ill.), 463 (ill.)
White House, *2:* 221, 277
White House Office, *1:* 75
Whitman, Christine Todd, *1:* 8 (ill.)
Whittemore, James D., *3:* 381
Wickard v. Filburn, 2: 251
William III, *1:* 24
Wilson, James, *1:* 46
Wilson, Woodrow, *1:* 9 (ill.); *2:* 290 (ill.)
    on Congress, *2:* 290
    on lobbying, *2:* 285
    on the Senate, *2:* 280
    State of the Union address of, *1:* 9; *2:* 187; *3:* 367

Index

Treaty of Versailles and, *1:* 147; *2:* 327
Wilson-Gorman Tariff Act of 1894, *2:* 254
wiretaps, *1:* 120
Wolfson, Louis E., *3:* 511
women, *1:* 70, 84; *2:* 257, 267
World War I
    declarations of war for, *1:* 54–55, 80, 149; *2:* 329
    Treaty of Versailles ending, *1:* 147; *2:* 327
World War II, *1:* 148 (ill.)
    declarations of war for, *1:* 55, 80, 149; *2:* 329
    executive agreements and, *1:* 147; *2:* 328
    National Security Council and, *1:* 108
    writs of habeas corpus and, *2:* 355; *3:* 510
writs of certiorari
    overview of, *3:* 432–33
    petitions for, *1:* 14; *2:* 192; *3:* 372–73, 440, 448, 464
    procedure for, *1:* 14; *2:* 192; *3:* 372–73, 440, 463–64
    votes required for, *1:* 16; *2:* 194; *3:* 375
writs of habeas corpus
    checks and balances and, *1:* 171; *2:* 354–55; *3:* 482–86, 510
    judicial power and, *3:* 409
    legislative power and, *1:* 6; *2:* 184; *3:* 364
    liberty and, *2:* 205
    in *Robertson v. Baldwin, 3:* 466–67
writs of mandamus
    Marbury v. Madison and, *1:* 162–63; *2:* 342–44; *3:* 424–25, 477–78, 497–98
    overview of, *1:* 171–72; *3:* 483
writs of prohibition, *1:* 171–72; *3:* 483

Youngstown Sheet and Tube Co., *1:* 166–67, 167 (ill.)

Zerfas, Herman H., *1:* 116
Zoellick, Robert, *1:* 8 (ill.)
Zylstra, Ival E., *1:* 116